AT HOME
ON THE
RANGE

AT HOME
ON THE
RANGE

Essays on the History
of Western Social and
Domestic Life

Edited by
John R. Wunder

Contributions in American History, Number 108

GREENWOOD PRESS
WESTPORT, CONNECTICUT
LONDON, ENGLAND

𝓛𝓒

Library of Congress Cataloging in Publication Data

Main entry under title:

At home on the range.

(Contributions in American history, ISSN 0084-9219; no. 108)
   Bibliography: p.
   Includes index.
   1. Agriculture—West (U.S.)—History—Addresses, essays, lectures. 2. Farm life—West (U.S.)—History—Addresses, essays, lectures. 3. Ranch life—West (U.S.)—History—Addresses, essays, lectures. 4. Frontier and pioneer life—West (U.S.)—Addresses, essays, lectures. I. Wunder, John R. II. Series
S441.A84   1985   338.1'0978   84-15719
ISBN 0-313-24592-4 (lib. bdg.)
ISSN 0084-9219

Library of Congress Catalog Card Number: 84-15719
ISBN: 0-313-24592-4
ISSN: 0084-9219

First published in 1985

Greenwood Press
A division of Congressional Information Service, Inc.
88 Post Road West
Westport, Connecticut 06881

Printed in the United States of America

10 9 8 7 6 5 4 3 2 1

Copyright Acknowledgment

Grateful acknowledgment is given for permission to reprint the following:

"The creation of Indian Farm Women: Field Matrons and Acculturation on the Kiowa-Comanche Reservation, 1895–1906" by Rebecca J. Herring has appeared in a revised form under the same title in *Oklahoma State Historical Review* 4 (Spring 1983): 47–58.

This agricultural history anthology is dedicated to a celebration of the life of Charles L. Wood, agricultural historian at Texas Tech University. At the age of 44, Chuck Wood died in Lubbock, Texas, after a brief, but heroic, battle with acute leukemia. The loss to his family, friends, students, and colleagues is incalculable. But unlike many who perish, historians or not, Chuck Wood left a legacy of wisdom in his writings—a legacy that this book will complement with new contributions in his chosen field of agricultural history.

Of Charles Wood, I remember him very well as a
very nice, quiet man in Agricultural History in
whose classes I gave a number of lectures on
agricultural history of the Chechen-Ingush Republic
(and with whom we were on a T.V. program once).
Also I enjoyed the warm hospitality in his house
after seeing the farms. . . .
He was the most considerate of persons.

Letter, Nina V. Potokova (Chairperson, Department of
History, Chechen-Ingush State University, Groznyy,
USSR) to John R. Wunder, November 3, 1981

Contents

Acknowledgments

This book would not have been possible without the authors herein who gave generously and lovingly of their time, energies, and scholarship. Of these persons, Rodolfo Rocha, James I. Fenton, Rebecca J. Herring, Byron Price, Deborah J. Hoskins, and Robert C. Williams were students of Charles L. Wood. Jacqueline S. Reinier, Janet Schmelzer, George Q. Flynn, and the editor were colleagues of Wood.

As important as the writers are the "stylists," helpers of form and substance. Vicki Pachall, Linda Lester, and Vicky Vaughan endured typing countless drafts and redrafts; Joan Weldon handled numerous administrative problems; and Francisco Balderrama assisted editorially. Particular acknowledgment should be paid to David J. Murrah, Michael Hooks, Rebecca J. Herring, Janet Neugebauer, and Tommie Davis—all from the Southwest Collection of Texas Tech University for their strong support of this project.

Several other persons aided greatly in this quest to recognize a historian of high merit. This aid came in an intangible form that sustained the effort throughout. Nina Potokova, historian from the Soviet Union and guest at Texas Tech University; Pamela Brink, Kansan par excellence, and Mary Hatfield; and Allan Kuethe and Briggs Twyman, interested and concerned colleagues, were most supportive. Susan Wunder, and Amanda

and Nell Wunder, my family; and especially Alma Wood, and
Mark, Greg, John, Marice, and Lisa Wood, Chuck's family,
made this book a deep and most meaningful experience.

John R. Wunder
Clemson, South Carolina

Introduction

Agricultural life in America has often been described in a static dimension. Social and domestic traits have been thought to be remnants of a beleaguered past. The worlds of the various centuries may have evolved in a continuous progression, but the people of agriculture were believed to have successfully resisted or hostilely accommodated cultural change.

These essays are brought forth to challenge the conceptualization of one-dimensional agricultural, social and domestic life experiences. Over time, cultural change has been the rule rather than the exception, and the forces of cultural change have been mighty. To build a ranch or a farm on virgin land required great fortitude, vision, and adaptability. Cultural adjustments were essential characteristics of the first ranchers and farmers.

Walter Prescott Webb noted that "the cattle industry, as carried on in the Plains country, rose in a natural manner and spread with amazing rapidity over the whole area to which it was adapted." Consequently, to Webb, "the ways of life in this region appear logical, reasonable, almost inevitable." But Webb also observed, "that no sooner had the cattle kingdom been set up as a natural institution adapted to its environment than the forces of the Industrial Revolution began to modify and destroy it."[1] In one paragraph, Webb identifies several key forces of cultural change for agriculturalists: environmental acculturation, collective strength, and technological demand. These forces helped transform frontier institutions into modern industries.

James Malin also found cultural change a common agricultural phenomenon, and he saw similar forces at work. He called for a restructuring of ideas concerning agricultural history that "would emphasize ecological competition of two or more cultures for dominance in given earth areas." Malin recognized the land involved not as new land, "but land that has been exploited for unknown generations, and that, in consequence of cultural invasion, became subject to a mode of exploitation different from that under a previous culture."[2] The land was old; the culture was adjustable; the technology of exploitation was new.

These concepts are readily seen in an account of a Kansas farmer's problem with fencing that was recorded by Charles L. Wood. A granddaughter recounted how her grandfather had been unable to encourage a wealthy neighbor to repair a common fence. The neighbor's expensive blooded stock continually ate and destroyed her grandfather's crops. Remembered the granddaughter: "Grandfather bought the oldest, ugliest, and poorest bull he could find, and put it in his own pasture. Needless to say, as time went on and Mother Nature took her course, the rich man's heifers and grandfather's old bull mingled together through the poor fence. When the following spring came, and the rich neighbor's cattle started to have calves, you never in your life saw such an ugly, mixed-up bunch of calves. The fence was fixed immediately, and stayed fixed."[3] Technology, nature, human experience—all these factors shaped the domestic and social life of the farmer and the rancher.

This collection of nine original essays and one edited document concerning agricultural life is divided into five sections: Initial Cultural Implantation; Agricultural Acculturation; Collectivism; Technology, War, and Cultural Change; and Agricultural Imagery and Reality. Each section explores the changing patterns of life for American ranchers and farmers from approximately the seventeenth century to the end of World War II.

NOTES

1. Walter Prescott Webb, *The Great Plains* (New York: Grosset & Dunlap, 1931), p. 227.

2. James C. Malin, *A Concern About Humanity: Notes on Reforms, 1872-1912, at the National and Kansas Levels of Thought* (Lawrence, KS: James C. Malin, 1964), pp. 221, 409-10.

3. Charles L. Wood, "Development of an Enclosure System for Five Kansas Counties, 1875-1895," *The Trail Guide* 14 (March, 1969): 2.

I

INITIAL CULTURAL IMPLANTATION

The road was level, just two ruts, blown deep by the prevailing southwest winds. The prairie was green and rolling.... We passed only one small settlement where we stopped for dinner at noon. The brackish alkali water was most unsatisfying. Canned milk was not much better. To us children it was a glorious feast. Mother, a 'city' lady, must have been pretty uncomfortable, but she laughed at all of the strangeness.... There were sod houses here and there. Cattle roamed about and there were no fences and no section lines.... Just at dusk we came into the town and drove down the main street. There were two stores, a blacksmith shop, a small hotel, a town well, and a few scattered houses. After a while we came to the ranch. There stood our new house, square and bare.

Helen Perry Edwards,
outside Englewood, Kansas, ca. 1942,
remembering an 1886 trip from Dodge City

Across the numerous American frontiers have marched the agriculturalists intent upon making their new life on a strange domain many had never known. By the end of the frontier era, all of the real estate inclusive of the United States had met the farmer, the rancher, and their agricultural assistants, the town builders. Some had been more successful at settlement than others. Everywhere these agriculturalists attempted to implant their known social and domestic experiences, and they found that adjustments were always necessary.

Ranchers have played a very important part in the history of American agriculture. From the first Europeans who arrived in the New World came the ranching industry. It was early introduced into Puritan New England and the Anglican South of the British colonies, but ranching truly flourished longer and attracted the attention of Americans in greater numbers in Texas and the Great Plains. Indeed, so important is ranching that some argue the ranching industry provided Americans with the necessary sagas for nationhood.

Perhaps most influential to the successful development of ranching in the United States were the first Spanish *rancheros* of the Rio Grande Valley. Rodolfo Rocha relates how the province of Nuevo Santander in the 1700s was settled with large and small ranching outfits. The people on this frontier outpost lived a hardy yet satisfying life. At home on the ranch required cultural adjustments in all phases of domestic life.

Similarly, farmers have journeyed with ranchers across the American landscape, and they have also contributed greatly to the story of American agriculture. The first farmers, Native Americans, and their European counterparts broke the land to raise crops and to build civilizations based on domesticated plant life. In the process they sought to impose their past cultural ideals on a new lifeway.

The late frontiers on the Great Plains found women and their men hard pressed. Many were faced with a dilemma of how to approach the harsh realities of this formidable agricultural environment. Old ways were known, proven, and used in humid lands; new notions were risky, untested, and yet more logical. How would these agriculturalists adjust?

James I. Fenton notes that Anglo women who had choices to make opted for imitative rather than adaptive solutions to problems endemic on the Plains frontier. Loneliness, wind, dust, drought, food preservation, and disease necessitated time-tested responses more often than not. Women proved to be more culturally bound than environmentally or spatially influenced.

Farmers and ranchers led a solitary life. As Helen Perry Edwards has related, it was not always comfortable. Yet these agriculturalists— the early rancheros and *vaqueros* and farm men and women—all found such a life a demanding and culturally dynamic one.

RODOLFO ROCHA

Early Ranching along the
Rio Grande

Ranching became Spain's method to extend her control into
Texas. Beginning in the early 1690s, a series of missions were
established in East Texas using ranching as the primary economic base. In the 1720s, the Spanish placed their most successful mission *ranchos* along the San Antonio River. Later, in
the mid-1750s, the area along the Gulf coast in Texas was
settled by awarding numerous land grants to prospective livestock ranchers. This latter area, organized as the province of
Nuevo Santander, developed its own unique ranching life-
style. A study of ranching in South Texas attests to its
peculiarity.

During the first quarter of the eighteenth century, the Spanish government in Mexico initiated procedures to colonize the
region known as the "Seno Mexicano," an area along the Gulf
of Mexico from the Panuco River to the Nueces River. It had
remained unsettled and unexplored for two-and-a-half centuries following the Spanish explorations of the sixteenth century. Several factors stimulated colonization. First, Spanish
authorities were dumbfounded to learn that the French under
La Salle had attempted to settle near Matagorda Bay. Proposed Spanish settlements in the Seno Mexicano would provide
a check against continued expansion by the French, and from
the Dutch and British who were active in the West Indies. In

addition, rumors of mineral wealth in the Seno Mexicano provided added motivation, and Indian threats in northern
Coahuila required reinforced settlements along the Rio
Grande. The Spanish by the mid-1750s had concluded to colonize what now appeared to be a vital area.

In 1746, the Spanish commissioned José de Escandón to head
the settlement of the new colony named "la provincia de Nuevo
Santander." He planned to lead Spaniards, *mestizos*, and *mu-
latos* from the northernmost settlements of Mexico to the new
colony, and on November 16, 1748, 2,515 colonists and 755
soldiers departed Querétaro bound for Nuevo Santander. By
1755, Escandón had founded twenty-four villas, six of which
lay along the Rio Grande: on the south bank were Camargo,
Reynosa, Revilla, and Mier; on the north bank were Villa de
Dolores and Laredo.[1]

Rancheros were the first pioneers on the Rio Grande frontier. Nicolas de la Garza started a *rancho* near the river some
twenty leagues above Camargo. Other ranchers came, and the
town followed. The first settlement on the north bank of the
Rio Grande was initiated by Don Juan José Vásquez de Borrego, a ranchero from Coahuila. The Villa de Dolores, founded in
August 1750, had three families, but increased in seven years
to 123 inhabitants who pastured 5,000 horses and 3,000 cattle.
A few years before the founding of the Villa, Escandón had
granted Borrego a total of fifty *sitios* (square leagues) of *ganado mayor* (cattle) and twenty-five *sitios* of *ganado menor*
(sheep), or about 270,624 acres. The Escandón settlements became the foundations for the *rancherías* established between
the Rio Grande and Nueces Rivers during the latter part of the
eighteenth century.[2]

Nuevo Santander, with abundant grasses and a dry climate
more suitable for ranching than farming, fast became stock
raising country, where thousands of cattle, goats, and sheep
grazed. The first rancherías were situated along the Rio
Grande from which water could be used to sustain the ranch.
The land was typically brush country covered with mesquite,
black chaparral, coma, huisache, brazil, amargoso, grangeno,

sapote and many other shrubs. An abundance of many types of cactus capped the area. In addition to the fertile meadows and rich farmland, the region had a large number of swamps, or *resacas*, which formed as the river cut its beds. Mosquitos bred in the resacas. Nonetheless, the abundant pasturage and wooded-area supported a rancho economy.[3]

Ranchos varied in size from hundreds to even thousands of acres. Many ranchos were segments of land without limits or landmarks. Large ranchos had as many as one hundred people. The majority had only from twenty to thirty inhabitants. Most people living on the rancho were *vaqueros* (cowboys) and their families. A prosperous rancho consisted of about 300 milk cows, forty bulls, 110 bullocks, 180 branding calves, 1,100 sheep and goats, twenty oxen, thirty horses, fifty mares, twenty colts, and assorted studs, mules, jackasses, jennies, and hogs, plus two carts. A moderate rancho had about eighty milk cows, thirty heifers, thirty bulls and bullocks, forty calves, fifteen tame horses, twenty-four mares, a stud, and some mules. A poor rancho had three cows, a heifer, horse, mare, three yoke of oxen and a cart.[4]

Usually ranchos were located in camping areas previously used by Native American inhabitants. Building sites on ranchos were selected with care, taking into consideration good terrace soil, firewood, shade trees, wind currents, and the availability of water.[5] The *casa grande*, or owner's house, was constructed of stone from the quarry on the river. Ranging in size from thirty to forty feet long; twelve to fourteen feet high; and twelve to fifteen feet wide, most casas grandes contained one room, with an occasional two-room structure constructed. The house had several *troneras* (loopholes) located on all four sides of the building that were used to fight off Indian attacks, and a bench-type structure about twenty-four to thirty inches high was built around the front of the building. Each casa had a door on opposite sides, and the house had windows on opposite sides of the doors. A room built adjacent to the house served as a kitchen on most ranches. Some houses had a fireplace situated on one of the broad-side walls. The huge fireplace was made of stone surfaced with lime plaster, and it had a *banqueta* (bench) adjacent to it, which was used for sitting, placing utensils, or sleeping.[6] One particular description of a casa grande elaborates:

Outside, the house appeared a mere plain, dead walls of adobes, having except the single door of entrance, no other openings than the spout-holes of the roof. Within was a single room, about forty feet long and fifteen broad, the floor of hard-trodden earth and the ceiling some sixteen feet above it, of bamboo, laid with cement, on small crooked unhewn rafters. As there were no windows and but two small, low doors, there was a great depth of gloom overhead. At one end, upon the whitewashed wall, hung a large old painting, the subject imperceptible except to the eye of faith; a crucifix over it; a small painting of a mermaid-like martyr, with long straggling, unsinged hair, rising, head and shoulders out from a sea of fire; and several coarse woodcuts of saints and friars. Near this, on a narrow shelf, was a blunderbuss, a horse-pistol and a thin prayer-book, the only literature in the house. At the end of this room were three broad beds, with elaborately worked cover-lids, used in the day as lounges. Two large chests . . . stood next to the beds, then a sort of settee, or highbacked bench, against the wall, wide enough to be used for a bed; then a broad, low table, used for a dining table when any one dined in the house, also as a bedstead for two at night. A little box or crib, in which a baby lay sucking its fists, swung near the floor by a hide rope from the ceiling. . . . Near the end opposite . . . was a back door. . . . The door opened upon a house-court and garden, which was enclosed by high and strong palisades. . . . In this courtyard were several walnut and fig trees, under which our horses were fastened, also, a high dome-formed oven, made of adobes, one of which is to be seen behind every Mexican house. . . . Various vegetables were growing in the garden, but more maize than all else.[7]

Furniture in a rancho can best be described as being "lo mas sencillo posible" (as simple as possible), made mostly of handcrafted mesquite. Doors, windows and beams were also fashioned from mesquite trunks. Although on some of the large ranchos, the *jefe* (owner of the ranch) did have a bed, most vaqueros did not. They simply slept on the floor on either a blanket or a piece of hide. Sleeping in a rancho in South Texas was not very comfortable, especially after a rain, because ferocious mosquitos came in by the thousands.

Besides a bed, every casa grande had one or more *castañas* (trunks). The castaña was used to store household belongings such as clothing, valuable jewelry, guns, and any other personal items. Houses also had a table. It usually was about twelve to fourteen feet long. Chairs were not used; benches made do. Both were homemade from mesquite. In some houses, especially in *jacales* (huts of a lesser construction than casa grandes), a smaller table, no bigger than a present-day card table, was used. Wooden shelves, sometimes inserted into the masonry wall, were commonly used for storage. Shelves were also built-in above doors. Troneras frequently served as shelves. In the jacal, the beam that sustained the roof midway through the house also doubled as a shelf. The banqueta along the side of the fireplace also served as shelving.[8]

Rancheros used miscellaneous furnishings inside their homes. The kitchen had a working table made from the side of a tree supported by a "Y" branch (fork) buried in the ground. Every kitchen had a *metate* (a curved stone, in the shape of an inclined plane, resting on three feet) used to grind maize to make corn tortillas. The size of the metate differed, but it usually was about three feet long, three inches thick, and two feet wide. Along with the metate was a *tejolote* (stone pestle) used to pound the *masa* (flour). Chile pepper and other spices were ground using a small *molcajete* (a mortar, either of burnished clay or stone). Women cooked in *casuelas* (pots) of all sizes. A *jarro* (jug) and its *vaso* (glass) were placed on the table. Jarros differed in size from one gallon to five gallons. Water stored remained *fresca* (cool) even on the hottest day. *Garrafones* (huge jugs) stored different types of liquors, especially wine and mescal. A *garrote*, a huge piece of mesquite with one end thicker than the other, was used to tenderize meat. The *zarzo*, a basket hanging from the ceiling, was used to store cheese, tortillas, or any food that "varmints" might like. The zarzo was made of *carrizo* (reed grass); it was twenty inches long, twenty inches wide, and about ten inches high. As far as table utensils, some ranchos had some forks, spoons, and *casuelas de sarro* (clay pottery) for plates. However, when people lacked utensils, which was the case in some jacales, the vaqueros used their tortillas to pick up food.[9]

Jacales provided temporary housing for the jefe while the casa grande was being built. On the other hand, a jacal constituted the permanent home for the vaqueros. The jacales were mostly adobe with dirt floors. They ranged in size from eighteen-to-twenty feet long and extended about nine feet wide. Most were single room structures, although some had a kitchen addition on the rear side. A door made from a piece of hide secured the house. Most jacales were constructed in a palisaded form consisting of a fence of closely spaced vertical pickets anchored into a continuous trench. The fence was placed slightly more than one yard in depth; it served as a base on which adobe plaster was spread on the inner and outer surfaces resulting in a tight and substantial wall. The walls were white-washed. A rough framework of mesquite wood served as the supporting frame for a sheltering grass-covered thatched roof. The jacal had two tree trunks making a "Y" that were used to support the roof. One was placed inside on one of the broad sides of the jacal and the other about three-quarters along the structure.[10]

For furniture, a jacal contained a simple table with two benches; on the bed, a *jorongo* (heavy blanket made of wool) served as bedding. The huge supportive *viga* (beam) served as a shelf. The stove in a jacal was nothing more than a large table with four or six bricks placed on the middle to form a wall and to support a grill of some type. If a jacal had a chimney, it was used as the stove. *Leña* (firewood) was used for fuel. Some jacales, however, did not have a private kitchen. Instead, a separate jacal alone served as a communal kitchen.[11]

Other furnishings found in the jacal included a castaña used to store valuable items and clothing. Some vaqueros made *gabinetes* (cabinets) to store plates or other utensils and food. In jacales without a gabinete, utensils were hung from the roof ceiling. Inside the jacal, a lasso was strung from one end to the other where jerky was left to dry.

Most jacales had a *corredor* (porch-type roof) where the vaqueros rested after work or where women sat during the day to sew, care for the children, or do work that could be done best outside under shade. A cot made of *carrizo* was usually found on one of the sides of the jacal. Vaqueros used it to "descansar en la tarde despues de un día muy largo" (rest in the evening after a long hard day). Pillows were usually homemade. Women took one leg from a trouser, cut it, then sewed one side, filled it with grass and sewed the other end to make a pillow.

Most of the ranchers did not reside permanently on the rancho. Families lived in the villas such as Camargo, Mier, or Reynosa. As a rule, most rancheros visited their rancho during the planting and harvesting or branding periods. They returned home after the work was done. The vaqueros protected their jefe's interest on the ranchos. Some ranchers eventually moved onto the ranchos later in the nineteenth century.[12]

The ranchero de Nuevo Santander wore his beard long with large *patillas* (sideburns). He wore a homemade sombrero, made of *piel*, or palm, with a wide brim and a chin strap, to protect his face from the hot, burning sun and he donned a pair of *chaparreras* (leggings) for protection from the chaparral and thorny thickets. His wardrobe included a tough, durable shirt made of wool in the winter and one made of *manta gruesa* (thick cotton) for the summer. These shirts did not have collars; a lace passed through buttonholes to fasten them. Cuff links were made of *huezo* (bone). During winter, he also wore a *chaqueta de piel* (leather jacket). His trousers were made from *gamusa* (chamois); and his underclothes were made from manta. He wore a good pair of boots.[13]

Riding long miles on a sturdy horse dictated the ranchero's possessions. He carried with him a *bolsa de cuero* (leather bag) filled with water; a cut of beef jerky, and a bit of *pinole* (parched corn, ground and mixed with sugar). A *sarape* across his back, a rifle slung over his shoulder, and a long *machete* or pistol completed his attire. His life as a man of the outdoors required him to be an excellent tracker and sharpshooter as well as a horseman highly skilled in the use of *la reata* (rope).[14]

The above description certainly is true of the ranchero; however, it also depicts the vaquero or *peon* who labored for the jefe. Other characteristics of the South Texas rancher and vaquero included their gentleness, peacefulness, restrained manners, and *machismo*, but with a pride of humble spirit. Even when dressed in rags, they were gentlemen, considerate of others with an unfailing courtesy, and abundant in displays of hospitality.[15]

An important characteristic of the ranchero was the relationship that he had with his workers. A good jefe treated his vaqueros well. He sat with them at the table and saw to it that all were well fed. He realized that his wealth depended on the product of the labor of his vaqueros. El jefe sometimes intervened in a family argument to settle the dispute. If a vaquero ignored his family, the ranchero withheld the man's wages and purchased for the family its food and clothing.[16]

A typical working day for the ranchero and vaquero began at sunrise. The first task was to feed the livestock, pigs, and chickens. Then the cattle were checked and the cows were milked so that the children could have milk with their breakfast. The ranchero then returned to the house where his wife had prepared his breakfast. After eating, he left to do his work in the cotton, corn, beans, or squash field; or work with livestock; or build, mend, or replace a structure on the rancho. He also had the task of going to fetch water in the *arrastra* (cart). He returned to the house at noon, if he were nearby; if not, he took his *bolsa de comida* (bag of food), which usually contained beef jerky and dried corn, with him. He returned for the evening one or two hours before sundown. Sometimes a vaquero was gone from the house for two or three days, especially in a large rancheria. In the meantime, *la ranchera* tended to these daily duties.[17]

Probably no other person experienced more the hardship of life on a South Texas rancho than the ranchera. She lived without many of the comforts of life, few clothes, few shoes and without the tools necessary for her to be at her best. But she managed. The ranchera rose along with her husband at sunrise. Her first task was to start the cooking fire for the day's meals. She made coffee and began to grind the maize for tortillas. After fixing breakfast for her husband and older children, she fed the babies. After feeding all the family, she washed clothes and bathed the little ones. She then went out to check the chickens and pigs. The rest of the morning was spent doing other housework. At noon, she prepared *la comida*; she ground the corn in the metate and killed a chicken for dinner. Tortillas were baked for every meal. After dinner, she continued her housework, mended and ironed clothes, or sewed a new shirt or dress. Later in the afternoon, she tended her vegetable garden as well as her flower bed, which surrounded her home. During the harvest time, the ranchera, in good health or not rearing children, helped in the field.[18]

A woman probably married very young, marriage vows usually being taken around the ages of fourteen to sixteen. Women usually married much older men. To a young girl, marriage promised a better life, although her dreams did not always materialize. Sometimes a girl found life much harder than before. When a husband beat his bride, she returned to her family. Her father then straightened out the dispute with her husband. Often, el jefe was asked to talk to the unhappy husband.

"Los niños no tenian niñez" (children did not have a happy childhood). Work was the rule for the children. They quickly learned the hardship of living in a remote area where work was never finished. By the time a child was five years old, he had been made responsible for some chore that contributed to the continuity of the family. Five-year-old boys collected firewood and milked cows, and girls helped keep house. Six- to nine-year-old boys worked herding small stock, sometimes including cattle. In the field they planted seeds, hoed or picked cotton, and cut large pieces of firewood. Sometimes the children had the task of making sewing thread or cleaning cotton. Boys took the wool to the *arroyo* (stream) for washing. The

young girls took care of the house garden. Older boys, twelve to
sixteen years, provided food by hunting game. Some young
boys frequently ran or rode from one rancho to another with a
message.[19]

In the absence of a mother, the oldest girl automatically took
over the household duties of the family. Children at the rancho
never became orphans. If a child lost his parents, he was
adopted by a family member or any other ranch family, usually
the first to learn of the child's predicament. The child became a
member of the family on equal status with the rest of the children. By age sixteen, a child was considered an adult.[20]

Children and women on the rancho were an important focus
of religious practices. As isolated as a rancho may have
appeared, it never lacked the presence of *Diosito* (the Lord).[21]
People were highly religious. Almost every night there was a
reading of the Bible and prayers of a *rosario, Ave Maria, Credo*
and *Padre Nuestro* (rosary, Hail Mary, the Creed, and an Our
Father). The oldest female of the house led the religious cere-
mony. If a rancho was large enough to have a *capillita* (chapel),
prayer and masses were held there.

A priest visited each rancho about once every one or two
months. The *padrecito* noticed that despite the lack of permanent priests and schools, the Spanish-Mexican ranchero
kept his faith. This was due to his extraordinary devotion to "la
Virgen de Guadalupe," whose image was found in virtually
every home. The respect and love for the priest who showed a
genuine interest was manifested in numerous ways: people
asked for his benediction, kissed his hands upon arrival and
departure, and spoke of him with great affection. Upon the
padre's arrival he was quickly invited to eat. At night, the
priest was offered the best bed in the rancho, no matter who
owned it. People gave him their undivided attention, and his
requests were seldom if ever denied.

Once the priest had been welcomed, he went about admin-
istering the blessings of the Church: attending the sick, baptiz-
ing children, performing marriages, and praying for those who
had died since his last visit. He summoned the children for

catechism classes. He visited every jacal inviting every person to attend mass.

Mass was held in the casa grande or in the largest jacal if there was no capillita. People decorated the house to be used. A table was converted into an altar. It was decorated with all the jewels and *santitos* (statues of saints) that people had in the rancho. Every jacal had several statues of saints and at least one crucifix. During mass, people always prayed for a better life. Everyone, especially women, dressed their best for the mass.

As a rule, people had a pair of clothes. A man had two shirts and trousers; a woman had two dresses. A semi-prosperous ranchero and his family had a *domingal* (Sunday attire) that was worn on special occasions such as attending mass. Everyone had a black dress-outfit worn during mourning which included a pair of stockings, a dress or a shirt and handkerchiefs. Some women went about barefooted. People changed their clothes on the average of every three days. Certainly, great care was taken with one's clothes. Most clothes were homemade by the women. Rancheros who traded with other provinces brought cloth to the rancho to be sewn into dresses or shirts. When the women were not sewing, they usually were cooking.[22]

Ranchos in South Texas hardly lacked food. Most ranchos had an abundance of corn, beans, *papas* (potatoes), various meats, venison, pork, and fish.[23] Rancheros enjoyed vegetables, salads, and fruits for their meals. Various vegetables were found in the ranchos including tomatoes, okra, pumpkin, squashes, onions, garlic, mustard, bell peppers, *chile pasillo*, and beans. For seasoning, people made use of *cilantro, mansanilla*, oregano, anis, *cominos*, and *peregil*. Corn and sugar cane were grown as were melons and watermelons. Mint, used in teas, was a favorite around the rancho. Some of these plants were cultivated year-around. For green salads, a number of native plants were consumed. *Verdolaga*, a heavy-leaved plant, was used as watercress is now used; *quelite*, a wild growing plant, was served as greens. Wild gherkins growing along creek beds were utilized. Cactus plants were cooked in all the ranchos. For dessert, rancheros ate pecans, oranges, figs, mulberries, *guayabas, tamarindos* and quince. *Bastimento* or *tortillas de rez* or *manteca* (corn tortillas made with pork) were also baked in every rancho as a favorite cookie. *Instamal* and *manteca de rez* or *puerco* and *sal* were mixed into a thin cookie shape and baked in an oven.[24]

Meat was always plentiful in the rancherias along the Rio Grande. Rancheros cooked beef, mutton, lamb, pork, and chicken. Game such as *javalina*, quail, turkey, dove, rabbit, deer, and duck were regular treats. During a fiesta, a steer was barbecued. *Cabrito* (kid-goat) was also a favorite meal for the people in the rancho. Jerky was prepared by slicing beef into thin, lean strips that were placed on a rack, or *lasso*, to dry in the sun. Beef supplemented with onions, red peppers, potatoes, corn, cabbage, *cilantro* and other ingredients made a delicious *caldo de rez* (beef stew).

For breakfast, the ranchero usually had tortillas, fried beans, chile, cheese, and *machacado* (eggs mixed with beef jerky) and *café* or *leche* (milk). Sometimes, instead of machacado, the breakfast consisted of *papas con huevos* (fried potatoes with eggs) or *chorizo con huevos* (Mexican sausage with eggs). Meat, either beef or chicken, caldo de rez, *arroz* (rice), beans, cheese, a salad, and café was the menu for dinner. Supper consisted of some variety of meat, served with beans and tortillas plus the day's left-overs.

Cheese was consumed in large quantity in the ranchos. *Queso de cabrito* was a favorite. It was made from the *quajo* (rennet) from goat milk with salt and water added. The clabbered milk was put in a bucket and covered with a cloth and left to harden. Mesquite bark was used to make rings to hold the cheese. *Queso molido* (ground cheese) was used to make *enchiladas.*[25]

Chorizo (spicy sausage) was also a delight of the ranchero, especially with eggs for breakfast. Chorizo was made by cutting *carne de puerco* (pork meat) into small cuts and spread into a large tub. Various spices and chiles were added to the meat cuts. The mixture was then packed into *tripas* (intestines of a cow) that were hung in a lasso to dry. Tiny holes were made into the tripa to allow the remaining water to drip out. Like cheese, chorizo was cooked with just about every meal.[26]

Besides café and milk, lemonade and a variety of teas were made in the rancherias. The elderly drank teas since most had medicinal values. *Piloncillo* (brown cane sugar) was used as sweetener for coffee and teas. It was also consumed as a candy. Women made several candies such as *dulces de calabaza* (pumpkin), *dulces de coco* (coconut), and *dulces de leche quemada* (carmel).[27]

Every rancho in South Texas had an *horno* (an exterior smoothly plastered adobe brick dome oven) used to bake bread. It averaged about four feet high and three feet wide with a diameter of three to four feet. It also had a *plancha* (a five-foot-long stick with a flat spatula ending) used to insert the firewood and bread to be baked. Women constructed the horno and had full control over its use. To prepare it for cooking, firewood was lit and inserted into the horno, and left to heat for about six hours until red hot. The firewood was removed once the desired temperature was reached. Dough prepared for baking was inserted and, depending on the intensity of the heat, the bread took a few minutes to bake. Bread and cookies were especially prepared for a fiesta.[28]

People in the ranchos enjoyed life. They celebrated as much as possible with much gusto; people seemed to be always ready to find an occasion to celebrate. For entertainment at their celebrations, rancheros and vaqueros played several musical instruments including the fiddle and the accordian, and especially the guitar. Songs were sung to one's *novia* (sweetheart) or a favorite relative. People frequently found occasions to dance. Fiestas were celebrated during weddings, during *el día del santo* (day of one's saint) or during a birthday or a baptism. Most fiestas lasted several days with everyone pitching in to keep the party alive. During the fiestas, there were roping contests, horse races, and cock fights. Tequila and mescal were favorite drinks.[29]

For some reason, people in the rancho lived a *vida muy sana* (a very healthy life). There were no doctors in the rancherias, but *curanderos* sufficed. Just about every rancho had a curandero or one lived at the next ranch. The curandero was an herb-healer. Many types of herbs were used for medicinal purposes: *yerba buena* (mint) for heart ailments, *savila* (aloe vera) to reduce swelling, *yerba aniz* to calm nerves, and *cenizo* (sage) to reduce coughing. The curandero was either an old man or an old lady. Usually an elderly woman was called to help in the delivering of babies.[30]

La provincia de Nuevo Santander was Spain's last frontier in Texas. Due to land and climatic conditions, ranching became the main economy rather than farming. The area remained rural and thus very provincial. Rancheros and vaqueros enjoyed a particular life-style tied to the necessities of the rancho. Housing and household goods remained simple. The ranchero, vaquero, ranchera, and children each made a specific contribution to the continuity of the rancho. Though living in South Texas was demanding, people still had time to attend to their spiritual needs. They also found time to celebrate various occasions during which they dressed their best and ate heartily. Early rancho life offered much to the South Texan.

NOTES

The initial research for this paper was made possible by a grant from the National Endowment for the Humanities in 1977, and it was sponsored by the Texas Tech University Museum. During a six-week tour of an area 200 miles south and 150 miles north of the Rio Grande, Mexican and Mexican-American rural life was studied through interviews, photographs, and observations. This article is based mostly on the data collected during this six-week field study.

1. For the best account of the Escandón expedition, see Lawrence F. Hill, *José de Escandón and the Founding of Nuevo Santander, A Study in Spanish Colonization* (Columbus: Ohio State University Press, l926). See also Herbert E. Bolton, *Texas in the Middle Eighteenth Century* (Austin: University of Texas Press, 1970; first edition in 1915), pp. 291-302; Florence J. Scott, *Royal Land Grants North of the Rio Grande, 1777-1821* (Waco: Texian Press, 1969).

2. Mercurio Martínez, "Old Buildings and Historical Sites—Zapata County," Zapata County Historical Survey Committee, Zapata County File, Institute of Texan Cultures, San Antonio, Texas; Willard B. Robinson, "Colonial Ranch Architecture in the Spanish-Mexican Tradition," *Southwestern Historical Quarterly* 83 (October 1979): 125; Florence J. Scott, *Historical Heritage of the Lower Rio Grande: A Historical Record of Spanish Exploration, Subjugation and Colonization of the Lower Rio Grande Valley and the Activities of José Escandón, Count of Sierra Gorda Together with the Development of Towns and Ranches under Spanish, Mexican and Texas Sovereignties, 1747-1848* (Rio Grande City: by author, 1965), p. 99; and *Royal Land Grants*, pp. 8-9.

3. Sandra L. Myres, *The Ranch in Spanish Texas* (El Paso: Texas Western Press, 1969), p. 15; and "The Spanish Cattle Kingdom in the Province of Texas," *Texana* 4 (Fall 1966): 237; Emilia Schunior Ramírez, *Ranch Life in Hidalgo County After 1850* (Edinburg, Texas: New Santander Press, 1971); Bernard Doyon, *The Cavalry of Christ on the Rio Grande, 1849-1883* (Milwaukee: Bruce Press, 1956), p. 127; Robinson, "Colonial Ranch Architecture," pp. 125-30; Bolton, *Texas in the Middle Eighteenth Century*, p. 163.

4. Paul S. Taylor, *An American-Mexican Frontier* (Chapel Hill: University of North Carolina Press, 1934), p. 11; Doyon, *Cavalry of Christ*, pp. 120, 124; David M. Vigness, "Nuevo Santander in 1795: A Provincial Inspection by Félix Calleja," *Southwestern Historical Quarterly* 75 (April 1972): 474-75; Carlos E. Castañeda, *Our Catholic Heritage in Texas* (Austin: Von-Boeckmann-Jones, 1936-1958), pp. 417-420.

5. Eugene George, ed., *Historical Architecture of Texas: The Falcón Reservoir* (Austin: Texas Historical Foundation, 1975), pp. 20-24.

6. Ibid., p. 47; interview with Henry Martínez, 14 June 1977, Laredo, Texas; Robinson, "Colonial Ranch Architecture," pp. 132, 139.

7. George, *Falcón Reservoir*, pp. 51-52.

8. Ibid., p. 44; Ramírez, *Ranch Life*, n.p.; Robinson, "Colonial Ranch Architecture," p. 131.

9. Eliseo Paredes-Manzano, *Homenaje a los Fundadores de la Heroica e Leal Matamoros en la Sesquicentenario de su Nuevo Nombre* (H. Matamoros: Impresos Alfa, S.A., 1976), p. 29; Ramírez, *Ranch Life*, n.p., Robinson, "Colonial Ranch Architecture," pp. 139-40.

10. Paredes, *Matamoros*, p. 28; Ramírez, *Ranch Life*, n.p.; Robinson, "Colonial Ranch Architecture," p. 130.

11. Ramírez, *Ranch Life*, n.p.

12. Scott, *Historical Heritage*, pp. 101-102.

13. Paredes, *Matamoros*, pp. 22-24.

14. Ibid., pp. 22-25.

15. Ibid.; Oran R. Scott, "History of Hidalgo County, 1749-1852" (M.A. thesis, Texas Christian University, 1934), p. 6.

16. Interview with María Cardenas, 7 July 1977, at Brownsville, Texas.

17. *Background Information for the Planning Lesson for a Unit on Mexican Origins of the Cattle and Ranching Industries*, Spanish Ranch File, Institute of Texan Cultures, San Antonio, TX; Paredes, *Matamoros*, pp. 22-24; Ramírez, *Ranch Life*, n.p.

18. Paredes, *Matamoros*, pp. 26-33; Ramírez, *Ranch Life*, n.p.

19. Ramírez, *Ranch Life*, n.p.

20. Virgil N. Lott and Mercurio Martínez, *The Kingdom of Zapata* (San Antonio: Naylor Company, 1953), p. 25.

21. Doyon's *Cavalry of Christ* has an excellent account on religion in South Texas.

22. Ramírez, *Ranch Life*, n.p.; Paredes, *Matamoros,* pp. 28-29.

23. Elena Zamore O'Shea, *El Mesquite* (Dallas: Mathis Publishing Co., 1935), p. 2; Lott and Martínez, *Zapata*, p. 102; George, *Falcón Reservoir*, p. 24; Doyon, *Cavalry of Christ*, p. 123; Paredes, *Matamoros*, p. 31; Ramirez, *Ranch Life*, n.p.; Maude T. Gilliland, *Rincón: A Story of Life in a South Texas Ranch at the Turn of the Century* (Brownsville, Texas: Springman-King, Co., 1964), p. 6.

24. Interview with María Cardenas.

25. Ibid.

26. Ibid.

27. Ibid.

28. Ramírez, *Ranch Life*, n.p.

29. Ibid.; Paredes, *Matamoros*, p. 43.

30. Ramírez, *Ranch Life*, n.p.

Critters, Sourdough, and Dugouts: Women and Imitation Theory on the Staked Plains, 1875-1910

Historians Walter Prescott Webb and Robert F. Berkhofer, Jr., have sought to explain the impact of moving to frontier areas on the people themselves. Each has noted that all settlers faced basic challenges to the way of life they had known, and that frontier men and women responded to these challenges. How they responded and why they chose a particular response has not been the subject of historiographical agreement.

An environmental explanation, the adaptation theory, views space, rather than culture, as the dominant factor in frontier institutional change. Webb wrote that when settlers reached the ninety-eighth meridian, they encountered the Great Plains, "an environment with which they had no experience." There, civilization halted for a generation until it developed technology sufficient to deal with the problems that this level, treeless, and semi-arid region presented. "Practically every institution that was carried across it," he believed, "was either broken and remade or else greatly altered."[1] He specifically mentioned methods of travel, weapons, farming techniques, and laws. To Webb, these institutions—including women's special sphere, the home—required a major adjustment or adaptation to the new environment, an adjustment most influenced by that environment.

In contrast, Berkhofer has posited an imitation theory that reverses Webb's order of determinants for institutional change by assigning culture the main role, and space or environment a secondary one. To explain institutional change in a frontier regional framework, Berkhofer wrote, "the prevailing cultural system is . . . far more fundamental than physical environment."[2] People who moved West, including the men and women settlers of Walter Prescott Webb's Great Plains, relied mainly on their cultural heritage that they brought from the East. According to Berkhofer, this accumulated knowledge, traditional ways of doing things, and material culture handed down by ancestors were crucial to survival.

Both of these theories concerning cultural adjustment to frontier conditions require the assessment of how pioneer agricultural women experienced the initial settlement of frontier areas. Whether frontier women adapted or imitated in order to survive is the inquiry of this research, and a case study of one particular region, the Staked Plains, and its first female settlers has been chosen as the vehicle for examining which of these theories offers a more plausible explanation for frontier institutional acceptance.

The Staked Plains was possibly the one region that best fit Webb's classic description of the Great Plains. Labeled by many the "Great American Desert," it is centered in northwest Texas—a vast tabletop that is level, treeless and semi-arid.[3] The first wave of non-Native American settlers moved onto the Staked Plains, or Llano Estacado, in the 1870s after the surrender of the Comanche and Kiowa to the United States Army. Coming first in rivulets and later, as land companies heavily promoted the region, in torrents, these newcomers, mostly cattlemen, encountered a desolate, forbidden region of vast grasslands, conspicuous mainly because until then all but the native American had avoided it. With these first settlers were, of course, the women—wives, would-be wives, daughters, and future farmers, ranchers, and merchants.

The problems facing pioneer women on the Staked Plains, a region barren of human-made features, were apparent from the outset. Mary Blankenship recalled that upon arriving there at the turn of the century from the Southeast and encountering the caprock, that conspicuous wall defining its eastern edge, she was scared. Moving up the escarpment's narrow, rock-laden, seldom-used wagon road that cold, January morning, her wagon fought a strong head wind that filled its tarpaulin to bursting capacity. Worse yet, on those occasions when the trail turned and the wagon faced the wind broadside, it would skid toward the canyon, causing her to clutch her baby even tighter and say a little prayer. As she neared the top, the wind blew debris into the mules' faces, making them balk.[4]

Safely atop the caprock, however, she paused for her first impression of the great expanse, some 20,000 square miles. It was, she decided, bleak, "stretching for miles and miles ahead . . . into a vast table land, bald and as big as all-outdoors." Its stirrup-high grass, so typical of the region, was "like an endless wheat field ready for harvest."[5]

When her party halted that night for camp and searched for fire wood, she received her next surprise: only mesquite trees, a waist-high shrub-like growth, were available. And though they made an excellent fire, their boughs contained so little wood it was necessary to dig deep in order to extract their roots, a difficult task at best. Blankenship's initiation to the Staked Plains was a rather rude awakening. Hardly had she passed inside its edge and already she had been exposed to three of the recurring problems plaguing women there: abundance of wind, and dust, and lack of fuel.[6]

But she was not alone. Others also saw the region as something less than ideal. "As long as I live, I'll never see such a lonesome looking country," lamented Mollie Luttrell in 1889. "Why, you could see for miles and still not see a thing."[7] The youthful, self-conscious Opal Berryman, a preacher's daughter, was more adversely affected, angrily announcing that

All the bitter dislike that had assailed me the day we ascended the caprock and caught our first staggering view of this great sweep of borderless land, came back to me now. Six months we had been on the

Llano Estacado and the country was no different. Not a tree worthy of the name graced the knotty fabric of the ground. Never a brook or pool of clear blue water, or a shady spot where grass grew green and soft. Every indigenous plant of any size bore spines and thorns. In order to exist, small animals must take refuge underground. A child dare not wander more than a few yards from home lest he become hopelessly lost. To drop exhausted made one a living sacrifice to the fierce red ants, whose gravelly mounds were never more than a few yards apart. In this harsh land what chance did an ugly, awkward child have ever to be anything but ugly and awkward?[8]

But for those women who saw the region in negative, physical terms, an enemy of sorts, there were others who did not. Mrs. T. W. Tomlinson, a Southerner with an eye for pristine charm, recalled philosophically that she could hardly describe her "first impressions of that beautiful, vast, lonely country. One could fill such a small part of the vacant space around us."[9] Acknowledging that the region contained puzzling and strange features "delightful in their novelty," Mrs. Warren W. Welsell, a Northerner and wife of a rancher, was favorably impressed, too.[10] Edith Duncan Pitts did not think she could "remember anything more beautiful than [her] first sight of the plains." Arriving there in spring "when nature was at its best," she found the grass green and the flowers in bloom, and it seemed to her "an ideal place in which to build a home."[11]

The comments of these women—the first group who saw the Staked Plains as unpleasant, even hostile and the second, pleasant, even beautiful—suggest the subtle impact that their cultural heritage had upon them, how it determined, to some extent their reactions. Consider the diverse impressions of Blankenship and Pitts. Negatively impressed, the former was the serious-minded wife of a farmer; positively disposed, the latter was a buoyant spirit married to a rancher. Of course, the fact that they arrived at different times, the first in winter, the second in summer, was a factor bearing on their outlook, yet despite this, their cultural heritage—especially their dispositions—colored their viewpoints. Blankenship was geared to see the unpleasant, it seems. Had she arrived in spring, it is unlikely she would have seen things much better. Too little there was familiar.[12] Pitts, on the other hand, would have found something to be enthusiastic about even if she arrived in winter. Her interview shows her to be an eternal optimist.[13] Regardless, both women were most influenced, the evidence indicates, by the cultural heritage that they brought to the Staked Plains from the East.

Loneliness, ample evidence indicates, was their main problem, the hardest thing to bear. Una Brooks, who studied these women settlers, wrote that many became desperately homesick, some returning home.[14] Blankenship echoed this claim and recalled that at times she wondered if she and her family "were the only people inhabiting the earth."[15] For others, the Staked Plains environment took on an even more ominous aspect. One woman dreaded moonlit nights falsely fearing that Indians might steal her horses. The last bands of Comanche and Kiowa had been forced on reservations some fifteen years earlier, but loneliness made it difficult for her to be totally rational. This mentality is not difficult to understand because fear and loneliness were boon companions. To illustrate, the eerie cries of packs of lobo wolves made another woman's "hair stand on end," her "blood turn cold," and quickly ran her indoors.[16]

Nevertheless, just as there was not total agreement among these women in their initial impressions of the region, not all women considered loneliness a serious problem. Writers in the 1930s for the Works Progress Administration heard from a typical sampling of these women a common theme: they were "never lonesome."[17] The WPA's claim seems questionable in its applicability to the Staked Plains. However, one woman apparently did thrive in this setting, exclaiming that "You can't imagine the quiet, serene happiness that we (she and her husband) experienced those four years. There was a peace that is lacking in modern civilization."[18]

The evidence further indicates that those few who reacted to loneliness in this way were emotionally tough and highly motivated. They wanted to see their husbands and themselves succeed. Still, there were other reasons for this unusual attitude. One woman who lived along one of the several trails that traversed the region saw people regularly so was not lonely. Closer to the main reason for claiming not to be lonely, however, is the fact that over the years the mind has a tendency to filter out the unpleasant. Pitts understood this when she said, "life is so beautiful after all: for memory gathers only the bright spots from our lives."[19] Women who said in their memoirs that the Staked Plains was a lonely region would be, in effect, condemning themselves. One must remember that it was there they had raised a family, shared hardships with friends, and become successful, and one does not easily give up the positive aspects of such experiences just because of an initial period of difficulty.

For most women, loneliness was a serious problem. Its best solution, they believed, was Anglo-American companionship— ideally one's family, a few close friends, and at least one adult female. Without feminine conversation, women felt unfulfilled. But in the absence of these people, the cheerful Pitts, unhappily sealed in her winter "tomb of loneliness," was glad to see even the infrequent Indian who came through, even the occasional Mexican who "rode so silently," neither of whom was particularly popular among other Staked Plains settlers.[20] To lift her loneliness, one woman actually sought the company of cattle. She would go to their watering places and talk to them about themselves, discussing various matters of mutual concern. Their contentment served as a balm for her nerves.[21] Mary Ann Goodnight, wife of the Panhandle cattle baron, had a similar experience. One day a cowboy rode into camp with three chickens in a sack. "No one can ever know what a pleasure they were to me, and how much company they were to me," she recalled. "They would come when I called them and they would follow me wherever I went and I could talk to them."[22]

Still, animals could not completely replace people. A common solution was to climb atop the windmill tower to see who might be in the area. One woman near Lubbock did, hoping against hope to see someone—anyone. Even if a person was moving away from her, she felt better.[23] But only human companionship could bring lasting relief. In the absence of family, those occasional visits by neighbors to check on her and her child were welcome.

Further exacerbating women's loneliness was the absence of trees. Nurtured among them back East, these female settlers sorely missed them on the Staked Plains and at the first opportunity planted some. Trees held birds whose songs broke the stillness, softened the sun's harsh glare. One woman planted eighteen acres of assorted fruit trees.

Mrs. J. B. Pottinger from Tennessee "became desperately homesick, especially for the trees—she missed them so." Late one winter a tree salesman passed through, taking ill at her homestead. She nursed him back to health and saved his saplings by temporarily planting them. In appreciation, he gave them to her because it was too late to deliver them. Later that year when a good harvest was in, her husband suggested that they return to their native Southeast on vacation. Mrs. Pottinger, who had earlier begged him to return, then protested, "Why, I can't go, I've got my trees to take care of."[24] And she stayed. Her efforts and those of many like her to recreate a bit of their familiar Eastern woodlands well demonstrate Berkhofer's imitation theory in action.

Wind and its principal byproduct—the sandstorm—were women's second most serious concern on the Staked Plains. Webb wrote that the "level surface and the absence of trees give the air currents free play. On the whole, the wind blows harder and more constantly on the Plains (of which this area is a part) than it does in any other portion of the United States, save on the seashore."[25] But for a further appreciation of the difficulties these twin torments could inflict on women, the words of Letty Mason, Dorothy Scarborough's tragic figure in her novel *The Wind*, are instructive. These malefactors were

hard on the women. Folks say the West is good enough for a man or a dog, but no place for a woman or a cat.

The wind is the worst thing. . . . It's ruination to a woman's looks and nerves pretty often. It dries up her skin till it gets brown and tough as leather. It near bout puts her eyes out with the sand it blows in em all day. It gets on her nerves with its constant blowing—makes her irritable and jumpy.[26]

In the end, they destroyed Letty, but her case was both fiction and extreme. There is no known instance of the wind and sandstorms causing a woman's death in the region.

Yet the hot, dry, southwest wind and horrendous sandstorms did bother pioneer women, particularly during the spring months. Brooks believed that they possibly accounted "for the nervous, high-strung, 'figety,' ever-active individuals found among women on the Plains today."[27] Though suspect, this claim's validity is not important. Wind and sandstorms like other environmental features disturbed these women, but in a less dramatic way than they had disturbed Dorothy Letty. Mrs. Lou Stubbs of Lubbock remembered that her doctor told her that the day after a sandstorm "certain women were just a nervous wreck," would walk the floor, even cry.[28] In one case, the woman had to be given a sedative. Interestingly, Stubbs also played the devil's advocate, claiming that if a woman remained indoors during a sandstorm, she would not suffer. Of course, most women did stay inside, but there can be little doubt that they experienced some anxiety, if not genuine fear. In Stubbs' own case, she believed that she had developed an immunity to dust.[29]

Regardless, wind and sandstorms presented very real, if not life-threatening, problems. Inside, women covered tables with sheets to keep out the dust, only removing them for meals that still had a continual taste of gritty sand. The sand settled in a thin layer on everything. One woman even complained that sandstorms generated "illusions," or static electricity, which shocked her when she lit her stove.[30]

But if the wind and sandstorms were troublesome inside, they were often violent outside. Anything not securely anchored was likely to be blown over—tents, outhouses, stock sheds, even windmill towers. Once a feather mattress, miles away from the nearest house, was found tumbling across the plains; another time a newly arrived woman left her household goods outside the first night, only to find them the following morning blown from the yard a mile away into a draw. Small animals fared no better. Should they be outside, the ever-present hen flock would be almost turned inside out, or blown away, their wings acting like sails. In any case, the nature of this problem does not lend itself to a discussion of theory. Then, as now, women and men could only ride out wind and sand-storms.

More compliant, however, was another of Staked Plains women's difficulties: obtaining and preserving essential sup-plies, namely, food and water. Much of the root of this problem lay in isolation; initially, there were few towns, and those there were lay off the Staked Plains. A trip to even the nearest early settlement, Colorado City, was a major event in women's lives. It taxed the mettle of the hardiest pioneer. Tomlinson recalled that, whether she went or stayed, she looked on trips with dread because they were a "real hardship."[31] Blanken-ship, who lived near present-day Lubbock, estimated that a round trip to Colorado City took eight to fourteen days.[32] But until the early 1880s, the next nearest towns were Wichita Falls, Texas, and Dodge City, Kansas, farther yet.

Women acquired supplies with typical pioneer ingenuity. In-itially they brought to their farm or ranch a year's supplies, namely, such staples as flour, sugar, and coffee. When these were exhausted, they made resupply trips, once or twice a year, as necessary, with the distance to market for many people being shortened by the intrusion of railroads into the region. The Texas and Pacific Railroad traversed the southern edge of the Staked Plains in the early 1880s, the towns of Big Spring, Stanton, and Midland developing in its wake. The Fort Worth and Denver line crossed the region to the North, along the Red River in the late 1880s, resulting in the hamlet of Amarillo. Although railroads shortened the distance to market, women still had to wait until the next resupply trip.

Preserving food was another aspect of the supply problem. Because refrigeration was not yet functional on the West

Texas agricultural frontier, women had to use other means. Meat was kept fresh several ways. One method was for four families to join in a cooperative effort whereby each, in turn, slaughtered a steer, cut it in four pieces, and gave each family a quarter. In this way fresh meat was provided for a week. Another method, used by women whose families were more isolated, was to cut beef into smaller sizes, cover each of them with cheese cloth, sprinkle them with black and cayenne pepper to keep flies off, and suspend them from the windmill tower, high enough to protect them from wolves. The jerking process, of course, had been used on earlier frontiers. A last method, one possibly involving more originality than the other two, was to place successive steaks in a huge crock, each interspersed between layers of buttermilk. Grace Warwick recalled that "meat put up in this way would last all summer" and when finally used, be as tender as chicken.[33] It was possible to preserve vegetables, too. Crocks of sauerkraut with beets and onions were placed inside a box, then buried in the ground. Excess butter could be kept all summer by placing it in barrels of brine, and when cold weather returned, by working it repeatedly until the salt was eliminated.[34]

Each homestead kept a small flock of chickens to provide eggs and meat. Chicken meat was convenient in size and required no preservation. May Cobea said that the "chicken should be immortalized in bronze."[35] And there was the ever-present jar of sourdough, which contained a small portion of fermented dough used to leaven the next day's bread. But, again, sourdough signaled nothing new, long having been in use.

Obtaining sufficient water was another related aspect to collecting the essentials. A woman's main concern was to have enough for cooking, bathing, washing, and drinking. As institutional as the sourdough jar became inside the dwelling was the row of wooden barrels for hauling and storing water on the outside. Luttrell told of helping bring a wagonload one winter, and due to the trail's roughness and the barrels having no tops, being thoroughly splashed and nearly frozen.[36] Water acquired under such trying circumstances was dear. One suspects that the Saturday night ritual of bathing in a zinc tub normally used for washing clothes may have been more honored in the breach than in the observance. But there is irony to the scarcity of water, for beneath much of the region lay an abundant supply of table water, a vast, cheap reservoir of precious liquid known as the Ogallala aquifer. Not until the late 1880s, when windmills became a somewhat familiar sight, would this source begin to be tapped. Another dimension of the water problem was how to make a harsh, impurity-laden water agreeable to the taste. Women solved this problem by simply adding lemons brought from railroad towns. Cobea claimed that the water was rough on a person, but a dash of lemon made it fit to drink.[37]

The task of providing their families with adequate housing was nearly as important as maintaining an adequate water supply. Living quarters were always at a premium on the Staked Plains, most families progressing through a series of construction phases. First, women lived in temporary structures: a wagon shell set on the ground, possibly a tent. As soon as circumstances permitted, however, they had more permanent structures built. Their first, stable living quarters likely consisted of a half or full dugout. The final step in this progression was the wooden frame house.

Regardless of what stage in this progression women found themselves, each structure presented challenges. The difficulties inherent in a wagon shell or a tent were obvious. The dugout, a crude, twelve-by-twelve structure, was made of native materials: stones from the breaks for those fortunate to live along a stream, and a roof supported by a single center pole and topped with beargrass "shingles" and sod. When it rained, fortunately an infrequent occurrence, the dugout leaked. One woman claimed, however, that beargrass, or "yucca," turned water, preventing leaks.[38] A locally made gypsum paste used to whitewash the walls and floor gave a fine finish and kept out vermin. Through pioneer ingenuity, as well as trial and error, Cobea learned that gypsum paste, which normally crumbled and melted during damp periods, could be heated while in powder form and, when applied as paste, would be as hard as cement and impervious to water.[39] Using gypsum as a plaster is another instance of technological innovation.

The lack of space inside the dugout denied women their essential privacy. This problem was moderated by suspending sheets from the ceiling, thus partitioning off an area for themselves. Another solution for cramped space was to use the trundle bed, a "sawed-off" sleeping convenience that was rolled under an ordinary bed when not in use. Several other pieces of crude but functional furniture graced the rooms, with boxing crates supplementing regular chairs.

But these difficulties paled in comparison to that of having to share the dugout with animal life. Being below ground level, it served as a magnet for assorted "critters". Snakes were the worst. Babe in arms, Pitts was horrified to find a large rattler coiled on the floor of her dugout.[40] A Gaines County woman killed 186 in one year.[41] Besides snakes, other creatures visited: mice, water dogs, lizards, scorpions, terrapins, bedbugs, fleas, and insects of every description.

There were creatures of more imposing caliber. Pitts, her husband, and several friends were sharing a special meal when a steer walked across her dugout roof and, unannounced, dropped in—one leg dangling through the ceiling—and unloaded so much dirt that shovels were needed to throw it out.[42] Clearly the dugout was an inferior dwelling. As soon as possible, women moved into a presumably better shelter, the wooden frame house.

Built of precious lumber shipped in from a railroad town, this twelve-by-twenty-four foot structure was little more than a shack. It did offer, however, an improvement because, raised some inches off the ground, it denied entrance to low-level intruders. Otherwise, it was little better than the dugout, leaking water when it rained and admitting sand through its many cracks during sandstorms. After the "awfullist storm," Luttrell cried because her "palace" leaked.[43]

As primitive as the dugout and wooden frame house were by modern standards, they were important to women on the

Staked Plains. Moreover, in a region with few hotels, they served as "traveller's inns" for people passing through. Blankenship lodged many a stranger for a night and sent him on his way in the morning with a shoe box of fried chicken and tea cakes.[44] Even if the settlers were out, one was expected to go inside, use what was needed, and be on the way. No note of explanation was expected; the only restriction was to clean up any mess. This practice underscores the fact that in a frontier agricultural region of small population, cooperation by all was necessary for survival.

Handling emergencies due to illness and injury was another domain requiring the action of women. Again isolation was the culprit. Customarily, distaff settlers prepared for their venture West by learning first aid and simple remedies from their doctor while still in the East. They read the standard "how-to-do-it" text of the day, *The Doctor's Book*. It, along with the *Bible*, was often the only reading matter in Staked Plains homes. Women also took such patent medicines as existed: Pinckney's bitters, Doan's liver and kidney pills, as well as Hood's sarsaparilla. Of course, home remedies filled out the medicine cabinet.

Babies were likely to be born without benefit of doctors, for seldom could they reach an expectant mother in time. Distances were great, trails dim, making finding the woman in time difficult. Doctors found their way across the uncharted Plains largely devoid of familiar landmarks by following directions given them, by accompanying messengers, and by the light of stars and moon at night. But by the time the doctor arrived, the mother likely had delivered her child. Sometimes there was a midwife in attendance, but women often did without help. One "delicate, frail-looking woman delivered all three of hers, sat up in bed and washed them as best as she could."[45] Another woman whose child had been borne sickly with the nearest doctor fifty miles away, said that her "life was just a terror."[46]

In fact, these women always felt some concern for themselves and their children because if an illness did not respond to their limited arsenal of remedies and medicines, if an injury was serious enough, someone must make a life-or-death dash for a doctor. To aid this messenger, a relay system was devised whereby each homestead kept an extra horse in the pasture so that the runner could exchange the jaded mount for a fresh one as often as necessary until medical aid was reached. On the way back the messenger reversed the procedure, ending up with the original horse. Based on cooperation and common sense, this relay system is yet another example of Berkhofer's theory of imitation in action. More than 2,000 years earlier, Romans used such a system to whittle down distance to manageable size; later in the American experience, the Pony Express mail delivery system copied it.

Fighting range fires also presented women with a clear threat to life and limb. Waist-high, burning grass, swept along by high winds, were, according to Cobea, the "greatest dread of pioneer women."[47] A range fire could call for quick action, such as when an alert mother climbed atop a windmill tower with her baby, in time to escape the fire's menacing flames. Another resourceful mother set a firebreak in time to clear an area large enough to save her brood.[48]

More often, however, the danger was not so immediate. If this were the case, women would assume their usual role, that of providing food and water for the men on the fire line. On occasion, women would more directly fight fires, such as the instance near Midland when several joined their men, commandeered all the local store's brooms, and, using these "housewifely tools," put a particularly dangerous one out. No floors were swept in that locale for some time until slow freight brought in replacements.[49]

Fires exacerbated the constant shortage of fuel for heating, washing, and cooking. Few trees grew in short-grass country; those that did were too precious to burn. Consequently, alternatives had to be found, until late in the century when railroads would bring in coal. Almost anything that would burn was tried: mesquite roots and shinnery, a dwarf oak found along sandy stretches to the south, were used when possible. Barring their presence, corn cobs—even bones—were used.

For women, however, the mainstay of the 1880s was the lowly cow chip. Euphemistically called "surface coal" and "grassoline" and classified according to color and size, dried cow chips provided a cheap, abundant, and fairly efficient fuel. But chips were controversial, and women engaged in considerable debate as to their relative merits and their proper use. Bothered by their odor, some women would use them only for washing and heating; others, less squeamish, burned them for cooking as well. The task of gathering them was the sphere of women and children. As one might imagine, they approached this onerous chore with varying degrees of reservation. Feisty young Opal Berryman labeled such work as "not ladylike," an indignity.[50] Conversely, Blankenship—though she initially tip-toed around them—learned to appreciate them, observing philosophically that just as the windmill pumped her water, the cow cut her wood.[51] One particularly daring soul, faced with oncoming winter and a chip-shed already full, stowed the excess beneath her bed. Cow chips remained an important fuel, for even after the railroad brought in coal, many could not afford to buy it; and for those who could afford coal, chips were a good substitute during coal shortages.

In conclusion, the solutions that pioneer women on the Staked Plains applied to their problems support Berkhofer's theory of imitation better than they do Webb's theory of adaptation. Memoirs indicate that when confronted with the problem of loneliness endemic to this vast, treeless, sparsely populated region, they drew upon the familiar, the cultural baggage they had brought with them, by planting the trees that were so much a part of their past. Jerking meat and sourdough to preserve food, running zig-zag relays with frequent changes of horses to handle medical emergencies, and sleeping in trundle beds to conserve room inside living quarters—these solutions further demonstrate imitation. All these were imitative because they were techniques that had been time tested. Of course, some solutions showed more pioneer ingenuity than others: the use of local materials in lieu of those normally available—gypsum and beargrass for waterproofing dugouts and cow chips for replacing scarce firewood, for example. But none of these were a major change or adaptation attributable mainly to environment; women brought their pioneer ingenuity with them, too. These women's reliance on prior solutions is understandable. Survival on a harsh agricultural frontier did not allow for long-term experimentation. Fear and loneliness, shortages and disease—all could cause emotions and subsequent actions that limited inventiveness to no more than that which was absolutely necessary. People everywhere and throughout time are like that.

NOTES

1. Walter Prescott Webb, *The Great Plains* (New York: Grossett & Dunlap, 1931), p. 8.

2. Robert F. Berkhofer, Jr., "Space, Time, and Culture, and the American Frontier," *Agricultural History* 38 (January, 1964): 24.

3. Webb, *Great Plains*, pp. 8-9, 205-6.

4. Mary A. Blankenship, *The West Is for Us*, ed. Seymour V. Connor (Lubbock: West Texas Museum Association, 1958), p. 25.

5. Ibid., p. 27.

6. Ibid.

7. Interview with Mollie Luttrell, Oral History File, Panhandle-Plains Historical Museum Archives, Canyon, Texas (hereinafter cited as PPHA).

8. Opal Leigh Berryman, *Pioneer Preacher* (New York: Thomas Y. Crowell Co., 1948), p. 83.

9. Interview with Mrs. T. W. Tomlinson, July 4, 1922. Oral History File, PPHA.

10. Interviews with Mrs. Warren W. Welsell, June 22, 30, and July 1, 5, 1936. Oral History File, PPHA.

11. Interview with Edith Duncan Pitts, n.d., Oral History File, PPHA.

12. Blankenship, *West Is for Us*.

13. Interview with Pitts, PPHA.

14. Una M. Brooks, "The Influence of the Pioneer Women toward a Settled Social Life on the Llano Estacado" (M.A. thesis, West Texas State Teachers College, Canyon, Texas, August 1942), p. 38.

15. Blankenship, *West Is for Us*, p. 70.

16. Interview with Tomlinson, PPHA.

17. Interview with C. May Cobea, n.d., Oral History File, PPHA.

18. Mary L. Cox, *History of Hale County, Texas* (Plainview, TX: n.p., 1937), p. 217.

19. Interview with Pitts, PPHA.

20. Ibid.

21. Temple Ann Ellis, *Texas Plains Pioneers* (Southwest Collection, Texas Tech University, Lubbock: Microfilm E47), unnumbered page.

22. Mrs. Clyde W. Warwick, *The Randall County Story: from 1541 to 1910* (Hereford, Texas: Pioneer Book Publishers, Inc., 1969), p. 97.

23. Blankenship, *West Is for Us*, p. 44.

24. Interview with Herbert and Carolyn Timmons, Amarillo, Texas, April 1942, cited in Brooks, "Influence of Women on Llano Estacado," p. 39.

25. Webb, *Great Plains*, p. 21.

26. Dorothy Scarborough. *The Wind* (Austin: University of Texas Press, 1925), pp. 20-21.

27. Brooks, "Influence of Women on Llano Estacado," p. 46.

28. Interview with Lou Stubbs, August 27, 1957, Oral History File, Southwest Collection, Texas Tech University, Lubbock, Texas.

29. Ibid.

30. Ellis, *Texas Plains Pioneers*.

31. Interview with Tomlinson, PPHA.

32. Blankenship, *West Is for Us*, pp. 39-40.

33. Warwick, *Randall County Story*, pp. 98-99.

34. Historical Survey Committee, *The Gaines County Story* (Seagraves, Texas: Pioneer Book Publishers, Inc., 1974), pp. 270-71.

35. Interview with Cobea, PPHA.

36. Interview with Luttrell, PPHA.

37. Interview with Cobea, PPHA.

38. Warwick, *Randall County Story*. p. 98, and Interview with Mrs. Hext, Canadian, Texas, May 5, 1932. Oral History File, PPHA.

39. Interview with Cobea, PPHA.

40. Interview with Pitts, PPHA.

41. Historical Survey Committee, *Gaines County Story*, p. 277.

42. Interview with Pitts, PPHA.

43. Ibid.

44. Blankenship, *West Is for Us*, p. 74.

45. Warwick, *Randall County Story*, p. 99.

46. Interview with Sophia Connell, June 1938. Oral History File, PPHA.

47. Interview with Cobea, PPHA.

48. Interview with Herbert and Carolyn Timmons, PPHA.
49. Ibid.
50. Berryman, *Pioneer Preacher*, p. 9.
51. Blankenship, *West Is for Us*, pp. 37-38.

II

AGRICULTURAL ACCULTURATION

Somebody had to lurch out on the front to open the way for others. You must remember that we was deprived of many conveniences and privileges that others had in eastern country. . . . No one knows the hardships the first settlers went through to make the country what it is, but I don't regret in the least. If my time were not so near spent, I would like to press on out to the front again. I like to live in the West.

Mellissa Martin Everett,
Garden City, Texas, 1923

Coming to terms with a new life oftentimes requires sacrifices of the most fundamental nature. They go to the core of a culture. Forces emerge that shape and reshape the way things are done and the way one thinks about the world. Such was certainly true for agriculturalists, and the persons most likely to be immediately confronted with cultural stress were the women.

Of course, Native American women were not to be left alone to decide on their own cultural options. As Rebecca J. Herring writes, the United States government sought to acculturate Indian women into farm wives with the use of the field matron. Federal officials believed imitation of the tried traditions of the Anglo agricultural past was desirable for the Comanche and Kiowa non-agriculturists who knew it was not always the best avenue toward survival on the Great Plains.

Other women on the farming frontiers seemed more willing to embrace the strong currents of past cultural practices. Everyday living for women on the southern Plains frontier provoked attempts to recreate the traditional sphere of Anglo women. According to Jacqueline S. Reinier, women on one of the last agricultural frontiers turned to the known aspects of domesticity for solace. Environment did not enhance or stimulate change from the previous sex roles of its inhabitants.

Native American and Anglo women were forced or chose to adjust to the agricultural frontier with significant dosages of the familiar.

REBECCA J. HERRING

The Creation of Indian Farm Women: Field Matrons and Acculturation on the Kiowa-Comanche Reservation, 1895–1906

"No uncivilized people are elevated till the mothers are reached. The civilization must begin in the homes."[1] With these words penned in 1889, Merial A. Dorchester, Special Agent in the Indian School Service, recommended that "provision be made by congress for the appointment of 'field matrons' whose business it shall be to visit the Indian families and teach the mothers to cook, to make and mend garments, to elevate the homes, and thus make helpful dwelling places."[2] Her suggestion was accepted, for within two years the United States House of Representatives appropriated funds for the new Indian Service position of Field Matron.[3] By 1895, Field Matron Lauretta Ballew was at work on the Kiowa-Comanche Indian Reservation in southwestern Oklahoma Territory helping to create Indian farm women.[4]

What motivated the United States government to initiate this policy of female Indian adult education during the last decade of the nineteenth century? What type of Anglo women would agree to live alone among an unfamiliar, and often feared, people? How did these women perceive the Indians among whom they went to work? What were their duties, and were they carried out? And finally, did this educational work bring the desired results? As is true of most historical questions, these have no simple answers. In the following exploration of the creation, goals, implementation, and results of the Field Matron program, emphasis will be placed on the Kiowa-Comanche Reservation and the women who served there between 1895, when the first Field Matrons were appointed, and 1906, when the final distribution of commonly held reservation lands occurred.

It was obvious to observers of late nineteenth-century America that marked differences existed between the dominant Anglo culture and minority Native American cultures. Rather than acknowledge those differences as acceptable and of equal value in a nation fashioned from diverse cultural backgrounds, Americans tended to view Indian life as deficient.[5] Anglo society, on the other hand, was considered to be superior, having reached a higher stage of development in cultural evolution.[6] This supposed inequity in levels of civilization served as moral justification for the widespread conviction that "Native Americans must be reformed according to White criteria and their labor, lands, and souls put to 'higher uses' in line with White goals."[7] Certain that Native and White peoples could never live in harmony if each group retained its cultural identity, and led by feelings of social responsibility toward a seemingly inferior race,[8] those in control of Indian affairs concluded that "the only practical and humane answer to the Indian problem was to assimilate the Indians into Anglo-American culture."[9]

Nineteenth-century America was a Christian, agrarian nation, prospering on principles of universal education and private ownership of land. Consequently, it was obvious to Indian Service policymakers that the most direct manner of assimilating the Indians into American society was to transform them into educated, Christian, landowning farmers. Once thus "civilized," Indians would become American citizens, eligible for full participation in the governing of the nation.[10] Within one or two generations, these people would shed tribal identities and be absorbed into mainstream agricultural America.[11]

Intent upon this civilizing mission, the U. S. government agreed to provide funds for teachers, farmers, blacksmiths, carpenters, physicians, millers, and engineers in most treaties written in the last half of the nineteenth century.[12] Academic education, as well as religious training, was often contracted to mission societies or denominational organizations. These groups were to provide training in agricultural, mechanical and domestic arts, as well as rudimentary educational skills and religious instruction. They were also required to furnish board, clothing, medicine, medical care, and school supplies. The government would supply land, school buildings, and a small stipend per annum per student. In addition, the government sometimes issued annuities of domestic animals, tools, and food directly to the schools.[13] Missionaries were the logical choice for the work of Indian acculturation because most people involved in Indian work believed "that nothing but Christianity could elevate the Indians; that there was no hope for them in education or civilization, except as these were employed as instruments of the Gospel."[14] Christianity, therefore, was an indispensable factor in the assimilating process.[15]

Following the Civil War and emancipation, many former anti-slavery workers turned their energies to the movement for Indian rights. Using the same tactics that had proved successful in their fight for abolition, these humanitarian workers, both male and female, wrote articles, gave lectures, and formed organizations advocating fair treatment for Native Americans.[16] Although they were from diverse geographical, occupational, and religious backgrounds, these reformers had common characteristics: "Nearly all were middle-class idealists who believed in the basic rights of all men to freedom from oppression," they accepted Darwin's theory of the survival of the most fit in a social context, they believed in the concept of the "noble savage," they held faith in the possibility of social improvement, and they were convinced that saving the Indians from extermination was "an obligation of all people who professed Christianity."[17] In constant communication with Indian policymakers, these philanthropists advocated the inauguration of a reservation system, followed by the swift assimilation of Indian people into American society. They felt that these goals could be most efficiently accomplished through larger appropriations, agricultural education, Christianization, and a bureaucratic organization to administer these programs.[18]

Nineteenth-century reformers held one other belief in common, the conviction that women were natural civilizers. In America, "republican women" supposedly were charged by God with the care and education of the nation's youth, as well as with the guardianship of national morals.[19] In light of this view of the Anglo woman's role in American family and society, it was natural to assume that the Indian woman held much the same position in Indian family and society. Consequently, when reformers searched for an effective method to acculturate Native Americans quickly, their attention turned to the Indian woman. Dorchester, in her 1891 report to the Commissioner of Indian Affairs, maintained that "it is very clear to those most closely studying the Indian problem' that the elevation of the woman is . . . the key to the situation. . . . The children start from the plane of the mother rather than that of the father. Therefore, the great work of the present is to reach and lift the woman and the home."[20]

American women were the most logical candidates to carry out this civilizing effort. Their services were requested as field workers, as well as in the realm of organizational support.[21] In 1877 Kiowa-Comanche Agent J. M. Haworth recommended in his annual report that the reservation be divided into districts, "with a man and wife and a teacher" appointed to each. The man was to teach the Indian men to farm, and his wife to teach the Indian women domestic skills necessary to be good farm wives.[22] This suggestion, however, was not acted upon for fourteen years. It was not until the 1890s, when Indian families began to inhabit permanent houses on their allotments,[23] that "the need of instruction in housekeeping was more urgent."[24] Repeated requests by reservation and special agents for Field Matrons to work with Indian women and returning Indian school girls[25] were finally answered in 1891.

On March 3, 1891, Congress authorized $2,500 "to enable the Commissioner of Indian Affairs to employ suitable persons as matrons to teach Indian girls in house-keeping." Matrons were to be paid not more than sixty dollars per month.[26] A slow start, this appropriation allowed for the hiring of only three to four women for one year to serve the entire Indian Service. By executive order issued April 13, 1891, the classified Civil Service was expanded to include matrons and three other field positions in the Indian Service.[27]

Field Matrons apparently were to be ideal women, imbued with sterling characteristics, and willing to work long hours for low wages. Applicants to any Indian Service position were to be "conscientiously desirous of aiding in the work of improving the physical, domestic, social, intellectual, and moral condition of the Indians, . . . in character above reproach, intellectually well-equipped, . . . energetic, industrious, firm, affable, kind, patient, considerate, dignified, possessed of great self-control and business ability and willing to adapt themselves to the contingencies of the service."[28] Beyond these exemplary attributes, Matrons were to be "in robust health, . . . have at least a good English education, and be able to speak and write the English language correctly, . . . have good executive capacity, [and] be neat, orderly, . . . [and] well acquainted with all kinds of domestic and household duties."[29] Although it demanded the services of model women, the U. S. Government was willing to pay only $500 to $720 per year, and sometimes less.[30]

Applicants were to be tested in orthography, penmanship, personal and housekeeping questions, elementary English composition, elementary grammar, arithmetic, elementary geography, and elementary United States history.[31] Matrons were to be considered in order of examination grade. Because of the geographical isolation of most agencies, and subsequent lack of qualified women in those areas, however, preference was given to wives of school superintendents already located at the reservations.[32] This problem of a limited supply of able women also was circumvented by providing for the hiring of part-time Assistant Field Matrons, paid less than $300.00 per year, and thus exempted from Civil Service testing. These positions could be filled by missionary wives and educated Indian schoolgirls already living on the reservation.[33]

The duties of Field Matrons, as enumerated by Commissioner D. M. Browning on December 1, 1893, were to "visit Indian women in their homes and to give them counsel, encouragement, and help in the following lines":

1. Care of a house, keeping it clean and in order, ventilated, properly warmed (not over-heated), and suitably furnished.
2. Cleanliness and hygienic conditions generally, including disposition of all refuse.
3. Preparation and serving of food and regularity in meals.
4. Sewing, including cutting, making and mending garments.
5. Laundry work.
6. Adorning the home, both inside and out, with pictures, curtains, home-made rugs, flowers, grass-plots, and trees, construction and repair of walks, fences and drains.

   In this connection there will be opportunity for the Matron to give the male members of the family kindly admonition as to the "chores" and heavier kinds of work about the house which in civilized communities is generally done by men.
7. Keeping and care of domestic animals, such as cows, poultry, and swine; care and use of milk, making of butter, cheese, and curds; and keeping of bees.
8. Care of sick.
9. Care of little children, and introducing among them the games and sports of white children.
10. Proper observance of the Sabbath; organizations of societies for promoting literary, religious, moral, and social improvement, such as "Lend a Hand" clubs, circles of "Kings Daughters," or "Sons," "Y.M.C.A.," Christian Endeavor, and Temperance Societies, etc.

In addition to these specific responsibilities, Field Matrons were to be flexible and creative in their work with Indian women, "stimulating their intelligence, rousing ambition, and cultivating refinement." They were to serve as advisers to returning schoolgirls, encourage education, and open their homes for counseling and instruction. In other words, they were to train Indian women in all the skills necessary to be model American farm wives. They were to work not less than eight hours per day Mondays through Fridays, and four hours on Saturdays. Finally, they were to write monthly, quarterly, and annual reports to the agent and the Commissioner of Indian Affairs.[34]

When the Kiowa-Comanche Reservation was formed by the Medicine Lodge Treaty on October 21, 1867,[35] provisions were made for buildings, physicians, skilled craftsmen, and teachers to assist in the civilization process.[36] Apparently this attempt to begin immediate assimilation activities failed, for as late as 1890 few children attended school and fewer adults lived the settled lives of Christian farmers.[37] Considered to be the "worst" Indians by some contemporary observers, the Kiowa, Comanche, and Kiowa-Apache were logical candidates to receive the services of the Field Matron program. On July 9, 1895, Lauretta E. Ballew, a Baptist missionary, was approved as Field Matron to the Kiowa at a salary of $60.00 per month.[38]

Although insufficient information exists for a thorough quantitative study of Field Matrons employed at the Kiowa-Comanche Agency between 1895 and 1906, a survey of the Agency records reveals several trends. These women, most of whom lived on or near the reservation prior to their appointments, appear to have had similar religious backgrounds, similar attitudes toward their work and the people among whom they worked, and were of similar ages and marital status.

The average age of women tested for the position of Matron by the Civil Service Commission in 1892 was thirty-three.[39] Field Matrons appointed to the Kiowa-Comanche Agency, however, tended to be somewhat older. The five women for whom information is available, averaged forty-five years of age at the time of their appointments.[40] In fact, youth seems to have been a liability. Theodore P. Smith writing to Agent Frank D. Baldwin in 1897 agreed to reassign a Miss Mendenhall, stating that "I appreciate what you say as to the unfitness of the position of Field Matron for a young woman of her years, and I will try to send an older person to take her place."[41]

Many Field Matrons were single, often former missionaries, school matrons, or school teachers. Assistant Field Matrons, however, tended to be married women, quite often missionaries' wives with no young children at home. Family obligations, it seems, could eliminate a woman from consideration. Rosa D. Deavenport and a Mrs. Brewer were denied positions because it was "entirely impracticable to appoint a person to that position who has family cares to make demands upon her time, and thought, and strength."[42]

All Field Matrons appeared to have had strong Protestant beliefs, and approached their work among the Kiowa, Comanche, and Kiowa-Apache with a missionary spirit. Ballew, the first full-time Field Matron at the Agency, originally went to work with the Kiowa in 1892 as a missionary appointed by the Woman's Baptist Home Mission Society of Chicago.[43] Almost all of the Assistant Field Matrons appointed at the turn of the twentieth century were wives of missionaries working with the various reservation Indian groups. Ella M. Carithers, whose husband served at the Reformed Presbyterian Cache Mission School, became an Assistant Field Matron in 1898.[44] Mary A. Clouse, appointed in 1903, was the wife of the Baptist missionary to the Kiowa at Rainy Mountain.[45] Anna M. Deyo, also hired in 1903, was married to Elton Cyrus Deyo, the Baptist missionary near Fort Sill.[46] Magdalena Becker, whose husband was an assistant missionary for the Mennonite Brethren, began her work as Assistant Field Matron in 1904.[47]

With the exception of Ballew, these women seldom separated their duties as Field Matrons and federal employees from their duties as missionaries sent by religious organizations. They seem to have continued their missionary work exactly as they had prior to becoming Assistant Field Matrons, with the additional task of writing a monthly report in return for receiving a monthly check of $25.00. Their reports are filled with accounts of their mission work. In June 1904, Clouse reported that she assisted in five funerals, fifty-eight religious services, a camp meeting at the mission, and several baptisms.[48] Likewise, Deyo, in November 1903, gave an elaborate account of the Indian members of her congregation packaging and sending Christmas gifts to the Hopi in Arizona.[49]

While the missionary wives tended to see matron work as merely an extension of mission work, full-time Field Matrons were more inclined to approach their tasks professionally. Ballew, although a former missionary, carefully reported the number of women to whom she taught each domestic skill. She reviewed the progress of individual women in her district, and requested materials such as churns, fabric, buckets, washboards, and brooms with which to work.[50]

Although the Indian Service originally stated that it planned eventually to hire educated Indian women as Assistant Field Matrons,[51] there is little indication this goal was successfully achieved. Julie Given and two girls named May and Amie apparently worked for short periods of time for $5.00 per month.[52] A request in 1898 for two Indian girls to work as Field Matrons for $50.00 per month was rejected, even though the money was to come from the sale of hides.[53] Nonetheless, Laura D. Pedrick, a returned Kiowa Carlisle student who married an Anglo man, was appointed Field Matron in early 1899.[54] She worked in this capacity for several years, carefully reporting her accomplishments in a meticulous, often repetitive, but always sincere, manner. She seems to have been particularly concerned with encouraging those with whom she worked to accept Christianity. "I endeavor always to lead my brothers and sisters of the Indian race to an exceptance [sic] of the higher and true religion. I am continually striving to have them throw away their old beliefs and superstitions that have so long kept them in the dark."[55] Her tenure in this position, however, was a turbulent one. Agent William T. Walker fought to block her appointment, and complaints were lodged against her as a result of the tribal divisions that occurred over the question of allotment.[56]

Field Matrons tended to view the Indian people with whom they worked in a manner similar to most late nineteenth-century reformers and missionaries—that is, Indians were not inherently bad, but merely products of their environment. Although deficient in many qualities necessary in a "civilized" society, they were honest, loyal, and brave, and thus capable of being culturally transformed. With careful guidance and the proper instruction, the Indian people could be elevated to become productive members of American society.[57] This patronizing attitude, in choice of words as often as in ideas expressed, is particularly evident in the Kiowa Field Matron reports.

Ballew often graded the accomplishments of the Indians with whom she worked against an ideal Anglo model. When their progress pleased her, she stated that "White people could not have done any better."[58] She likewise excused their faults by maintaining that "we can't expect them to progress as fast as the White people,"[59] and that "it takes time, patience and persiverence [sic] to raise them out of the old Indian rut."[60] When she considered their actions to be inexcusable, however, she conceded that "of corse [sic] we have some, who never will amount to anything, with all we can do for them,"[61] or accused them of being "like grown up children and never will learn."[62] It should be noted that she never referred to an Indian woman as a friend, nor indicated that any relationship, other than professional, existed between herself and the Indians among whom she lived.

Field Matrons at the Kiowa-Comanche Agency again like most nineteenth-century reformers, held the firm conviction that what they were doing was right,[63] and that they alone knew what was best for the Indian people. They were particularly dismayed at the Indians' habit of leaving their homes and farms and camping near each other for weeks at a time. "This is a hindrance to the Field Matrons' work and I think bad for the Indians. . . . It is damaging to their farms, and has a bad effect on the children,"[64] Carithers reported of the Kiowa-Apache in 1905. Likewise, Deyo considered their "constantly travelling and camping from place to place is very demoralizing to the Indians."[65] Ballew planned work for women every day of the week in order to "break up this unnecessary going to town and running around everyday."[66] They all considered the Indians' nomadic life "an evil and it is the duty of the Field Matron to try to show the Indians that it is a mistake."[67]

This confidence in their knowledge of right and wrong led the Field Matrons, particularly the missionary wives in the early twentieth century, to make continual demands to higher authorities for legislation to force the Indians to conform to Anglo mores. It is possible that after more than a decade of work it had become obvious to the Field Matrons that the Indians were not going to recognize the superiority of Anglo culture and adopt its habits voluntarily as had been expected.[68] Since "the last persons presumed to know their own larger interests were the Indians,"[69] they would have to be made to comply. Clouse, concerned that "they did not seem to have any moral feeling on the subject,"[70] agreed with Deyo "that school boys and girls be compelled to marry legally."[71] Becker and Deyo asked that "gambling be suppressed" because homes, work, and children were neglected in its pursuit.[72] Clouse requested that "a compulsory educational law" be enacted,[73] and Deyo continually demanded that "the Indians be made to stay home, and away from these towns where saloons, degradation and death await them."[74] She even went so far as to insist "that every Indian would be obligated to plant a crop and then stay at home and attend to it."[75] It appears that these women's requests were sometimes heeded, for in 1905 Deyo expressed her happiness that the Indians had not been allowed to camp near the traders and had stayed home.[76]

Field Matrons were charged to teach Indian women skills and ideas necessary to be efficient American farm wives and mothers. Evidence indicates, however, that their actual duties often overstepped these boundaries to include any service that the Matrons felt to be advantageous to the Indians. They provided nursing services, teaching cleanliness, vaccinating against disease, and dispensing medicine.[77] They prepared bodies for burial and, in the absence of missionaries, performed funerals.[78] They interceded in disputes, often defending or translating for Indians in court.[79] They offered advice on all aspects of life, including financial matters, home decoration, education, proper companionship, and fashion.[80] They wrote letters for, and in behalf of, their Indian acquaintances.[81] In later years, they maintained birth and death records and delivered payment checks to Indian families.[82] Finally, apparently in between their numerous other duties, they were responsible for the maintenance and upkeep of their own homes.[83]

It is evident why the Field Matron program was instituted in the final decade of the nineteenth century. The tendency toward social reform, the belief that Indian assimilation was necessary, the conviction that an agricultural society provided the best form of democratic civilization, and the faith that women (both Anglo and Indian) were moral guardians of society, merged and gave birth to this unique branch of the Indian Service. Women teaching women attacked the problem of assimilation at its foundation, namely, in the Indian home where children, the anticipated first generation of Indian citizens, were being trained and nurtured. The results of the program, however, are not as readily apparent.

In judging the success or failure of the Field Matron program one must consider its goals on two levels. On the first, the Field Matrons were hired to teach Indian women the domestic skills necessary to perform the duties of turn-of-the-century American farm wives. If one can believe the reports of Anglo people closely involved in the program, it was at least partially successful in this area. The Field Matrons reported slow but constant progress in teaching and then convincing the Indian women to adopt Anglo, or "civilized," habits[84] Martha Leota Buntin, whose father was appointed Kiowa Agent in 1922, reported that by 1930 there were fewer practicing medicine men, that all Indians lived in houses, that eighty percent of the houses were screened, that sanitary water supplies were available, that reports of tuberculosis had decreased, that a better attitude existed toward education, and that Indian women were raising chickens, making butter, tending gardens, and practicing many other skills encouraged by the Field Matrons.[85]

Teaching household arts, however, was secondary to the overall goal of assimilation. Practicing Anglo domestic and agricultural skills, when combined with belief in Christianity, in some mystical way was to transform the Indian people from nomadic "hunters and warriors into [settled] farmers and stockmen."[86] This anticipated change did not occur. In the words of William T. Hagan, "the Comanches came no nearer to escaping their dependence on the government. . . . Notwithstanding the lip service paid to the concept of assimilation, Comanche children continued to attend government schools, they and their parents were treated by government doctors, and they patronized government-licensed traders." The Indian Office, later the Bureau of Indian Affairs, did not die from disuse as expected, but grew in scope.[87] The Kiowa, Comanche, and Kiowa-Apache in southwestern Oklahoma did not assimilate and disappear into American society as predicted, but were transformed "into apathetic wards of the United States."[88] Why the assimilation policy failed so miserably, and in what way the Field Matron program contributed to, or resisted, that failure, are questions yet to be answered.

NOTES

1. "Report of Special Agent in the Indian School Service," in Commissioner of Indian Affairs *Annual Report*, 1889, in *House Executive Documents*, 51st Cong., 1st sess., no. 1, part 5, vol. 2 (Serial 2725): 346 (Hereafter referred to as C.I.A. *Annual Report*, 1889 (Serial 2725).)

2. Ibid.

3. Indian Appropriations Act, approved March 3, 1891, in U. S. *Statutes at Large*, 26: 1009.

4. Browning to Baldwin, August 5, 1895, Kiowa Agency Employee Records, 1895; Browning to Baldwin, June 27, 1895, Kiowa Field Matrons Files; Indian Archives Division, Oklahoma Historical Society. (Hereafter referred to as K.E.R., K.F.M., and O.H.S.).

5. Robert F. Berkhofer, Jr., *The White Man's Indian: Images of the American Indian from Columbus to the Present* (New York: Alfred A. Knopf, 1978), pp. 25-26, 113, 173.

6. Robert Winston Mardock, *The Reformers and the American Indian* (Columbia: University of Missouri Press, 1971), pp. 4, 183.

7. Berkhofer, *White Man's Indian*, p. 113.

8. Mardock, *Reformers and Indian*, p. 4.

9. Henry E. Fritz, *The Movement for Indian Assimilation, 1860-1890* (Philadelphia: University of Pennsylvania Press, 1963), p. 19.

10. William T. Hagan, *United States Comanche Relations: The Reservation Years* (New Haven: Yale University Press, 1976) p. 140; George Posey Wild, "History of the Education of the Plains Indians of Southwestern Oklahoma Since the Civil War" (Ph.D. dissertation, University of Oklahoma, 1941), pp. iv, 41; Berkhofer, *White Man's Indian*, p. 4; Mardock, *Reformers and Indian*, pp. 4, 31, 55, 183.

11. Berkhofer, *White Man's Indian*, p. 155; Mardock, *Reformers and Indian*, p. 4; Wild, "Education of Plains Indians," p. 191.

12. Fritz, *Indian Assimilation*, p. 19; Hagan, *Comanche Relations*, p. 38.

13. Fritz, *Indian Assimilation*, pp. 56-57, 65-66; Wild, "Education of Plains Indians," pp. 150-52.

14. Wild, "Education of Plains Indians," p. 123.

15. Mardock, *Reformers and Indian*, p. 2.

16. Ibid., p. 1; Berkhofer, *White Man's Indian*, p. 156.

17. Mardock, *Reformers and Indian*, pp. 2-4.

18. Ibid., p. 55; Berkhofer, *White Man's Indian*, p. 169.

19. Catharine Beecher, "The Peculiar Responsibilities of American Women," p. 173; Alexis de Tocqueville, "On American Women and American Wifes," p. 117; both in Nancy F. Cott, ed., *Root of Bitterness: Documents of the Social History of American Women* (New York: E. P. Dutton and Co., Inc., 1972). For a discussion of women's role in nineteenth-century American society, see Barbara J. Harris, *Beyond Her Sphere: Women and the Professions in American History* (Westport, Connecticut: Greenwood Press, 1978), pp. 41, 49, 56-57, and Nancy F. Cott, *Bonds of Womanhood* (New Haven: Yale University Press, 1977), pp. 63-100.

20. "Suggestions from the Field," in Commissioner of Indian Affairs *Annual Report*, 1891, in *House Executive Documents*, 52nd Cong., 1st sess., no. 1, part 5, vol. 2 (Serial 2934), 542.

21. C.I.A. *Annual Report*, 1889 (Serial 2725): 346.

22. Annual Report, Haworth, 1877, Kiowa Agent's Reports, O.H.S., quoted in Wild, "Education of Plains Indians," p. 69.

23. As the final step in the Indian assimilation policy, the Kiowa, Comanche, and the Kiowa-Apache were alloted 160 acres of reservation land each, the surplus land sold to Anglo farmers and speculators. It was hoped that private property ownership would speed the Indians' awareness of the superiority of agrarian life, and that contact with Anglo farmers would encourage the acceptance of Anglo culture. See Hagan, *Comanche Relations*, pp. 166-67; Martha Leota Buntin, "History of the Kiowa, Comanche, and Wichita Indian Agency" (M.A. thesis, University of Oklahoma, 1931), pp. 152-54.

24. Wild, "Education of Plains Indians," p. 247.

25. In an attempt to speed assimilation by training Indian children to be American, Kiowa, Comanche, and Kiowa-Apache schoolchildren were sent to off-reservation boarding schools such as Carlisle in Pennsylvania. Quite often the returning schoolchildren, after years of isolation from Indian culture, found that they were accepted in neither Anglo nor Indian society. Field Matrons were charged to befriend returning schoolgirls and encourage them to retain the Anglo habits learned in school. See Alice Marriott, *Greener Fields* (New York: Thomas Y. Crowell Company, 1953), pp. 14, 19.

26. U. S. *Statutes at Large,* 1891, 26: 1009.

27. U. S. Civil Service Commission *Annual Report*, 1890-91, in *House Executive Documents*, 52nd Cong., 1st sess., no. 1, part 8 (Serial 2942): 2, 46. (Hereinafter referred to as C.S.C. *Annual Report*, 1890-1891 (Serial 2942).)

28. Ibid., 216.

29. Ibid., 217.

30. Ibid.

31. U. S. Civil Service Commission *Annual Report*, 1890-91, in *House Executive Documents*, 52nd Cong., 2nd sess., no. 1, part 8 (Serial 3097): 155, 212-15. (Hereinafter referred to as C.S.C. *Annual Report*, 1890-1891 (Serial 3097).)

32. C S.C. *Annual Report*, 1890-1891 (Serial 2942): 47-48; Paul Stuart, *The Indian Office: Growth and Development of an American Institution, 1865-1900* (Ann Arbor, MI: University Microfilms International, 1978), p. 49.

33. C.S.C. *Annual Report*, 1890-91 (Serial 3097): 90; Larrabee to Agent, December 31, 1907, K.F.M., O.H.S.

34. Field Matron Report Forms, K.F.M., O.H.S.

35. Buntin, "History of Indian Agency," pp. 20-22.

36. Wild, "Education of Plains Indians," p. 60; Hagan, *Comanche Relations*, p. 38.

37. Buntin, "History of Indian Agency," pp. 89, 112; Wild, "Education of Plains Indians," p. 39.

38. Browning to Baldwin, August 5, 1895, K.E.R., O.H.S. *Home Mission Monthly* Vol. XVI, No. 11 (November 1894): 455.

39. C.S.C. *Annual Report*, 1890-1891 (Serial 3097): 118-19.

40. Descriptive Statement of Changes in the Force of the Agency Employees, December 20, 1900, July 9, 1903; Personal Record of McFarland, December 6, 1910, Givens, n.d.; K.F.M., O.H.S.

41. Ibid., Smith to Baldwin, May 8, 1897.

42. Ibid., Browning to Baldwin, June 27, 1895; Jones to Baldwin, April 25, 1898.

43. John Preston Dane, "A History of Baptist Missions Among the Plains Indians of Oklahoma," (Ph.D. dissertation, Central Baptist Theological Seminary, Kansas City, 1955), p. 45.

44. "Loyalty Oath," August 4, 1903, K.F.M., O.H.S.; Wild, "Education of Plains Indians," pp. 169-70.

45. Descriptive Statement of Changes . . . , July 9, 1903, K.F.M., O.H.S.

46. Ibid.; *Indian Pioneer Papers*, Vol. 24, pp. 225-27, Western History Collections, University of Oklahoma.

47. Becker to Randlett, August 30, 1904; Loyalty Oath, Magdalena Becker, December 15, 1904; K.F.M., O.H.S.

48. Ibid., Quarterly Report, Clouse, June 1904.

49. Ibid., Monthly Report, Deyo, November 30, 1903.

50. Ibid., Ballew, September 30, 1898; Ballew, Mendenhall, 1895.

51. C.S.C. *Annual Report*, 1890-91 (Serial 3097): 90.

52. Given to Agent, September 15, 1895; Monthly Report, Ballew, September 30, 1898; K.F.M., O.H.S.

53. Ibid., Jones to Baldwin, April 2, 1898.

54. Ibid., Jones to Walker, January 31, 1899; Hagan, *Comanche Relations*, p. 222.

55. Monthly Report, Pedrick, June 30, 1904, K.F.M., O.H.S.

56. Ibid., Jones to Walker, January 31, 1899. Allotment for the Kiowa-Comanche Reservation was ratified in 1900. Leaders of the three tribes involved, Quanah, Apiatan, and Apache John, accepted the ruling. Lone Wolf, a Kiowa, and Eschiti, a Comanche, refused to accept the decision and attempted to have the agreement nullified

through the courts. At the same time, on the reservation, disputes took place between the two factions. The anti-allotment group failed in their efforts, and allotment began in late July 1900. See Hagan, *Comanche Relations,* pp. 262-64.

57. Mardock, *Reformers and Indian*, pp. 3-4.

58. Monthly Report, Ballew, December, 1896; May 31, 1899, March 31, 1902; February 28, 1907; K.F.M., O.H.S.

59. Ibid., September 30, 1901.

60. Ibid., September 30, 1898.

61. Ibid., June 30, 1905.

62. Ibid., January 31, 1902.

63. Mardock, *Reformers and Indian*, p. 2.

64. Annual Report, Carithers, July 25, 1905, K.F.M., O.H.S.

65. Ibid., Monthly Report, Deyo, July 1, 1905.

66. Ibid., Ballew, March 31, 1907.

67. Ibid., Annual Report, Carithers, July 25, 1905.

68. Berkhofer, *White Man's Indian*, p. 150.

69. Ibid., p. 153.

70. Monthly Report, Clouse, March 31, 1905, K.F.M., O.H.S.

71. Ibid., Deyo, July 1, 1904.

72. Ibid., September 1, 1904; Becker, February 28, 1907.

73. Ibid., Clouse, September 30, 1904; January 31, 1905.

74. Ibid., Deyo, December 1903; January 3l, 1905; November 1, 1905; September 30, 1906.

75. Ibid., November 30, 1906.

76. Ibid., January 30, 1905.

77. Ibid., Pedrick, December 1900; March 31, 1902; December 31, 1903, Ballew, March 31, 1907.

78. Ibid., Deyo, February 1, 1905; Quarterly Report, Clouse, June 1904.

79. Ibid., Reeside to Baldwin, August 31, 1897; Ballew to Randlett, August 1 and 15, 1899; Monthly Report, Pedrick, December 31, 1903; March 31, 1904; Clouse, December 31, 1907.

80. Ibid., Ballew, September 1896; Dickens, January 31, 1901; Pedrick, June 30, 1901; September 31, 1903, December 31, 1903, Carithers, March 31, 1906; Deyo, October 31, 1903.

81. Ibid., Deyo, February 1, 1904; Bauk to Buntice (?), 1903; Buntin, "History of Indian Agency," p. 130.

82. Monthly Report, Ballew, March 31, 1902; May 31, 1902; K.F.M., O.H.S.

83. Ibid., Given to Johnson, November 2, 1895.

84. Ibid., Monthly Report, Ballew, September, 1896; April, 1897; July 30, 1897; September 30, 1898; March 31, 1899; May 31, 1899; January 31, 1901; June 30, 1901; September 30, 1901; October 31, 1901; Becker, May 31, 1906; Deyo, May 1, 1904; Annual Report, August 15, 1904; Carithers, August 11, 1906.

85. Buntin, "History of Indian Agency," pp. 177-87.

86. Hagan, *Comanche Relations*, p. xiii.

87. Ibid., p. 286.

88. Ibid., p. xiv.

Concepts of Domesticity on the Southern Plains Agricultural Frontier, 1870–1920

Definitions of "domesticity" and "the woman's sphere" in nineteenth-century America have been the subject of recent scholarly scrutiny. Nancy Cott has discovered that prescriptive literature published early in the century described woman's proper "sphere" as the domestic setting where her superior moral influence could restrain the vices of her husband and mold the character of future citizens, her children. Although most areas of public life were closed to nineteenth-century women, their "sphere" did include the church, the schoolroom and the religious or benevolent voluntary association.[1] Katherine Kish Sklar's biography of Catherine Beecher has explained how Beecher elaborated these role definitions and extended them to single women by exalting the American mothers and schoolteachers who would play a special role in transmitting cultural values to the rapidly expanding Western frontier.[2] Anne Firor Scott has demonstrated how the institution of slavery made acceptance of "woman's sphere" particularly urgent for Southern women. During and after the Civil War, Southern women were forced by necessity to extend their "sphere" beyond the domestic setting; some worked for wages, some enjoyed widened opportunities for education, and others participated actively in women's clubs and organizations. Nevertheless, even those who advocated female suffrage did not significantly challenge nineteenth-century definitions of femininity, arguing that women could use the vote to enhance their role as wives, mothers, and the nation's moral guardians.[3]

Recent studies in women's history have investigated whether emigrating nineteenth-century agricultural women followed, altered, or abandoned these definitions of "woman's sphere" under the pressures of migrating and building new homes on the frontier. In his study of midwestern farm families who crossed the plains on the Overland Trail to the Pacific Northwest, John Mack Faragher described "woman's sphere" in the rural setting, suggesting that feminine ideology that filtered into the Midwest essentially reinforced traditional agricultural sex roles and division of labor. Even on the trail, he found that sex roles did not change but were transferred to the new agricultural environment.[4] Julie Roy Jeffrey has reached a similar conclusion. On agricultural frontiers, she found "wide acceptance" of nineteenth-century domestic ideology, concluding that "frontier women gave many indications of their desire to hold on to the conventions of female culture no matter how unfavorable the circumstances seemed." She attributed even the early granting of female suffrage in Western territories to conservative expediency rather than to an altered vision of feminine contribution and responsibility.[5]

Other historians, however, have suggested that the experience of women who settled the Great Plains might present a special case. Some time ago, Walter Prescott Webb argued that settlers who ventured into the "level, timberless, and semiarid" region west of the ninety-eighth meridian "were thrown by Mother Necessity into the clutch of new circumstances." Women, he conjectured, who left the humid regions they had known and were forced to cope with the isolation of the vast, empty prairie, the lack of wood and water, and problems caused by excessive dust and wind, found the Plains "peculiarly appalling."[6] Mary Hargreaves has emphasized the loneliness and the domestic hardship experienced by women who settled the northern plains.[7] And, disagreeing with the con-

clusions of Faragher and Jeffrey, Christine Stansill has argued
that plains women, who lived in sod huts and dugouts and
lacked cultural supports, "failed to reinstate their own sphere"
because of "the duration as well as the severity of cultural
disruption" that they experienced.[8]

All of these studies, from Cott to Faragher to Stansill, have
added to our knowledge about frontier women. Some discussed
those women who settled the Great Plains, but none specifically concentrate on the Southern plains. Might the experiences of farm, ranch, or town women who settled the Southern
plains of western Texas and eastern New Mexico be different?
Would they be influenced by feminine ideology? What cultural
values would they transmit to their particular agricultural
frontier?

This case study is based on materials left by forty women
who participated in the agriculturalization of one of the United
States' later frontiers, the high Southern plains.[9] It seeks to
examine whether this plains environment did so disrupt the
lives of women that they found establishment of conventional
female culture especially difficult. These forty women lived in
twenty-five Texas and three New Mexico counties which constitute a level, treeless, semi-arid plains region that the Spanish labeled the Llano Estacado.[10] They were born or arrived
during the years when this last frontier was being settled,
largely between 1880 and 1910. Only two of the forty women
migrated in the late 1870s; ten arrived in the 1880s, eight in
the 1890s, eleven in the first decade of the twentieth century,
and only one after 1910. Although their birthdates ranged
from 1840 to 1903, most of the women were born between 1860
and 1890, with the largest number of their birthdates clustered
between 1869 and 1878. Three of the women were born in
Europe, three in the northeastern United States, and three in
neighboring plains states; but most of them, the remaining
thirty-one, came from east or central Texas, the border states,
or the South.[11]

Twenty-one of the women were wives and daughters in what
could be called "ranching" families; their husbands or fathers

were owners of large or small ranches or workers in the cattle industry. Ten of these "ranching" women married cowboys. Eleven of the forty were wives and daughters of "homesteaders"; two briefly had been homesteaders themselves before they married. These families generally engaged in a combination of stock farming and production of a small cotton crop. The remaining eight women best could be described as "townswomen"; their husbands or fathers were merchants, lawyers, judges, or town founders.

Eight of the forty women were born in or set up housekeeping in a dugout, and only one, from Kansas, in a sod house. After an initial period of living in either a tent or a covered wagon, the rest of them lived in wooden houses of one or two rooms. Several of them were educated; five had been schoolteachers and one had been a governess. Of the forty, only one never married and only three gave up pioneering on the southern plains and returned "home." Unfortunately, the sources do not provide enough information to determine numbers of children and their birth intervals.[12]

The experience of these forty pioneer women certainly was influenced by the plains environment they sought to settle. Once they climbed the escarpment of the Llano Estacado, they encountered a vast, empty grassland, with few rivers, sparse rainfall, and almost no trees, that was swept by hot dry winds in summer, blizzards in winter, and dust storms in the spring. However, this late frontier was opened when Eastern technology already was well advanced. By the late 1880s, railroads reached Amarillo in the north, and Colorado City in the south; many of these pioneering families began their trek west by rail. Technology could provide not only barbed wire and windmills, but also canned goods and sewing machines. Families could order manufactured items from mail-order catalogues.[13] By 1910, the automobile brought relief from rural isolation. Mary Perritt Blankenship arrived in Hockley County in 1902; ten years later her life changed dramatically when her family purchased their first Ford.[14] By 1910, the "frontier" period was essentially over in West Texas, although it lingered into the

1920's in eastern New Mexico.[15] These forty women, then, were pioneers under unique circumstances. Largely of Southern background, they attempted to build homes under the difficult conditions created by a plains environment, at a late date when industrialization was of some help.

Southern plains women worked long and hard to recreate in their new homes the values of the particular cultural setting in which they had been socialized. Technology aided them, when they could make use of it, and temporary modifications were made to cope with the plains environment. The better educated pioneer women tended to focus on their role as educators rather than as experts in domestic production. One of the three women from the northeastern United States made a deliberate and conscious attempt to transplant northeastern feminine ideology. Margaret Adams McCollum Mooar was born in New York state and, according to her daughter, Lydia Louise, was "a highly educated lady both academically and musically" before she married John W. Mooar, a buffalo hunter who settled down to become a prominent rancher in Scurry County.[16]

Margaret Mooar chose to spend much of her time at her town home in Colorado City, Mitchell County, where she became an active club woman. In 1892, she helped organize the "Up-to-Date History Club", which attempted to keep abreast of national issues concerning women. Members of the Up-to-Date Club were proud of being the first federated women's club in West Texas. They felt their spirits ennobled by their plains environment, those "vast prairies . . . in whose lap this child club of the West has been rocked and nourished—broadminded, full souled, big and generous hearted." Euphemistically, they considered themselves "as active in body, mind, and soul as the gentle zephyrs" that blew through their West Texas town.[17] Catherine Beecher would have lauded Mooar's civic emphasis on molding citizens through motherhood rather than seeking the vote: "In this day when we hear so much of woman's sphere," wrote Mooar, "let us not forget that it is eminently her [concern] to teach her sons and daughters to be patriots."[18] Members of the Up-to-Date Club gave reports on English and American history, on activities of the Texas Federation of Women's Clubs, and on eminent nineteenth-century women such as Margaret Fuller. On George Washington's birthday, they dressed up in colonial costumes and made speeches praising Washington's mother whose good influence clearly had molded his noble character.[19]

Although less up-to-date on northeastern feminine ideology, West Texas pioneer women born in Europe worked as diligently to transmit learned cultural values to their new homes. Constance Aldous arrived from England in 1901 with a side saddle, a Singer sewing machine, and a tin bathtub, to keep house for her brother who had been herding sheep in Collingsworth County since 1887. A year later, she married a second English sheep herder, Albert Manby, fourteen years her junior. Constance Aldous Manby was a well-educated English "lady" who learned her limited domestic skills from her new husband. Throughout her years on their Elm Creek cattle ranch, she endeavored to instruct her only daughter, Mary, in English culture and values. In 1911, a governess came from England to occupy Mary with mornings of rigorous lessons and afternoons of reading and needlework. When this first teacher went to Canada to marry a cowboy in 1913, a replacement was quickly sent for from England.[20]

Juliana McGregor, born in Munich, came to live on her American husband's Haskell County ranch in 1904. Dismayed by the hot, dry West Texas environment, she sought to beautify it according to European standards. Her daughter commented: "Julie so loved things to be pretty that she took a wheelbarrow down into the canyons where she gathered up the lace-like white caliche rocks and built 'rockeries' in which she planted flowers so that they looked like fountains. She also lined the walk-ways around the house with the rocks and made flower beds. . . . She drew the well dry, bucketfull by bucketfull [sic] carrying water to her garden."[21]

Educated women of Southern and border state background, although less conscious than Margaret Mooar of feminine ideology, also worked diligently to transmit learned cultural values, especially to their children. Mollie Wylie Abernathy came to Lubbock County in 1902 with her first husband, James Jarrott, who sought to settle twenty-five families on a strip of land missed in the early surveys. After Jarrott's murder by a paid assassin, Mollie stayed, living on her four sections of land, eventually increasing them to eighteen, and building a thriving cattle ranch. Mollie's strength was not in domestic skills: "I never did any hard house work," she said, "I never did wash and iron, scrub and scour, but I cooked a little bit." Nevertheless, she prided herself on providing an education for her three children. Although not a Catholic, she sent them to a convent school in Stanton, Texas. "It was the nearest place I could find that would take my children and take care of them," she said; "they stayed there four years and they got wonderful training and a fine start in school." Mollie had attended Add-Ran College near Fort Worth; "I come from an educated place," she declared, and "I educated my children."[22]

After her marriage to Monroe Abernathy in 1905, Mollie lived part-time in the town of Lubbock where she became an active businesswoman in real estate and development, and a charter member of Lubbock's Business and Professional Women's Club. Like most of the forty women, she favored prohibition, but was unusual not only in her business career, but also in her advocacy of female suffrage. Her support of her beliefs neatly summarized the entire nineteenth- and early twentieth-century suffrage argument: "I was born a suffrager and almost a prohibitionist," she said. "When we were born, we were born equal. Women got as much sense as men. May not be the same kind, but it's usually a better kind."[23] And she acted on her views by organizing Lubbock chapters of the Women's Christian Temperance Union, and later, the League of Women Voters.

Other educated women born in Southern and border states also saw themselves essentially as educators. Texas-born Margaret Collins had been trained in a New York City conservatory of music. Shortly after she came to Cochran County as a governess at the Byrd Bar N Bar Ranch in 1905, she met and married Hiley T. Boyd, foreman on the nearby Slaughter Ranch. Her son later commented that single schoolteachers in West Texas generally married cowboys: "I . . . can't remember but one . . . or two at least that ever escaped some cowpuncher for the next twenty years." Margaret Collins Boyd was deeply concerned about the health, diet, and education of her three children in the isolated conditions of their ranch life. She put up hundreds of gallons of canned peaches, cherries, and plums in order that her children would have a proper diet even in drought years. Realizing that she was too busy with domestic chores to educate her children properly herself, she arranged for a "slight tax" in her area, hired and boarded a teacher, and set up a school in her front yard.[24]

Julia Sutton taught school for thirteen years in Oklahoma before she homesteaded as a single woman in Curry County, New Mexico, in 1907. Within a year, she married U. S. Land Commissioner, Thomas Carter. While raising five children and helping with the family's "trading post" after their move to DeBaca County, she organized an interracial, interdenominational Sunday school. Her daughter explained: "Julia always had been a teacher at heart. Here in this even further west location, she extended herself into bringing some form of culture to her community." In her later years, Julia was postmistress of her town and Democratic chairperson of her county while her husband served as Republican county chair.[25]

Yet, what of the southern Plains pioneer women less educated than these fortunate few? What cultural values did they endeavor to transmit? These women were not unlike the midwestern farm women described by John Mack Faragher; although they exhibited scant consciousness of feminine ideology, they were well trained in methods of domestic production and profoundly versed in traditional feminine lore. An excellent example would be Winnie Harris Rush, who carefully described the medical treatments, food processing, soap making, laundry procedures, and cloth production that she had learned during her Arkansas girlhood in the 1890s. Although her mother had a sewing machine, this introduction of technology followed a pattern frequently found in this group of forty women. It was the only such machine in the neighborhood and women came from miles around to use it: "People from all over the country would bring their sewing and sew all day, which was a little irritating. Some would bring their children to run the treadle."[26]

After her father's death in 1909, Winnie, her mother, and her brothers homesteaded in Curry County, New Mexico. The two women valiantly transmitted their rich domestic knowledge to the new environment. On the plains, they made some interesting temporary domestic adaptations. Winnie's mother worked hard to make their dugout more comfortable. She put wagon sheets over joists to create a ceiling, "covered the dirt walls with gunny sacks," and then "papered over that with remnants of wall paper that she had brought along. She brought some cement and plastered the whole floor completely." Winnie later marveled, "it is still a mystery to me where she got all the stuff to work with."[27]

Mrs. Arthur Duncan, one of the first women to come to Floyd County in 1884, lived with her husband and children in an abandoned sheep herder's dugout for seven years. She, too, attempted to make her new home "attractive and livable" by nailing towsacks covered with newspapers to the walls and building a partition that would divide her home into a kitchen and a "bedroom-parlor." She even managed to smile when a steer's leg penetrated the dug-out roof and spoiled the first meal for company she had prepared in three years. When the family moved to a two-room wooden house in Floydada in 1891, Mrs. Duncan was ecstatic: "A queen in all the splendor of her palaces," she said, "could not have glorified in her riches as much as I did in that home."[28]

Other Plains women in the Llano Estacado environment followed a similar pattern, working diligently to transplant domestic values and procedures, yet being forced by circumstances to make temporary adaptations. For example, on the West Texas homestead, the windmill became an important focus for women. Mary Perritt Blankenship, who came to

Hockley County in 1902, climbed the windmill tower when her husband was away, hoping for a glimpse of company. She hung a lantern on the windmill to direct her husband home, hung a towel to signal dinner for field hands, used the windmill tank for a cooler for milk, and the tower as a place to hang and dry beef. Before a church was built in her area, baptism took place in the windmill tank.[29] Emma B. Russell was born in a dugout in Dickens County in 1890. Her mother attempted to use the power generated by the windmill to churn butter, attaching the dash of the churn to the windmill rod. She had trouble, however, controlling the wind.[30]

Child care in the plains environment could be difficult for these busy pioneer women, and they evolved ingenious methods to make their task easier. Jane Lowe Quillan came to Hale County in 1888 when she was two. After her mother's death, she was raised by an aunt who insisted that Jane wear a bright red sunbonnet with two holes cut out for her braids so that she could not take it off. Then, whether Jane was in her playhouse by the cow lot or sailing homemade wooden boats in the pond in the pasture, her aunt could climb the windmill tower and spot her.[31] Nanny Jowell came to West Texas with her cattleman husband in 1886 and moved with him from place to place, frequently living in a tent, while he sought pasture land unsettled by homesteaders. Her great worry in caring for her young children was the constant presence of snakes; finally she hit on the solution of using a mule for a babysitter. With her two toddlers high on the mule's back, she could concentrate on her domestic chores. Later, she said, "Old Jen was a dandy. She raised all the kids. That's a fact."[32]

Another woman who practiced traditional domestic skills in an unusual way was Mrs. J. P. McDonald, wife of the foreman of the XIT Ranch, which covered ten counties in northwestern Texas. In 1904, she lived at the ranch headquarters, Las Escarbadas, where she cooked for the cowboys and measured out supplies for the line camps. McDonald was delighted with her domestic arrangements at XIT headquarters; later she commented: "I loved living in that house. It was cool in the summer and warm in the winter. . . . That was the nicest little ranch place that I've ever been in . . . everything was convenient." She lovingly described her 500 chickens, her splendid big black cookstove, her neat bins to keep supplies with the biscuit-rolling board that covered them, and her butter churn on a frame in which she made ten to fifteen pounds of butter a day. The cowboys helped her by clearing the table, and she, too, worked out arrangements for child care. While she cooked, either her husband cared for the children or three-year-old Raymond pulled baby Mary around the ranch yard in a little red wagon. Mrs. McDonald had learned home medical reme-dies, domestic skills, and methods of maintaining family har-mony from her Southern mother-in-law. "We have always had harmony," she said, "I know people can live together without fussing."[33]

These frontier women worked diligently to transmit learned cultural values and methods of domestic production to their new arid environment. Although they discovered ingenious ways of coping with the isolation of the empty prairie, the lack of wood and water, and the weather, their goal was always reestablishment of the conventions of female culture they had known. Although advanced technology was available to them, only a few with sufficient means were able to use it prior to 1910. A sewing machine mentioned in a memoir always was the only one in the county; women came from miles around to share in its use. Canned goods were considered a luxury and were not included in lists of supplies brought by wagon every six months. Some women thought that only cowboys and bachelors used store-bought canned goods; others were con-vinced that such provisions were unhealthy.[34]

With the exceptions of Mollie Abernathy, businesswoman; Julia Carter, homesteader and postmistress; and Martha Kil-lough Conaway of Mitchell County, who managed the family ranch after her husband's death, these women did not venture from nineteenth-century definitions of "woman's sphere." Although only Margaret Mooar consciously transplanted femi-nine ideology, most of the women implicitly followed it. Educated women of southern background concentrated on transmitting values and knowledge to children, as mothers and as schoolteachers. Less educated Southern women diligently transplanted their complicated methods of domestic production and their rich medical lore. Only three of the forty women even mentioned female suffrage. Instead of creating new gender definitions, they concentrated on recreating the world they had known. With the men who accompanied them, in a short span of thirty years, defying heat, wind, snakes, and dust storms, they transformed the vast and empty Llano Estacado into an extension of mainstream Anglo-American rural culture.

NOTES

1. Nancy Cott, *The Bonds of Womanhood, "Woman's Sphere" in New England, 1780-1835* (New Haven: Yale University Press, 1977).

2. Katherine Kish Sklar, *Catherine Beecher* (New York: Oxford University Press, 1973); and Catherine Beecher, *A Treatise on Domestic Economy* (New York: Schocken Books, 1977, first edition, 1841).

3. Anne Firor Scott, *The Southern Lady, From Pedestal to Politics, 1830-1930* (Chicago: University of Chicago Press, 1970). Another source for discussion of the complexity of the female suffrage argument, especially in the South, is Aileen S. Kraditor, *The Ideas of the Woman Suffrage Movement, 1890-1920* (New York: W. W. Norton Co., 1981).

4. John Mack Faragher, *Women and Men on the Overland Trail* (New Haven: Yale University Press, 1979), pp. 182, 187.

5. Julie Roy Jeffrey, *Frontier Women, the Trans-Mississippi West* (New York: Hill & Wang, 1979), pp. xiv, 73, 188-191.

6. Walter Prescott Webb, *The Great Plains* (New York: Grosset & Dunlap, 1931), pp. 9, 506.

7. Mary W. M. Hargreaves, "Women in the Agricultural Settlement of the Northern Plains," *Agricultural History* 50 (January 1976): 179-89.

8. Christine Stansill, "Women on the Great Plains, 1865-1890," *Women's Studies* 4 (1976): 87-98, 190-191.

9. The unpublished letters, diaries, scrapbooks, reminiscences, and oral history interviews of this sample of forty women can be

located through the unpublished bibliography, "Frontier Women in West Texas," located in the Southwest Collection, Texas Tech University, Lubbock, Texas (hereinafter referred to as FWWT, SWC).

10. These counties are located between the ninety-ninth and one hundred·third meridians, including the entire Texas Panhandle (measured by its western boundary) and a tier of two counties to the east. They range from Deaf Smith County in the northwest to Midland County in the southwest and from Hemphill County in the northeast to Shackelford and Stephens Counties on the southeast. Much of this area includes the high Staked Plains, or Llano Estacado, and the escarpment and more rolling countryside that surrounds it.

11. FWWT, SWC. The latter migration pattern from the South and border states through Arkansas to Texas conforms to those discussed in Blaine T. Williams, "The Frontier Family: Demographic Fact and Historical Myth," Harold M. Hollingsworth, ed., *Essays on the American West* (Austin: University of Texas Press, 1969).

12. FWWT, SWC.

13. The availability of manufactured items to West Texas families has been discussed by Deborah J. Hoskins in an unpublished seminar paper, "Material Culture on the West Texas Frontier," Department of History, Texas Tech University, 1981.

14. Mary A. Blankenship, *The West Is for Us*, ed. Seymour V. Connor (Lubbock: West Texas Museum Association, 1958), p. 94.

15. Zela Maye White Long, born in West Texas, homesteaded with her family in Roosevelt County, New Mexico, as late as 1920. Zela Maye White Long, "Biographical Information," FWWT, SWC.

16. Lydia Louise Mooar, "My Longest Day," p. 2, FWWT, SWC.

17. "Report of Up-to-Date Club," n.d., pp. 14-15, FWWT, SWC.

18. Margaret Mooar, "Report on Public Education," Up-to-Date Club, n.d., p. 4, FWWT, SWC.

19. "George's Birthday, The Up-to-Date Club Celebrates the Event with Exercises Befitting the Occasion," Newsclipping in Up-to-Date Club Minute Book, 1898, FWWT, SWC.

20. Constance Mary Manby Smith, "Life and Original Poems," 1961, FWWT, SWC.

21. Irene McGregor Ratliff, "From Heaven to Texas and Back," 1972, p. 9, FWWT, SWC.

22. Transcript, interview by Seymour V. Connor with Mr. and Mrs. Monroe Abernathy, June 4, 1956, Reel no. 2, p. 20, FWWT, SWC.

23. Ibid., June 7, 1956, Reel no. 4, pp. 25, 28.

24. Transcript, Interview with Hiley T. Boyd, Jr., n.d., FWWT, SWC.

25. "Life and History of Mrs. Julia Carter," 1970, pp. 7, 8, FWWT, SWC.

26. Winnie Harris Rush, "My Footprints in the Sands of Time," 1970, p. 13, FWWT, SWC.

27. Ibid., p. 25.

28. Mrs Arthur Duncan, "Recollections of a Pioneer Mother," n.d., pp. 3-4, 6, 9, FWWT, SWC.

29. Blankenship, *West Is for Us*, pp. 16-17, 19.

30. Transcript, Interview by Duncan G. Muckelroy with Mrs. Emma B. Russell, August 14, 1972, p. 9, FWWT, SWC.

31. Jane Lowe Quillan, "A Saga of the Plains," n.d., pp. 8, 12, FWWT, SWC.

32. Lucille Hughes, "Recollections of Mrs. J. T. Jowell," transcript from interview on June 21, 1938, p. 4, FWWT, SWC.

33. Transcript, interview by Duncan G. Muckelroy with Mrs. J. P. McDonald, February 3, 1973, p. 4; second Interview, March 7, 1973, pp. 3, 6, 14, 17, FWWT, SWC.

34. Rush, "My Footprints . . ."; interview by Melody McCarron with Mary Pirkle Sparks, April 1981, FWWT, SWC.

III

COLLECTIVISM

We believe in small farms and thorough cultivation.

We believe in large crops, which leave the land better than they found it, making both the farmer and the farm at once.

We believe the best fertilizer of any soil is the spirit of industry, enterprise and intelligence—without this, lime and gypsum, bones and green manure, marl and guano, will be of little use.

We disbelieve in farmers who will not improve—in farms that grow poorer every year—farmers' boys turning into clerks and merchants—in farmers ashamed of their vocation.

Farmers' Creed,
by Judge Charles F. Holly,
Sentinel, ca. 1853

The post-Civil War era brought new challenges to the very survival of American ranchers and farmers. Technology altered the relationship of agriculturalists to their lands; environmental disasters caused a necessary sensitivity to nature. Big business forced farmers and ranchers to adapt individually and organize collectively. Agriculturalists became culturally less self-reliant and less individualistic.

By 1865, the United States had expanded to the Pacific Coast encompassing the plush grasslands of the Great Plains. Cattleman and cowboy came here to traverse the open ranges. But contrary to common mythology, the leaders of the early American cattle ranching industry on the plains were more a community of individualists than a collection of fighting singletons. According to Byron Price, this was especially true in the Texas Panhandle where, under the guidance of Charles Goodnight, the Panhandle Stock Association helped large and small rancher alike to conquer economic hardship and avoid social turmoil. Cooperation characterized the ranching world.

Realizing that individual survival required group alliance, Texas farmers, according to Janet Schmelzer, created a statewide farm bureau. In its early years, the Texas Farm Bureau Federation attempted to model itself after the national organization, and it also sought specialization, paying particular attention to cotton farmers. Education and marketing experimentation were key elements for the social and economic well-being of Texas farmers.

Collectivism, then, was a unique cultural response of both farmers and ranchers to the forces of cultural change. Cultural as well as economic survival necessitated cooperation among agriculturalists.

Community of Individualists:
The Panhandle Stock
Association, 1879–1889

Recent works by historians, such as Daniel Boorstin and
Robert V. Hine, have focused on communal rather than individual frontier experiences.[1] The two authors have discovered expressions of community in a variety of Western institutions, including the cattle industry. Both have recognized
a basic dynamism between community and individual in a
business that has long symbolized independent enterprise.
Hine, for example, concludes that "only organization made an
open-range cattle system function," but that "cooperative
loyalties were overlaid by an imperious individualism, a spirit
that insinuated itself in many shapes."[2]

During the two decades that followed the Civil War, cattlemen banded together for mutual protection and benefit in
numerous local and regional alliances throughout the West.
Association did not, however, subdue the strong strain of individualism that permeated the character of free range ranchers. An unidentified editorialist writing in the *Texas Livestock
Journal* in the early 1880s observed that stockmen in the Lone
Star State were, "less closely united and less enthusiastic
about their organizations than any other class of businessmen
who might be mentioned."[3] Indeed, the strength of cattlemen's
organizations, their successes and failures, may be measured,
at least in part, by the commitment of individual members and

their willingness to subordinate personal interests to community goals. The short and stormy history of the first Panhandle Stock Association illustrates the complex interplay of individual and communal instincts during a decade in which the cattle business experienced both prosperity and disaster.

In the mid-1870s the removal of the Indian barrier to settlement opened the vast, unspoiled grassland of the Panhandle-Plains of Texas to cattlemen for the first time. In 1876, Charles Goodnight, in partnership with John Adair, an Irish investment broker, led the vanguard, driving a herd into the depths of Palo Duro Canyon and establishing the JA Ranch. By 1880, the herds of Goodnight and the more than fifty cattlemen who had followed him into the region numbered almost 100,000 head. Over 60 percent of these cattle belonged to seven individuals or partnerships, the JA herd, numbering about 15,000 animals, being by far the largest.[4]

The stocking of the range, however, was only beginning. In 1880, British investors organized the Prairie Cattle Company Ltd., signaling the beginning of large-scale foreign investment in the cattle business. Nearly a dozen joint-stock companies were established in England and Scotland during the next five years. These organizations, along with those financed with Eastern capital, eventually would dominate the cattle business on the Texas plains. Until that time, control of the industry remained in the hands of relatively small individual operators.[5]

Early arrivals had claimed the choicest range, immediately preempting huge tracts along rivers and streams. Those with sufficient capital resources purchased what land they could from railroads and land companies; others founded and sustained their fortunes on the free grass of the public domain. In the Texas Panhandle, as in other regions where the open range system of ranching flourished, cattlemen maintained order through a quasi-legal, sometimes ambiguous, set of range customs.[6] Although revered by romanticists as an almost ideal form of government, the code of conduct that governed ranchmen's activities in the days before barbed wire frequently was

breached when frontier conditions combined with eager entrepreneurs and competitive business practices to produce a vola-
tile mixture. According to one contemporary writer, stockmen's associations arose throughout Texas in the 1870s and
1880s in response to "the condition of cattle management as
pursued under the old system of 'every ranchman for himself,'
a grabbing up of all in sight, a disregard of other's rights, and
the selfish bullying and damaging way of running cattle, pursued in the years immediately following the late war."[7] The
Panhandle Stock Association was no exception.

When considered in a broader context, the creation of an
association of Panhandle cattlemen may be viewed as a single
component of the general movement toward order in that frontier region. Its birth closely followed that of Wheeler County,
the first county organized in the Panhandle, and coincided
with the establishment of the Thirty-Fifth Judicial District
there in 1881. All three institutions worked to halt the general
lawlessness that had prevailed in the absence of effective legal
machinery.

Credit for launching and nurturing the Panhandle Stock
Association throughout most of its brief existence belongs to
Charles Goodnight. In addition to owning the largest ranch in
the area, Goodnight possessed enormous energy and experience. The epitome of independence, he also recognized the importance of organization and unity in problem solving.[8]

To that end, Goodnight and a few other stockmen of his ilk
had, as early as 1879, met informally to discuss the prospects
for a permanent association. Two general meetings of cattlemen held in 1880, in Mobeetie, seat of Wheeler County, con-
firmed the need; in January of the following year, the Panhandle Stock Association officially organized. By joining together,
members pledged their "united efforts and influence to the
general advancement of the live stock interest, and to the
special protection of our joint and individual interests."[9]

The association offered membership to any reputable male
over age eighteen, who owned or managed stock in the Panhandle, upon payment of a small initiation fee and a two-thirds

vote of the membership. According to Goodnight, the association took in "any settler that would join us, whether he had one cow or ten."[10] Persons owning no cattle but desiring to join became non-voting members and were eligible to hold the posts of secretary or treasurer in the organization.[11]

Despite the initial enthusiasm for the association, its membership grew slowly. In August 1882, a Mobeetie newspaper and official organ of the association, reported that only about 25 percent of the ranchers in the Panhandle belonged. Less than fifty companies and individuals comprised the rolls of the organization as late as 1884. Most of these were substantial cattlemen located in the eastern Panhandle or just across the state line in Indian Territory. The Panhandle stockmen's organization drew very few members from among ranchers operating in the western reaches of the region. A brand book published for the association in 1884, for example, listed no members having a headquarters west of Potter and Randall counties.[12]

Several factors account for this geographic imbalance. At least initially, a majority of Panhandle stockmen occupied ranges on the rolling plains to the east and south of the caprock escarpment. Great distances coupled with poor transportation and communication must also be considered as negative forces, as must the individualism and independence of the cattlemen of the western Panhandle. As late as 1886, most of the ranchers surrounding the town of Tascosa belonged to no formal cattlemen's organization, though they did meet together periodically to discuss mutual problems and to cooperate during general roundups and range work. Otherwise, large operators such as the LX and LS seem to have preferred handling their own affairs.[13]

Beyond being merely unwilling to join the Panhandle Stock Association, many cowmen on the Llano Estacado apparently were openly hostile to it. "The Tascosa vicinity," asserted O. H. Nelson, twice president of the Panhandle organization, "was ultra-tough, the bully of the entire region."[14] He later told historian J. Evetts Haley that he believed some of the ranchers in that area declined to affiliate because they were among the biggest cattle thieves and therefore at cross-purposes with association goals. Although Tascosa sources are silent on the matter, there is at least some evidence to suggest that personal rivalries between western Panhandle stockmen and the leaders of the Panhandle Stock Association may have been a root cause of the conflict.[15]

The constitution of the Panhandle Stock Association vested the leadership of the organization in a president and two vice-presidents elected annually. This trio comprised the powerful finance committee charged with managing the business affairs of the association. Although a fourth person was later added to the committee, it has been suggested that the membership desired a small governing body because it permitted an easy quorum and expedited the handling of business. During the ten-year history of the association, relatively few men occupied these top leadership positions. The most frequent office holders included Charles Goodnight, O. H. Nelson, H. W. Cresswell, Nick Eaton, and Robert Moody, all of whom owned or managed large herds.[16]

Despite the apparent concentration of decision-making responsibility in the hands of a few powerful stockmen, a greater number of individuals directed association affairs at the local level. An examination of the composition of the multitude of special committees appointed to plan roundups, to lay out trails, to draft resolutions on important issues, to confer with other cattlemen's groups on matters of mutual concern, and to formulate other policy reveals fairly broad participation and interest among the rank and file. Moreover, regional meetings of the association called to deal with local issues appear to have been relatively better attended than the general assemblies held semi-annually at Mobeetie. Poor attendance at general conventions probably prompted an 1884 resolution to fine absentees $5.00.[17]

To ensure the democratic process, votes on association business were apportioned equally among members. The majority of stock owners steadfastly rejected the suggestion of several large cattle companies that voting privileges be commensurate with herd size. Charles Goodnight is reported to have been particularly chagrined at the idea and to have threatened to leave the organization if such a rule ever passed. Others undoubtedly would have followed him.[18]

The Panhandle Stock Association supported its diverse activities through small initiation fees and annual dues plus yearly assessments usually based on the value of each member's stock as enumerated for state tax purposes. Such levies commonly amounted to between 1¢ and 3¢ per head and generated thousands of dollars of revenue. Occasionally, cattlemen supported local projects through special assessments. This was the case in 1881-1882 when association members in the Clarendon vicinity voluntarily assessed themselves to provide a school and a doctor for that fledgling community. Besides payments directly to the association, many individual ranchers also spent heavily in the promotion of association (and their own) interests.[19]

Responsibility for the collection and appropriation of funds fell to the finance committee. The association constitution delegated broad authority to this three-man body and according to one historian, "its power was almost arbitrary."[20] Although it was required to submit an annual expense report, at least part of the financial dealings of this committee went unrecorded, especially those matters involving the suppression of cattle thieves.[21]

The finance committee, sometimes referred to as the Executive Committee or the Detective and Protective Committee, hired stock detectives on local ranges, supplemented the salaries of local law enforcement officials, and employed brand inspectors on trails and at shipping points. Members authorized the first inspectors in August 1881, providing one each at Kansas City, St. Louis, and Chicago for a period of four months during the heavy shipping season. They also designated commission merchants to receive and market any stray or stolen stock cut from herds by association inspectors. The following year brand inspectors were stationed at Dodge City and Cald-

well in Kansas, as well as at other points.[22] "The association
starts this fall with blood in their eyes," the *Dodge City Times*
reported in July. "They are determined that the interests of
each stock owner shall be protected."[23]

Since the hiring of inspectors, whose salaries ranged as high
as $100.00 per month, quickly proved burdensome, it became
advantageous to cooperate with other cattlemen's organizations in sharing such expenses. As a first step, the Panhandle
Stock Association, in 1883, agreed with the Western Kansas
Stock Growers' Association to share the cost of hiring three
inspectors. Association officials later concluded a similar
arrangement with the Northwest Texas Cattle Raisers' Association, paying $5 per head for all animals cut out by NTCRA
inspectors at St. Louis and Chicago.[24]

Brand inspectors recovered thousands of dollars worth of
stray and stolen stock annually. In a few shipments, the number of illegally branded cattle discovered by investigators
amounted to as much as 25 percent of the total. At least one
shipper, irate at the thorough manner in which an association
inspector had cut his herd, assaulted the man, severely injur-
ing him. Most inspectors, however, operated unmolested and
were quite effective in the performance of their duties.[25]

Closer to home, Panhandle cattle raisers attempted to protect their interests by supplementing the salaries of local law
enforcement authorities. By so doing they hoped to attract
quality individuals to the posts of county sheriff, district judge,
and district attorney as the region organized for judicial purposes. According to one association president, the standard salary of these positions, "would not have supported a man for a
month."[26] Subsidies paid to these officers varied from $500.00
to $1,500.00 or more per year. As District Attorney of Wheeler
County in the early 1880s, Temple Houston received a law
library as well as a salary supplement from the association.[27]

In contrast to brand inspectors and local lawmen, stock detectives operated with little fanfare. Their appointments and
activities were a closely guarded secret known only to the finance committee that paid them. Cattlemen had employed

range detectives to ferret out rustlers even before the formal organization of the Panhandle Stock Association. In December 1880, for example, cattlemen of the region sent former Wheeler County deputy sheriff, John Poe, to New Mexico with orders to assist Lincoln County authorities in the apprehension of Billy the Kid whose gang had been depredating among Panhandle herds. Poe, who bore a letter of introduction from Charles Goodnight, worked closely with Sheriff Pat Garrett until the Kid's death on July 14, 1881.[28] This modest success did not, however, reduce cattle thievery on the ranges of West Texas. As incidents of rustling multiplied throughout the early 1880s, the association employed detectives on all the major ranches in the eastern Panhandle. The frequent reports of these agents, who worked as cowboys, provided such comprehensive information that an association official later boasted that the finance committee, "knew more about what was going on than the ranch owners themselves."[29]

The Panhandle Stock Association was the first Texas cattlemen's organization to offer rewards for the arrest and conviction of cattle rustlers. A constitutional provision offered $250.00 to any party furnishing information leading to the apprehension of stock thieves and an equal amount to prosecute and insure the safe keeping of the accused. When Donley County ranchman, J. F. Evans, and Mobeetie lawyer, H. A. Lewis, drafted the document, they inserted the reward proviso against the advice of many experienced stock raisers. Most expected antagonism from the ranks of that fiercely independent breed of early Texas cowman who freely engaged in mavericking unbranded stock and other questionable range practices. Indeed, during the fight to suppress rustling, association officials regularly received complaints and threats, most of them anonymous. Intimidation of this sort had little effect, however, as resolutions designed to discourage cattle theft repeatedly passed during association meetings.[30] Years later, Evans, who had been elected the first president of the Panhandle Stock Association, remembered with pride that, "in the face of the bitterest opposition we hewed to the line, respecting no violator's standing or wealth."[31]

Early in the battle, the reward offered by the association proved to be a liability in court and had to be abandoned because a judge hearing a case involving the theft of stock belonging to one association member disqualified other members from serving as jurors. The reward, he ruled, prejudiced the entire membership in the outcome of the trial. At an association meeting on July 21, 1883, therefore, the collective reward was withdrawn, and it was recommended that members tender instead individual recompense of at least $1,000 for convictions. Few could be secured.[32]

In Donley County, for example, cattlemen failed to obtain a single conviction for rustling between 1882-1891. Although numerous cowboys and their employers sat in judgment during litigation involving cattle theft, all trials resulted in either a not guilty verdict or a hung jury. Many others never reached trial for lack of sufficient evidence.[33]

To circumvent what many cattlemen saw as an ineffective and unjust judicial process, the association took matters into its own hands from time to time and engaged in extralegal bargaining with suspected thieves. A committee typically confronted these nefarious characters with evidence of their criminal conduct and agreed not to prosecute if the accused left the region and did not return. Although this approach usually worked well, a few of the more outspoken members of the association advocated sterner measures including the formation of a vigilance committee to dispense summary justice. The suggestion never was consummated, but the threat apparently convinced a number of well-known rustlers to depart from the area.[34]

The fight against cattle theft during the early 1880s led to progressively formal organization and regulation of range work. Following an example set by the Northwest Texas Cattle Raisers' Association in 1877, the Panhandle Stock Association, in 1881, established roundup districts within its territory.

Ranchers located between the Main and North Forks of the Red River belonged to the North Fork and Red River Division. Those operating along the Canadian River separated into two divisions, the boundary between them being Adobe Walls, located in present-day Hutchinson County. The number of districts was later reduced to two by combining the Canadian districts.[35]

Each district planned and conducted its own cooperative roundups, which varied slightly in timing and organization from season to season. Stockmen within a division usually gathered at a designated meeting place and elected a district roundup superintendent who then appointed a committee to plan the operation. Most commonly, the superintendent delegated authority for the actual conduct of the roundup to individual foremen and owners while working their range. Occasionally, however, division members elected and paid a general superintendent and empowered him to arbitrate all disputes relating to the ownership of stock. Noah Ellis, for example, served as general superintendent for the North Fork and Red River Division in 1882 and received for his services $5.00 per day plus a special assessment amounting to $155.00 from seventeen participating ranchers.[36]

Association members considered the systematic roundup of individual ranges by combined outfits during specified periods preferable to haphazard individual efforts. Communal endeavor and organization minimized losses to thieves and to negligence and provided a framework for the arbitration of stock disputes. Disagreements, some of them the result of lax management, arose periodically, nevertheless. In July 1883, for example, the manager of the Francklyn Land and Cattle Company advised his superiors in New York that H. W. Cresswell, an association officer, had been, "raising old ned with Mr. [J. M.] Coburn for allowing his men to brand his calves," and that there was "no ranch in that country that has not suffered from the same careless work."[37]

Many of the range regulations imposed by the Panhandle Stock Association affected the cowboys who labored on the

ranches of the region. Some of the rules, such as the pro-
hibitions against card playing and drinking, were designed to
control personal behavior in the interest of general safety. Others were devised to cut expenses. One discontinued the custom
of feeding free any cowboy who happened by a chuckwagon at
mealtime. The 1885 resolution required ranchers to provide
their hands with evidence of employment during roundups and
to be responsible for paying for their meals.[38]

Restrictive policies of Panhandle ranchmen who forbade
their cowboys to build up personal herds and who discouraged
them from owning land have been cited by some historians
as key factors precipitating the Cowboy Strike of 1883. The
extent to which the members or the labor tactics of the Panhandle Stock Association may have influenced this walkout is
unclear, because none of the ranchers affected by the strike
belonged to the cattlemen's organization or were subject to its
regulations. Moreover, the strikers' only demand involved
wages, not land or cattle or working conditions. Apart from
Charles Goodnight, who is said to have offered his assistance
in helping break the movement, other association members did
not seem disposed to take an active role. Had the rebellion
lasted longer or spread eastward from its place of origin in the
Tascosa vicinity, affiliates of the Panhandle organization
might have been more vocal in their opposition. Few, if any,
sympathized with the strikers, and association members probably participated in the blacklisting of those involved once the
disorder had run its course.[39]

To cattlemen of the Panhandle-Plains, labor unrest seemed a
minor nuisance when compared to the perils of the drift of
Northern cattle and the spread of tick fever into the region.
These problems did not lend themselves to individual solutions. Cattle drifting by the thousands from as far away as
Kansas and southern Colorado threatened to decimate already
overstocked Panhandle pastures in the early 1880s. In 1882,
faced with this continuing dilemma, stockmen determined to
build a major fence well north of the Canadian River to halt
the drift. Like so many other ranching activities, this coopera-

tive effort was promoted by the association but conducted by individuals, not all of them members. Each cattle raiser or company with range lying along the proposed fenced line erected a part of the nearly 200-mile barrier. Its barbed presence proved an effective deterrent to Northern stock.[40]

The introduction of tick-bearing cattle from southern Texas was more difficult to check, and their presence among Panhandle herds was more devastating. Ticks transmitted a dreaded disease known variously as Texas or Spanish Fever. The vexing question of how to prevent outbreaks of this malady among Panhandle herds perhaps more than any other united cattlemen in a common cause.

Discussions of tick fever problems had dominated meetings of Panhandle cattlemen since 1880. Convening in Mobeetie in late July of that year, stock raisers passed resolutions recommending that South Texas herds bound for Northern markets use trails which avoided the eastern Panhandle and requested that cattlemen bringing Southern stock cattle into the region keep them separate from herds already there until a frost rid the new arrivals of the disease. Six months later Panhandle cattlemen petitioned Governor Oran M. Roberts for assistance. They encouraged him to help legislate and enforce a quarantine law or to mandate specific Northern trails for South Texas herds. These proposals fell on deaf ears.[41]

Unable to convince the Governor to act, the Panhandle Stock Association again resorted to extralegal protective measures. In 1881, determined members of the North Fork and Red River Division placed armed patrols along the southern edge of their territory to discover and divert fever-ridden herds around their ranges. Although the Panhandle Stock Association sponsored the effort, individual ranches such as the JA, Shoe Bar, RO, Matador, and Spur bore most of the expense of maintaining the line for about five years.[42]

The effectiveness of the celebrated "Winchester Quarantine" is debatable. Certainly many drovers were persuaded to take alternate routes that avoided the eastern half of the Panhandle. Others, however, slipped through, and at least one association member himself brought tick-infested Southern cattle to his ranch in defiance of the ban. The total number of cattle lost to the disease in the region may have reached 300,000 head between 1880-1885. During a single two-year period of the quarantine, one Panhandle company recorded losses of livestock valued at $200,000 or more. Many of these animals were expensive purebred stock brought from the Midwest and elsewhere to upgrade Panhandle longhorns.[43]

The lobbying effort of the association in the state legislature fared little better; South Texas lawmakers consistently outvoted their Panhandle counterparts. The Panhandle cattlemen's group did, however, find allies among other associations whose members were suffering similarly. At a meeting held in St. Louis in the spring of 1885, cattlemen's organizations in Colorado, Kansas, and Indian Territory rallied behind the Panhandle Stock Association and pledged to resist further incursions of fever-bearing herds from below the thirty-fourth parallel. Tensions mounted until South Texas drovers finally yielded to demands that they confine their herds to a specific trail. Assembling in Dallas in May of that same year, the major Texas stockmen's groups agreed to a route that passed east and north of the main Panhandle range.[44]

For a while, wary Panhandle ranchers maintained their vigilance, policing their pastures and turning aside violators. "The cattlemen here," wrote one from Mobeetie in May 1885, "are altogether in the matter and will use all means in their power to keep them on the route they have picked for them."[45] The need for association supervision of the primary cattle outlet to the North gradually diminished as trail driving succumbed to barbed wire fencing and legal quarantines.

The whole complex of open range ranching began to change in the mid-1880s. Forces threatening the tenure of the cattle kingdom of the Llano Estacado and the rolling plains east of the caprock closed in from all directions. Many were beyond the power of stockmen, either as individuals or as an association, to resist. Cattle prices declined rapidly forcing numerous companies into bankruptcy. The weather destroyed others as cattle perished by the thousands during a succession of winter storms and summer droughts between 1885-1887. The railroad, too, began its relentless advance across the Panhandle-Plains. An endless wave of new settlers followed in its wake, claiming parts of the public domain where longhorns once had grazed unencumbered.[46]

Since their earliest occupation of the Panhandle range, beleaguered stockmen had fought to secure enough land to operate profitably. Most had bought what they could from land speculators and railroad companies, but huge tracts of school land that usually consisted of alternate sections remained in the hands of the state. In 1883, the Land Board Act authorized the sale of up to seven sections of this land to individuals and the competitive leasing of additional range for ten years at a minimum of 4¢ per acre. When cattlemen of the region all bid the minimum and refused to compete for leases, the land board and the legislature attempted to revise the law by doubling minimum lease fees and restricting sales to bona fide settlers. The board also refused to lease certain watered property altogether. Only a long and difficult court fight, which lasted until 1887, forced the board to honor the original terms.[47]

Lawyers hired by the association conducted the five-year long struggle, successfully defending individual cattlemen and their organization against charges ranging from illegal occupation of state lands to conspiracy. A few particularly outspoken stockmen such as Charles Goodnight, O. H. Nelson, and J. F. Evans also played key roles. On the matter of leases, the association's position was complicated by a small but ardent group of "free grassers" within the organization who opposed leasing or any other policy that required paying for the use of the range. They succeeded in introducing a number of bills in the legislature to support their position. Although none passed, the activities of the free grass element divided an already weakened association.[48]

The leasing controversy, cattle rustling, Texas fever, and dismal economic conditions had laid a heavy burden on the pocketbooks and the morale of the association and its members. Goodnight's biographer asserts that the lease fight alone cost the veteran cowman at least $20,000.00.[49] Legal fees and lobbying efforts plunged the association heavily into debt, as well, and forced the group to reorganize.

In 1885, preliminary steps were taken to change the association when a committee was appointed to revise the constitution and by-laws of the body. The following year, members approved a new constitution and an amended state charter and closed out the business of the previous organization. Thirty-two members comprised the initial roster of the new association, and a five-man board of directors replaced the finance committee in the management of association business. Constitutional provisions reflecting financial retrenchment limited the annual expenditures of the board to a maximum of $5,000. C. B. Willingham, Robert Moody, Nick Eaton, H. H. Campbell, and Charles Goodnight, all prominent leaders in the old organization, were elected to positions on the board of the new one.[50]

Whatever enthusiasm or optimism that may have greeted the reorganization of the Panhandle Stock Association was short lived. Charles Goodnight, who had been elected president of the new association in April 1886, unexpectedly withdrew from the position in the early summer. Personal affairs may have played a part in his decision; he was on the verge of dissolving his decade-long partnership in the JA Ranch.[51] More likely, however, the source of Goodnight's disenchantment lay within the organization itself. "If the cattlemen of this country had any foresight," he wrote to a business associate shortly after his decision, "and were willing to spend their money in the way of shaping legislation I think we might accomplish what we need. But I have so little means that I can spare and if I had it I have no desire and no authority to expend money belonging to others."[52]

In August, Goodnight approached the Matador and several other ranches to join with him in forming a separate organization. When this idea bore no fruit, the pioneer cowman joined the neighboring Northwest Texas Association where he became a member of the executive committee. Goodnight's departure proved a serious blow to the Panhandle Stock Association, which had relied on his powerful and persuasive leadership in times of crisis. Other members, following their president's lead, left the ranks as well. In doing so, they placed an even greater financial burden on those who remained.[53]

In 1887, the fiscal outlook for both the cattle business and the association worsened. George Tyng, who had taken control of the bankrupt Francklyn Land and Cattle Company in 1886, wrote a New York trustee of the defunct corporation in March that "the embarrassments of cattlemen are more general than I have represented them to you. Maturing obligations and occupation of ranges by actual settlers are going to force sales of stock cattle."[54] One month later, a committee appointed to examine the accounts of the stockmen's association reported that Secretary E. J. Rising had "absconded" leaving the books in such poor shape that a satisfactory report was impossible. Best estimates at the time, however, placed association indebtedness at about $1,100.[55]

Despite the dismal economic picture, the Panhandle Stock Association limped on for two more years. The association continued to plan roundups and employ inspectors and legal counsel, and a new secretary attempted to sort out the books, collect overdue assessments and accounts, and clear the organization of its debts. As association levies required to defray operating expenses and settle past financial obligations became increasingly burdensome, members defected at an alarming rate. By 1889, the organization had folded altogether.[56]

Many factors contributed to the demise of the Panhandle Stock Association. Drought and depression certainly played key roles as did the close of the open range. The arrival of farmers, fences, railroad, and legal institutions altered forever the frontier environment that had briefly bound individual cattlemen into a regional community. Seemingly impotent against the forces that assailed it from all sides, the organization gradually ceased to serve effectively the interests of its constituents. Likewise, individual members proved unwilling and unable to sustain the body in times of severe economic hardship and social turmoil. The Panhandle Stock Association was truly a community of individualists typical of Robert V. Hine's modern version of frontier society and of the democratic frontier institutions so idolized by Frederick Jackson Turner. That the organization should ultimately fail on the eve of the passing of Turner's frontier seems both appropriate and inevitable.

NOTES

1. Daniel Boorstin, *The Americans: The Democratic Experience* (New York: Random House, 1974), pp. 18-29; Robert V. Hine, *Community on the American Frontier: Separate But Not Alone* (Norman: University of Oklahoma Press, 1980), pp. 164-71.

2. Hine, *Community on American Frontier*, p. 165.

3. *Fort Worth Texas Live Stock Journal*, 9 June 1883. For a discussion of the role of cattlemen's associations in the West, see William W. Savage, Jr., "Stockmen's Associations and the Western Range Cattle Industry," *Journal of the West* 14 (July 1974): 52-59.

4. Harley True Burton, *A History of the JA Ranch* (Austin, Tex.: Von Boeckmann-Jones Co., 1928), pp. 24-30; Seymour V. Connor, "Early Ranching Operations in the Panhandle: A Report on the Agricultural Schedules of the 1880 Census," *Panhandle-Plains Historical Review* 27 (1954): 47-69.

5. Ibid. The role of foreign capital investment in Panhandle ranching is discussed in detail in W. G. Kerr, "Scotland and the Texas Mortgage Business," *Panhandle-Plains Historical Review* 38 (1965): 53-71; Richard Graham, "The Investment Boom in British-Texas Cattle Companies, 1880-1885," *Business History Review* 34 (Winter 1960): 421-445; and L. F. Sheffy, "British Pounds and British Purebreds," *Panhandle-Plains Historical Review* 11 (1938): 55-68.

6. Boone McClure, "The Laws and Customs of the Open Range," *Panhandle-Plains Historical Review* 10 (1937): 64-79; Boorstin, *The Democratic Experience*, pp. 19-26.

7. *Fort Worth Texas Live Stock Journal*, 20 October 1883.

8. A complete study of Goodnight's life including his impact on the Panhandle Stock Association may be found in J. Evetts Haley, *Charles Goodnight, Cowman & Plainsman* (Boston: Houghton, Mifflin Company, 1936).

9. O. H. Nelson, "The Story of the First Panhandle Stockmen's Association," address delivered at the Annual Meeting of the Panhandle-Plains Historical Society, Canyon, Texas, 12 February 1926, p. 1, O. H. Nelson Papers, Panhandle-Plains Historical Museum, Canyon, Texas (hereinafter cited as Nelson Papers); *Dodge City* (Kansas) *Times*, 7 August 1880; *Ford County* (Kansas) *Globe*, 28 December 1880; Panhandle Stock Association, *Brand Book Containing the Brands of the Pan-Handle Stock Assoc'n, also Constitution and Resolutions Adopted by the Association, 1884* (Kansas City, MO: the author, 1884), p. 3.

10. As quoted in Haley, *Charles Goodnight*, p. 364.

11. Panhandle Stock Association, *Brand Book*, p. 5.

12. Ibid., pp. 10-31; *Dodge City* (Kansas) *Times*, 31 August 1882.

13. Connor, "Early Ranching," pp. 47-69; *Tascosa* (Texas) *Pioneer*, 12 June 1886; *Fort Worth Texas Live Stock Journal*, 30 May 1884, 24 April 1886; O. H. Nelson to J. Evetts Haley, 26 February 1927, interview, Nelson Papers.

14. As quoted in Wellington Brink, "Those 'Good Old Days' on the Plains," *Amarillo* (Texas) *Southwest Plainsman*, 17 April 1926.

15. O. H. Nelson to J. Evetts Haley, 13 July 1926, interview, Nelson Papers.

16. Panhandle Stock Association, *Brand Book*, pp. 2-3; Haley, *Charles Goodnight*, p. 363.

17. Reports of association proceedings including attendance, election results, and committee assignments were published regularly in newspapers in Texas and Kansas. Typical examples include *Fort Worth Texas Live Stock Journal*, 14 April 1883, 22 December 1883, 26 April 1884, 24 April 1886; *Ford County* (Kansas) *Globe*, 4 April 1882; *Dodge City* (Kansas) *Globe Live Stock Journal*, 4 May 1885; Panhandle Stock Association, *Brand Book*, pp. 3, 9.

18. Haley, *Charles Goodnight*, pp. 364-65.

19. Ibid., pp. 364, 372, 501; Panhandle Stock Association, *Brand Book*, p. 6; idem, minutes of meetings of the Board of Directors, meetings of 6 June 1887, 24 April 1888, manuscript volume, Panhandle Stock Association Papers, Panhandle-Plains Historical Museum, Canyon, Texas (hereinafter cited as Panhandle Stock Association Papers); *Ford County* (Kansas) *Globe*, 30 August 1881, 4 April 1882.

20. Haley, *Charles Goodnight*, p. 363.

21. Ibid.; Panhandle Stock Association, *Brand Book*, p. 6; J. F. Evans, "A Few Campfires Along My Trail" (unpublished typescript, J. F. Evans Papers, Panhandle-Plains Historical Museum, Canyon, Texas).

22. Panhandle Stock Association, *Brand Book*, p. 7; *Ford County* (Kansas) *Globe*, 30 August 1881; Nelson,"Stockmen's Association," p. 3. O. H. Nelson indicated in an interview many years later that the association had as many as fifteen to twenty detectives and inspectors on the payroll at one time; see Nelson to Haley, 26 February 1927, Nelson Papers.

23. *Dodge City* (Kansas) *Times*, 13 July 1882.

24. *Ford County* (Kansas) *Globe*, 30 August 1881, 19 June 1883; *Fort Worth Texas Livestock Journal*, 26 April 1884, 24 April 1886; Panhandle Stock Association, *Brand Book*, pp. 8-9; idem, minutes of meetings of the Board of Directors, meetings of 6 June 1887, 7 April 1888, Panhandle Stock Association Papers.

25. *Ford County* (Kansas) *Globe*, 19 June 1883; Nelson, "Stockmen's Association," p. 304.

26. Ibid., p. 5.

27. J. Evetts Haley, "The Grass Lease Fight and attempted Impeachment of the First Panhandle Judge," *Southwestern Historical Quarterly* 38 (July 1934): 19-20; idem, *Charles Goodnight*, pp. 367, 372. Association members also served in positions of authority as county commissioners and grand jurors; see Commissioners Court Record, vol. 1, p. 4, Office of the Donley County Clerk, Clarendon, Texas.

28. Sophie A. Poe, *Buckboard Days* (Caldwell, Idaho: Caxton Printers, Ltd., 1936), pp. 98-101; John L. McCarty *Maverick Town: The Story of Old Tascosa* (Norman: University of Oklahoma Press, 1946), pp. 83-91; Nelson, "Stockmen's Association," p. 4.

29. Nelson to Haley, 26 February 1927, Nelson Papers.

30. Ibid.; Panhandle Stock Association, *Brand Book*, pp. 6, 8; J. F. Evans to Wm. L. Evans, 10 March 1926, Mrs. Joseph H. Mitchell Papers, Panhandle-Plains Historical Museum, Canyon, Texas.

31. Ibid.

32. Nelson to Haley, 26 February 1927, Nelson Papers; Panhandle Stock Association, *Brand Book*, p. 8; *Fort Worth Texas Live Stock Journal*, 4 August 1883; H.T. Groom to Mr. [Frank G.] Brown, 22 July 1883, Francklyn Land & Cattle Company Papers, Panhandle-Plains Historical Museum, Canyon, Texas (hereinafter cited as Francklyn Land & Cattle Company Papers).

33. Burton, *JA Ranch*, pp. 86-87; Brink, "Good Old Days"; Nelson, "Stockmen's Association," pp. 4-5.

34. Ibid.; Haley, *Charles Goodnight*, pp. 375-76.

35. Chester V. Kielman, "The Texas and Southwestern Cattle Raisers' Association Minute Book," *Southwestern Historical Quarterly*

71 (July 1967): 95; *Fort Worth Texas Live Stock Journal*, 26 April 1884; *Ford County* (Kansas) *Globe*, 4 April 1882; Panhandle Stock Association, *Brand Book*, p. 6.

36. Ibid., pp. 5-7; *Fort Worth Texas Live Stock Journal*, 14 April 1883, 26 April 1884; *Ford County* (Kansas) *Globe*, 22 March 1881, 30 August 1881, 4 April 1882, 26 April 1884, 5 May 1885.

37. H. T. Groom to Mr. [Frank G.] Brown, 11 July 1883, Francklyn Land & Cattle Company Papers.

38. *Ford County* (Kansas) *Globe*, 4 April 1882; Haley, *Charles Goodnight*, pp. 350-51, *Fort Worth Texas Live Stock Journal*, 25 April 1885.

39. McCarty, *Maverick Town*, pp. 108-117; Gene M. Gressley, *Bankers and Cattlemen* (Lincoln: University of Nebraska Press, 1966), pp. 123-124; Boone McClure, "A Review of the T Anchor Ranch," *Panhandle-Plains Historical Review* 3 (1930): 34.

40. McCarty, *Maverick Town*, p. 161; Haley, *Charles Goodnight*, p. 365; G. C. Boswell, "Some Early Activities Around Mobeetie," West Texas Historical Association *Year Book* 12 (1936): 54; Nelson to Haley, 26 February 1927, Nelson Papers.

41. *Dodge City* (Kansas) *Times*, 7 August 1880; *Ford County* (Kansas) *Globe*, 28 December 1880.

42. J. Evetts Haley, "Texas Fever and the Winchester Quarantine," *Panhandle-Plains Historical Review* 8 (1935): 37-53; Burton, *JA Ranch*, pp. 89-91; William C. Holden, *The Espuela Land and Cattle Company* (Austin: State Historical Association, 1970), pp. 149-52; Nelson, "Stockmen's Association," pp. 6-8.

43. Ibid., p. 7; *Port Worth Texas Live Stock Journal*, 24 April 1886; Lester F. Sheffy, *The Francklyn Land & Cattle Company: A Panhandle Enterprise, 1882-1957* (Austin: University of Texas Press, 1963), p. 161.

44. Ibid.; Haley, "Texas Fever," pp. 44-46; *Fort Worth* (Texas) *Gazette*, May 13, 1885; *Dallas* (Texas) *Daily Times*, 16 May 1885; *Dodge City* (Kansas) *Globe Live Stock Journal*, 28 April 1885; *Fort Worth Texas Live Stock Journal*, 28 April 1885, 23 May 1885. It should be noted that some herds continued to use routes that passed through the western reaches of the Panhandle, an area not controlled by members of the Panhandle Stock Association. Ranchers in that area, however, rallied together in 1886 to resist Southern herds as well. See *Fort Worth Texas Live Stock Journal* 17 April 1886.

45. R. H. Arnold to Mr. [Frank] Brown, 20 May 1885, Francklyn Land & Cattle Company Papers.

46. Frederick W. Rathjen, *The Texas Panhandle Frontier* (Austin: University of Texas Press, 1973), pp. 240-43; Edward E. Dale, *The Range Cattle Industry: Ranching on the Great Plains from 1865 to 1925* (Norman: University of Oklahoma Press, 1960), pp. 117-18; John T. Schlebecker, *Cattle Raising on the Great Plains, 1900-1960* (Lincoln: University of Nebraska Press, 1963), pp. 6-13.

47. Haley, "Grass Lease Fight," pp. 1-27.

48. Ibid., Burton, *JA Ranch*, pp. 94-95.

49. Haley, *Charles Goodnight*, p. 401.

50. W.F. Sommerville to A. Mackay, 21 December 1885, Sommerville Correspondence, book 1, November 1885-May 1886, p. 138, Matador Ranch Records, Southwest Collection, Texas Tech University, Lubbock, Texas (hereafter Matador Ranch Records); *Fort Worth Texas Live Stock Journal*, 25 April 1885, 24 April 1886; Panhandle Stock Association, Constitution and By-laws [1886] manuscript vol., Panhandle Stock Association Papers. The association received its initial charter, No. 2721, on 2 June 1885; the amended one was granted on 26 April 1886. Both are filed with the Certifying Section of the Corporations Division, Office of the Secretary of State, Austin, Texas.

51. Arthur J. Weir to W. F. Sommerville, 16 July 1886, Sommerville Correspondence, book 1, May 1886 January 1887, p. 833, Matador Ranch Records.

52. C. Goodnight to Wm. Maquay, 5 January 1887, letterpress copybook, 26 June 1886-September 1893, JA Ranch Records, Panhandle-Plains Historical Museum, Canyon, Texas.

53. Arthur J. Weir to W. F. Sommerville, 16 July 1886, 18 August 1886, Sommerville Correspondence, book 1, May 1886-January 1887, pp. 833, 906, Matador Ranch Records.

54. George Tyng to Mr. [Frederic de P.] Foster, 1 March 1887, Francklyn Land & Cattle Company Papers.

55. Panhandle Stock Association, minutes of the Annual Meeting, 8-9 April 1887, Panhandle Stock Association Papers.

56. Idem, minutes of meetings of the Board of Directors, meetings of 11 April 1887, 6 June 1887, 25 June 1887, 7 April 1888, 24 April 1888, minutes of a Called Meeting, 16 June 1888, Panhandle Stock Association Papers; Burton, *JA Ranch*, p. 85.

The First Years of the Texas Farm Bureau Federation

From 1914 to 1919, the farmer reveled in unparalleled prosperity—and for good reason. With the outbreak of World War I,
agricultural products were in great demand. Abroad, overseas
markets bought American staples because European farmers
were devastated by the war and no longer producing. After the
United States declared war, Americans quickly sold their crops
as the need for military supplies skyrocketed. The result was
higher, inflated prices that farmers hoped would persist for
several years. Conditions were especially favorable for wheat
because the government guaranteed a minimum price of $2.00
per bushel.

The agricultural economy appearing unshakable, farmers
planted and harvested bumper crops without considering even-
tual consequences; they believed that all produce would surely
be sold at record profits. For instance, in 1919, cotton reached
the $2 billion level. Believing that these conditions would con-
tinue, farmers invested in additional acreage that had also
risen to inflated prices. Unwisely, they reasoned that if their
productive land holdings increased, so would their income. To
carry out such schemes, farmers mortgaged heavily with the
expectation of paying off bank loans on time and avoiding foreclosure. For five years they rode this crest of prosperity, hypno-
tized by momentary good times. After all, how could anything

go awry? High crop yield, high demand, and high profits—it seemed as though the farmer's dream had finally materialized.[1]

After 1919, the farmer discovered only too late that this prosperity was ephemeral—collapsing in a spiraling, surely calamitous downward plunge. A major contributor to this financial reversal was overproduction and underconsumption. At the end of the war, demand dropped sharply in domestic and foreign markets. As worldwide agricultural conditions recovered and as the Europeans planted staples in their homelands, American farmers still exported large quantities, but they now received fewer dollars per bale or bushel.

The real blow came in May 1920 when the federal government withdrew guaranteed price supports from wheat and other crops. From then on, agricultural prices plummeted during 1920 and 1921. For cotton growers, prices sagged every month from an average of 41.75¢ (at New Orleans) in April 1920, to 40.52¢ in June, 14.64¢ in December, and 11.08¢ in March 1921. Those producers who sold top-grade cotton were no better off because classifying or grading laws were weak; thus, both poor- and good-quality cotton were treated alike by buyers. And, at a time when they were earning less, farmers continued to pay more for non-agricultural commodities, the costs of which had remained high. By 1920, bleak were the possibilities of repaying bank loans or other debts accrued during those years when farmers had overtaxed their financial limitations. For many, the consequence was foreclosure; for others, tenancy.[2] As the Department of Agriculture reflected years later, the crops of 1919 and 1920 were "grown at great expense, and as a result of this enormous price decline in 1920 cotton producers (and others) faced disaster."[3]

Southern farmers especially needed help. Possibly, they could rely on the government. After all, since 1913 they had benefited from the Woodrow Wilson administration. In 1914 and again in 1916, a Cotton Futures Act defined grades to ensure equitable monetary returns for all cotton. In an effort to keep the producer advised on market conditions, a cotton quotation service, which issued weekly reports, was created in 1919. Another advancement was the Warehouse Act of 1916, establishing government-licensed store houses. In these buildings farmers could deposit crops until prices rose to a satisfactory level. That same year, the Federal Farm Loan Act started a credit system through Farm Loan Associations whereby more money became available to borrow at lower interest rates. Just as important but unrecognized for its long-range value, the Smith-Lever Act of 1914 initiated the extension service of county agents and home demonstrators who dispersed agricultural information. Related to this program, the Smith-Hughes Act of 1916 funded grants-in-aid to vocational and agricultural schools. Generally, the emphasis of both these laws was education, instructing the people of rural areas on better farming techniques as well as social and economic advancements.[4]

After 1920, however, the political environment was transformed dramatically. With the election of Republican President Warren G. Harding, a symbol of the changing times, conservatism swept across the country. Accordingly, progressivism was ostracized, Wilsonian idealism discarded, and social, economic, and political reform shelved. Under Republicans, laissez-faire and industrial, planned economic policies reigned supreme. The government allied with big business. Only occasionally could agriculture depend on federal support, and even then such help was minimal.

In the past, when agriculture was in a depression and when government was unresponsive, farmers organized. The decade after the Civil War, especially after the so-called Panic of 1873, exploded with agricultural groups attempting to rectify poor economic and political conditions. Shortly after 1867, the Grange, or Patrons of Husbandry, spread across the country. Due to their persistence and pressure on state legislatures, as one historian has noted, they "enjoyed considerable political influence." In fact, they directed much of their energies toward correcting and eliminating railroad malpractices.[5] At the same time, they "developed an ambitious marketing program" of collective cotton selling, hoping to guarantee higher prices.[6] As the Grange declined after 1875, the Greenback Party rose. Politically active, the Greenbackers wanted more federal paper dollars circulated so that debts could be repaid with inflated currency. According to John Hicks, the party was "designed primarily as a vehicle through which debt-ridden farmers . . . could express their views."[7] Appearing almost concurrently, the Farmers' Alliance (Northwestern and Southern) began as a non-partisan association that emphasized educating farmers. Eventually turning political, the members pushed for railroad regulation and the free and unlimited coinage of silver.[8] Of all the late nineteenth-century movements, however, Populism was by far the most potent. Populists went directly into the political arena forming a party and running candidates in 1890 and 1892. Rurally oriented, the Populists incorporated into their platform legislative suggestions aimed at aiding the farmer. For instance, they advocated a government-controlled bank system, government ownership and operation of railroads, and the sub-treasury plan.[9] But as Populism waned in the early twentieth century, two other groups reverted to controlling production and, thus, to increasing prices. The older was the Southern Cotton Association, which survived from 1885 to 1905. After 1902 the Farmer's Union employed the ideas of the Association, augmenting them with crop diversification, as well as cooperative buying and selling, and cooperative warehouses.[10]

Although these movements had surely benefited agriculture, farmers were on their own by 1919 and 1920. They could not rely on past associations that no longer existed or were now impotent. The conditions were prime for a new national organization, and in 1919 the American Farm Bureau Federation filled this void. Representing hundreds of local bureaus, the federation evolved from other institutions already established. Since 1914, county farm bureaus had existed, each one working as an independent unit with regional agricultural colleges and the United States Department of Agriculture (USDA). Their primary objective was to educate the farmer.[11] One of the most important components to the success of a bureau was the county agent, a position rising out of the USDA and the Morrill Land-Grant College Act of 1862.[12] Generally, agents disseminated the "accumulated knowledge of these scientific institutions [agricultural societies and the USDA] to the individual farmer."[13] Over a period of time, they began to cooperate with farm bureaus which provided a central nucleus for distributing information. Periodically, all the agents within a state met at the agricultural college and invited the county farm bureau presidents to attend. Thus, the natural outgrowth of such gatherings was the state farm bureau federation.[14]

The greatest impetus to the expansion of local farm bureaus across the country was the Smith-Lever Act of 1914. Generally, the act coordinated the extension service activities of state agricultural colleges and the USDA in "the giving of instruction and practical demonstrations in agriculture and home economics." To carry out this program, the federal government appropriated funds annually to extension services if states agreed to match the amount. Due to the technical wording of the act, money for extension services could come from the private sector. State extension directors, therefore, entered "into agreements with county officials and farm bureaus or like organizations with reference to financial support" of county agents. Thus, a county agent was an integral figure of the USDA, the agricultural colleges, and the farm bureaus because he was paid by all three bodies.[15]

As more state farm bureau federations appeared, a national organization was necessary to unite these separate branches. The first attempt was in Ithaca, New York, where farm bureau and USDA extension representatives from nine states met in 1919. In order to solicit more interested parties, another meeting occurred in Chicago in November 1919. At this time, the American Farm Bureau Federation (AFBF) became a reality. But the task was not easy. Five hundred strong, convention delegates were split at the outset over the basic foundations of the AFBF. The Northerners, Easterners, and Southerners urged that education and a small budget be primary goals. The largest group, the Midwesterners, focused on legislative and commercial activities that required an extensive and expensive budget. Eventually, everyone settled on broad-based principles: to develop state federations; to improve conditions for economic production, conservation, marketing, and transportation of farm products; to further the enactment of constructive agricultural legislation; to advise with public agricultural institutions in determining nationwide policies; and to keep all members informed.[16]

Concerning finances, the AFBF adjusted the national fee to 50¢ per member with other dues left to the discretion of individual county farm bureaus. With this compromise intact, the government of the AFBF was formed. The main body was a Board of Directors composed of one official and one representative for every 20,000 members, all of which had to be "bona fide farmers." Elected from this board was an executive committee composed of twelve men (three from each of the four national geographic regions—north, west, central, and south) who had "charge of the administrative affairs." In addition, a House of Delegates, each state being appropriated one delegate, met with the board and exercised identical powers, except the right to vote on AFBF matters. To conduct all business, an elected president, "the executive head," presided over each body aided by a vice-president, treasurer, and secretary.[17]

In 1920, after the convention, twenty-eight state federations ratified the constitution that officially launched the AFBF. Later that year, the membership elected as president James Howard of Iowa. Once other offices were filled, Howard, the board, and the executive committee ordered the instituting of such departments as transportation, trade relations, distribution, statistics, legislation, and cooperation. And, of course, they set up a political office in Washington, D. C., so that lobbying efforts would be carried out effectively. Over the next year, stimulated by energetic compaigns, the national membership climbed to 1,060,000 in 31 states and 797 counties.[18]

From the beginning, the objectives of the AFBF were clear cut—to advance every facet of agricultural life. Economically,

AFBF members defended the right to organize, to bargain collectively, and to market cooperatively, thus insuring a "just profit" for equal labor. Equally important was education. Farmers deserved better homes and health as well as social and religious atmospheres. Moreover, they needed assistance in crop and livestock production from a county agent who was well informed on new scientific techniques. On the legislative front, AFBF officials defended the agricultural sector. Avowing to be nonpartisan, they lobbied in Congress and state legislatures for such measures as prohibiting tenantry, regulating food packers, and setting fair transportation rates. Because the AFBF represented such a large constituency, they periodically conducted opinion polls of the membership to measure farm sentiment on pending national issues.[19]

While safeguarding the general well-being of the farmer, AFBF members remained in tune with the 1920s. In fact, they aptly reflected the post-war conservatism that swept across the United States. For instance, in honoring World War I veterans, they wanted Armistice Day to be a national holiday; they also pledged to help soldiers return to civilian life. As patriots, they stood for the Constitution and "one Flag," and they denounced radicalism, calling for the expulsion of "Bolshevism and all other anarchistic tendencies." Law and order advocates, they defined "disrupting and criminally wasteful strikes" as "unjustifiable." And in echoing the "Return to Normalcy" slogan of the Harding-Coolidge ticket, they espoused "Christian tolerance" and the "return to the homely virtues and beliefs of the yesterdays."[20]

Although the AFBF surely knew the national direction it was headed with regard to the farmer, the primary working part of the organization became the county farm bureau. Within a community, farmers who wanted social, economic, and educational advancements formed a county bureau. First, they elected a president, secretary, treasurer, and executive committee who solicited membership, managed bureau affairs, and collected dues, ranging from $5.00 to $10.00. Accepting men and women on an equal basis, they guided the formation of cooperative marketing associations, but did not directly "engage in commercial activities."[21] As for educational programs, they delegated that responsibility to county agents of the state agricultural college extension service and to the States Relation Service of the USDA. This bond was cemented securely because local bureaus contributed to the salary of the agent. Working in concert with the bureau, the extension service conformed to the definition under the Smith-Lever Act. Required to help all farmers whether bureau members or not, county agents were, however, prevented from directly participating in such bureau affairs as starting membership drives, conducting meetings, or collecting dues.[22]

During the 1920s, not only growth, but also political achievements measured the success of the AFBF. Operating from the Washington office, Gray Silver, the bureau representative, vigorously lobbied on behalf of agriculture.[23] Much of the time he attended House and Senate hearings or buttonholed congressmen. In 1921, he put together the Farm Bloc, an alliance of Western Republicans and Southern Democrats. This political affiliation secured numerous legislative victories including the Emergency Tariff (1921), the Fordney-McCumber Tariff (1922), the Grain Futures Act (1921), and the Capper-Volstead Act (1922). Of all these laws, Capper-Volstead was the guardian of the bureaus; this act legalized agricultural marketing agencies (or cooperatives) and exempted agricultural associations from antitrust laws—if all members were farmers.[24]

Building upon the stability of the AFBF, state federations appeared across most of the country. Although many Southern states resisted the intrusion of bureaus, Texas farmers were receptive but cautious.[25] In 1919, when the AFBF met in Chicago, Texas delegates were not present; they were skeptical about the success of such an undertaking. Moreover, they desired more detailed information on AFBF objectives before committing themselves. At this time, however, three Texans, T. O. Walton, Walton Peteet, and W. B. Lanham, were in the vicinity attending a meeting of the Association of Land-Grant Colleges. Every so often, they investigated the AFBF proceedings, listening to various speakers and delegates espouse the virtues of this new farm group. Thus, they became convinced that such a state and national organization could well serve Texas farmers. At their urging, in late 1919, Texas A&M University officials and several prominent farmers held a meeting in Waco to set up the State Council of Agriculture and Home Economics. Electing John Orr of Dallas as president and H. L. McKnight as secretary, the delegates created a federation of county bureaus "modeled very closely after the Farm Bureau movement but under a different name."[26]

Loosely organized, the State Council contained many weaknesses, resulting in instability. For the plan to succeed, money was necessary; and yet, no individual membership fees were set. Ironically, county units "were roughly allotted a certain amount" for operating expenses, but funds from the State Council were practically nonexistent. Moreover, county agents were responsible for educational functions; they were also expected to work for the State Council by soliciting members and finances. Preferring to help farmers improve agricultural techniques, they soon resented all other activities that seemed to monopolize their time. By late summer, the future of the State Council was in jeopardy.[27]

Meanwhile, throughout Texas, county farm bureaus influenced by the AFBF model appeared. One of the most important was the Dallas County Farm Bureau, which adopted a constitution and by-laws in May 1920. Led by county bureau president Schuyler Marshall, these members were the first to organize in Texas on a fee basis "with the purpose of working out the farmers' problems." Later in August, when the Bell County Farm Bureau was conducting a membership drive, the AFBF sent Charles G. Stonebreaker as a representative to direct the initial operations.[28]

Recognizing that the AFBF was growing in popularity and realizing that the State Council required a solid foundation, officials accepted AFBF help. Once this decision was made, the AFBF assisted in forming the Texas Farm Bureau Federation. Since the best model was the Illinois Bureau, five members from Cook County arrived in Texas to help in the state bureau organization. And county agent, C. O. Moser of Dallas, aided by national office representatives, launched the first membership drive based on a $10.00 fee for five years.[29]

After August 1920, events moved rapidly to stabilize the Texas Farm Bureau Federation. To provide some coherency, the officers of the State Council continued in the leadership roles until elections could be held. In September, they established the state headquarters in Dallas. They also appointed Moser as the secretary-manager who was "to run an efficient office and field force," "to launch a membership campaign," and "to secure 100,000 members." But two major obstacles had to be overcome before the TFBF would succeed. Over the preceding year, two associations constituted stiff competition in Texas—one was the American Cotton Growers and the other was the United Cotton Growers. In October and November, the leaders of all three organizations decided that the TFBF would absorb the other two, which then pledged total cooperation. Since the American Cotton Growers and the United Cotton Growers were primarily marketing groups, it was agreed that a Committee of Twenty-One be appointed to devise a plan that would continue such functions.[30]

In January 1921, the TFBF held its first annual meeting. Convening in Dallas, delegates, who had been chosen from already existing county bureaus, ratified the constitution and by-laws. They set the economic, social, and political direction of the TFBF. The federation was to "assert the rights and defend the interests of the agricultural producers of Texas" and to promote the "most wholesome and satisfactory conditions of rural life." More specifically, cooperation was to be exercised in every aspect of marketing, especially to ensure a "fair profit" and a "fair price." The TFBF would analyze market conditions, secure better credit facilities, strive for equitable transportation charges, and lobby as the "spokesman and champion" of Texas agriculture. As dictated in the AFBF constitution, the TFBF would work in conjunction with the USDA, the Texas Department of Agriculture, and Texas A&M University in order to carry out its programs.[31]

As for the mechanics of the TFBF, the constitution was clear cut. Any "white farmer, landlord, or tenant . . . having a bona fide and direct interest" in the organization could join. Since funds were necessary to the existence of the TFBF and the related county bureaus, members paid annual dues of $10.00. This sum was apportioned as follows: $5.00 to the County Bureau, $5.00 to the state federation from which 50¢ went to both the *Farm Bureau News* and the AFBF.[32]

Overall, the statewide organization operated on three levels. The smallest section, the Community Farm Bureau, elected a chairman, a vice-chairman, and a secretary, and then met "to work out the problems pertinent to the community" through project leaders (farmers and farm spouses) who supervised educational activities. Utilized as guides, county farm and home demonstration agents would handle "production, improvement, social, economic, and cooperative projects." As the middle section, the County Farm Bureau, headed by a board of directors, a president, a vice-president, a treasurer, and a secretary, with the county agent as an adviser, attended to "the general routine work"—publicity, economic and cooperative projects such as pooling, cooperative buying and marketing through systematic grading, standardizing, and classing, as well as through uniform breeding. Project leaders, along with county and home demonstration agents, carried on these tasks.[33]

The state federation was still the central agency. As directors of this main body, a president, a vice-president, and a treasurer presided over a board of directors that consisted of eighteen members (chosen by congressional districts) plus the President of Texas A&M University, the director of the Cooperative Extension Service, and the presidents of the commodity sections, who were the ex-officio members. At annual state conventions, these officers were responsible for holding elections, submitting reports, and handling "customary business." Although these officers considered uniting all bureaus into a state unit to be an important objective, they also concentrated on the problems of farm labor, immigration, and colonization. And since the extension service was a vital coworker, the state federation buttressed agricultural education at all times. But the "chief work" of the TFBF was "to set up, maintain, and develop commodity marketing sections."[34]

The TFBF did have certain self-imposed power limitations. For instance, marketing, community, county, or state divisions could not directly "engage in any commercial activities," but could "encourage, develop, and promote" such associations through the commodity marketing sections of the TFBF. Moreover, the TFBF could not "hold stocks or bonds" in organizations performing commercial activities.[35]

Although solidifying the TFBF was a primary achievement, far more significant for its long-term success was the formation of the commodity marketing association in 1921. The Committee of Twenty-One, which had met in December 1920, submitted a cooperative marketing plan to the TFBF convention. Under the persuasion of Aaron Sapiro, a California marketing expert, delegates voted for the creation of the Texas Farm Bureau Cotton Association (TFBCA). Designed as "a remedy for the ills of the marketing of farm and ranch products," the TFBCA, a branch of the TFBF, was based on agreements between cotton farmers and the federation. Each member signed a contract turning over all cotton bales for five years to the TFBCA and to no one else. Such restrictions were vital to guarantee "that the Association will stick, that it will be able to deliver the goods, that it will prevent the weak-knee'd from sliding out and hurting the strong, and that it will function." To insure a sufficient cotton supply to this cooperative, the contract required that a total of 1,000,000 bales be guaranteed by July 1, 1921, before the TFBCA was incorporated. If only 500,000 bales could be secured, the members could approve incorporation nevertheless.[36]

Endeavoring to end "dumping," to market cotton orderly, to eliminate "wasteful methods," and to ensure "greater profits," TFBCA officials attempted to correct many weaknesses inherent in cotton marketing. They graded, stapled, and weighed each bale, and then sold in lots such classified cotton; this system ensured "a true value," in terms of quality, and a fair price. At the same time, they encouraged farmers to grow "uniform and standard varieties" for pooling by offering information on better "production methods and problems." In an effort to eliminate middlemen, they stored cotton in their own cooperative warehouses, selling collectively and "only when the market demands it." And as if copying provisions of the Warehouse Act of 1916, they authorized a farmer to borrow money from the TFBCA based on the value of his stored crop.[37]

A self-governing section of the TFBF, TFBCA affairs were controlled by elected officials. A board of directors was composed of twenty-three men. The membership was to elect twenty directors from cotton-growing districts; the other three were to be nominated by the governor, the president of Texas A&M, and the president of TFBF; the first twenty-three directors were to immediately take charge of TFBCA business, especially the sale of the 1921 crop.[38]

For both the TFBF and the TFBCA, a vigorous membership campaign began March 1, 1921. Walton Peteet, Director of Commodity Marketing, headed this operation. Comprising a large field force, members canvassed many areas of the state, especially cotton-producing regions. Since a commission was paid for each recruited farmer, they oftentimes made "extravagant statements" as well as "impossible promises," in order to convince people to join. Even so, following the association slogan of "Organized for Business," county farm bureau officials and county agents scoured the 130 farm bureaus in the state for new members. One month before the deadline, they had secured 250,000 new members for the cotton association. By July 1, the total was 500,000. Although this amount fell short of the 1,000,000 mark, the TFBF officials were satisfied; moreover, they now could incorporate and operate the TFBCA.[39]

Although the association was growing, TFBF officials faced severe difficulties, almost from the beginning. The most critical problem they soon discovered was that expenditures far exceeded the income from new memberships. Consequently, they shut down many TFBF activities. Under criticism that the directors were too extravagant, they reduced office expenses and clerical personnel. One of the greatest consumers of the budget was establishing and maintaining the various commodity marketing associations, such as the TFBCA, until they were self-sufficient. Once the money issue had surfaced, critics quickly challenged the objectives of the TFBF. Some charged that the bureau acted "as a nursemaid" for cooperatives. Others complained that introducing better farming methods and living conditions should be primary goals.[40]

The TFBCA became the target of the angrier, more bitter charges, primarily because it was the most expensive yet least profitable agency during 1921-1922. Farmers expressed dismay that profits on cotton were unusually low. In turn, they blamed the directors, who were seen as farmers with little business expertise. Even though, at the onset, many expected bank loans for the support of the association to be easily obtained, banks "were very shy," willing to extend credit only with complicated and binding provisions attached. Without question, the overhead was exorbitant, especially since TFBCA officials earned high salaries. And when the association sold the 1921 cotton crop of 92,737 bales, the price was only 2¢ or 3¢ better than the average. Everything indicated that the association could not sustain itself. Not until the War Finance Corporation supplied the necessary credit did business affairs stabilize for the TFBCA.[41]

Despite such shortcomings, TFBCA officials made considerable strides over the next few years. In 1922-1923 they reduced expenses and made the association "more business like." Moreover, they sold cotton for approximately 5¢ more per pound than average market prices. They also centralized the warehousing of cotton in Houston and utilized cheaper grading and classing methods. Similarly, they secured uniform cotton seed prices in the state by informing county bureaus of current market values and, in an effort to stabilize cotton production, they educated many farmers on the financial benefits of crop diversification.[42] Undeniably, the TFBCA was a central component of the TFBF.

Yet the TFBF was the core, the nucleus of the Texas farm bureau movement. To ensure stability and effectiveness, TFBF officials, directed by John Orr, Walton Peteet, and in the early stages C. O. Moser, undertook a major reorganization. Centralizing the operations of the Federation late in 1921, they started a permanent field service consisting of seventeen district supervisors who acted as coordinators between county bureaus and the state association and promoted educational, political, social, and economical objectives. Through 1921 and 1922, they instituted plans that would solve financial problems. At first, they reduced office costs by cutting salaries and personnel; then they incresed income by annual membership drives that required fees to be paid in cash, not in promissory notes. From these $15 dues, they set aside $5 expressly for educational programs and only $2 for operating expenses.

At the same time, they pursued avenues by which the several bureau departments became self-supporting. For instance, the publicity department gradually accumulated enough advertising to cut printing costs and to purchase a printing machine. Later, it expanded the number of subscriptions by soliciting nonbureau members to buy the *Farm Bureau News*, a weekly publication. To ensure accurate accounting, the state federation hired a treasurer, T. K. Motherspaw, who would then head the fiscal department. Eventually, he simplified the bookkeeping of the bureau and encouraged all county bureaus to adopt his system. The new Fire Insurance Department offered policies to members at rates 25 percent cheaper than standard premiums. Considered a "valuable service," the cotton seed department instructed planters on superior seeds and production methods.[43]

In an effort to aid and include all members of a farming area, TFBF officials created the Women's Farm Bureau Division. Women would compile poll lists of possible membership drive leaders, including anyone, male or female, who managed a farm. Recognized as having some influence in a community, and encouraged by TFBF officials they attended county bureau meetings. Women joined the bureau, oftentimes following the advice of one reputable local woman, the Home Demonstration agent. They volunteered their services through women's clubs that held fund drives for church construction, library book buying, or other philanthropic causes. But primarily, they worked in membership drives persuading farmers and ranchers that the Federation served educational and economical needs. Not too surprisingly, though their help was greatly appreciated, they did not obtain the total confidence of some TFBF leaders who questioned the capability of the female to "master the contract sufficiently . . . as to make their work effective."[44]

Later, after many of the bureau departments had been functioning smoothly, other departments such as finance, legislative, transportation, legal, and research were put into the planning stages; further expansion was in commodity marketing. Receiving loans from the War Finance Corporation, fourteen various crop and livestock associations (including wheat, wool, hay, watermelon, alfalfa, tomatoes, poultry, dairy, potatoes, onions, and rice) were installed by the end of 1922. By that time, Texas was "in the front rank of cooperative marketing states." Moreover, the TFBF buttressed such affiliated associations through membership campaigns, financial guidance, and legislative work.[45]

During the early years, the TFBF was active in the legislative arena. Whenever national farm bills were pending in Congress, TFBF officials worked closely with the AFBF. For instance, when freight rates were strangling Texas bureau commodity associations, the TFBF joined forces with the AFBF traffic department arguing their case before the Interstate Commerce Commission and the Texas Traffic Association. And when congressional committees in Washington, D.C., debated new tariff provisions, they requested the AFBF to speak against lifting all duties on vegetable oil coming into the country. Using "all the influence at our command"—meaning the AFBF and Texas congressmen including Senator Morris Sheppard—they requested that bidders selling hay and wheat to the Army must have the produce "on hand or under contract." Such new requirements would in effect prevent low market prices based on low bids for government contracts. In the Texas legislature, TFBF officials backed a model cooperative marketing law that legalized their associations. Furthermore, they won pink boll worm laws that called for the research and extermination of this destructive cotton insect.[46]

In every aspect of TFBF work, Texas A&M and the Extension Service offered "the fullest kind of cooperation." They advised farmers who had trouble selling produce to secure advice from one of the commodity marketing associations. At various times, they permitted the Federation to hold crop production conferences on the campus. Moreover, the educational functions, the information dissemination, and the assistance in organization were completely under the supervision of the extension service district agents, county agents, and specialists. As one representative stated at a Bureau directors' meeting: "[The TFBF] is the type of an organization that we have been hoping for for many years. The Extension Service is standing squarely behind it and are helping it all they can, and are asking the same help from the Farm Bureau in reciprocation."[47]

For several years, Texas farmers had felt the fluctuating market cycles after 1919. They, too, enjoyed the post-war prosperity until overproduction and underconsumption drove prices down in 1920. During 1922-1924, conditions brightened, but only minimally. In 1923, because crop production dropped, profits rose slightly. Even so, these times were marked by financial and market instability. During the 1920s, Texas farmers, although not suffering as severely as farmers in other agricultural states, still needed help. For many, the TFBF became the answer. Despite certain shortcomings, it represented one large organization that could work on behalf of individual farmers, fight for appropriate legislation, and remedy some of the marketing disorders. By 1921, the TFBF claimed 70,000 members in 130 counties (19,146 in the TFBCA). But long-term success depended upon legislative victories, financial improvements, and continuing membership growth not only in the Federation, but also in the commodity marketing associations. Without question, by 1924 the TFBF had survived well, with many farmers joining the ranks. Only time and cooperation among the members were to determine the future of the TFBF.[48]

NOTES

1. For more information on agricultural conditions in the 1920s, see Gilbert Fite, *American Agricultural and Farm Policy Since 1900* (New York: Macmillan Company, 1964); Theodore Saloutos, *Farmer Movements in the South, 1865-1933* (Lincoln: University of Nebraska Press, n.d.); U. S. Department of Agriculture, *Bulletin No. 1392* (Washington, D. C.: 1926).

2. Fite, *American Farm Policy*, pp. 3, 9, 10; Saloutos, *Farmer Movements*, pp. 254, 257; *Bulletin No. 1392*, pp. 3-4.

3. *Bulletin No. 1392*, pp. 3-4.

4. Ibid. One other law was the Clayton Anti-Trust Act (1914) which allowed farmers to act together only in nonprofit organizations.

5. Roscoe Martin, *The People's Party in Texas: A Study in Third Party Politics* (Austin: University of Texas Press, 1970), p. 22; John D. Hicks, *The Populist Revolt* (Lincoln: University of Nebraska Press, 1961), p. 96.

6. *Bulletin No. 1392*, pp. 2-3.

7. Hicks, *The Populist Revolt*, p. 96.

8. Ibid., pp. 96, 105; Martin, *The People's Party*, pp. 21-27.

9. For a discussion on Populism, see Hicks, *The Populist Revolt*; and Richard Hofstadter, *The Age of Reform: From Bryan to F.D.R.* (New York: Vintage Books, 1955).

10. For more information on agricultural conditions and movements, see Theodore Saloutos and John D. Hicks, *Agricultural Discontent in the Middle West, 1900-1939* (Madison: University of Wisconsin Press, 1951); Samuel Berger, *Dollar Harvest: The Story of the Farm Bureau* (Lexington: Heath Lexington Books, 1971), pp. 89-95; *Bulletin No. 1392*, pp. 2-3.

Cattlemen's associations also developed in response to crises in their industry, but their strength was at the state level. For the history of the origins of one of the more important state organizations, see Charles L. Wood, "Cattlemen, Railroads, and the Origin of the Kansas Livestock Association—the 1890's," *Kansas Historical Quarterly* 43 (Summer 1977): 121-139.

11. For a discussion of the AFBF up to 1940, see Christiana McFadden Campbell, *The Farm Bureau and the New Deal: A Study of Making of National Farm Policy, 1933-1940* (Urbana: University of Illinois Press, 1962); Orville Kile, *The Farm Bureau Movement* (New York: Macmillan Company, 1921); Berger, *Dollar Harvest.*

12. The Morrill Land-Grant College Act of 1862 provided every state with 30,000 acres of public domain. This land-grant was to be used for educational and agricultural purposes, leading eventually to land grant colleges and extension services.

13. Gladys Baker, *The County Agent* (Chicago: University of Illinois Press, 1939), p. 1.

14. U. S. Department of Agriculture, *Yearbook of Agriculture, 1954: Marketing* (Washington, D.C.: Government Printing Office, 1954), pp. 248-253.

15. Section 2 of the Smith-Lever Act read:

That cooperative agricultural extension work shall consist of the giving of instruction and practical demonstrations in agriculture and home economics to persons not attending or resident in said colleges in the several communities, and imparting to such persons information on said subjects through field demonstrations, publications, and otherwise and this work shall be carried on in such manner as may be mutually agreed upon by the Secretary of Agriculture and the state agricultural college or colleges receiving the benefits of this Act.

See "Memorandum of Understanding [1921]," Texas Agricultural Extension Service Historical Files, Box 4-48, Soil Conservation and Farm Bureau Federation Scrapbook, Texas A&M University Archives, Texas A&M University, College Station, Texas (hereinafter cited as Box 4-48); "Putting the Farm Bureau to Work," Texas Agricultural Extension Service Historical Files, Box 7-21, Farm Bureau: 1919-1924, Texas A&M University Archives, Texas A&M University, College Station, Texas (hereinafter cited as Box 7-21); Baker, *The County Agent*, p. 38.

16. Kile, *The Farm Bureau Movement*, pp. 77, 91-97, 113-123; *Semi-Weekly Farm News* (Dallas), July 27, 1920, p. 1; "What is the American Farm Bureau Federation?" Box 7-21.

17. For document collections on the AFBF, see American Farm Bureau Federation Files, AFBF Headquarters, Chicago, Illinois; Department of Agriculture Papers, National Archives, Washington, D. C.; "What is the American Farm Bureau Federation?" Box 7-21.

18. *Semi-Weekly Farm News* (Dallas), November 19, 1920, p. 1; "What is the American Farm Bureau Federation?" Box 7-21.

19. "What is the American Farm Bureau Federation?" Box 7-21.

20. Some historians have emphasized the anti-radical nature of the AFBF. See Eric Goldman, *Rendezvous with Destiny: A History of Modern American Reform* (rev. ed.; New York: Vintage Books, 1960). Goldman pointed out that James Howard was "single-mindedly devoted to the proposition that the political role of the farmer was to get high prices and cheap credit" (p. 229). And Howard was to have been "a rock against radicalism" (p. 229). In *Dollar Harvest* Berger stated that the AFBF "became a bulwark against the radical farm movements after World War I" (pp. 89-95). See also "Putting the Farm Bureau to Work"; "What is the American Farm Bureau Federation?" Box 7-21.

21. A. C. True to T. O. Walton, November 12, 1920, Texas Agricultural Extension Service Historical Files, Box 7-20, Farm Bureau: 1919-1922, 1924, Texas A&M University Archives, Texas A&M University, College Station, Texas (Hereinafter cited as Box 7-20).

22. "Memorandum of Understanding [1921]," Box 4-48. As provided in the Smith-Lever Act, the extension service in each state was under an executive director who represented the college and state agricultural departments. Next were the state agents, extension specialists, county agents, and home demonstration agents.

23. Historians have disagreed over the intent of the AFBF. Hofstadter in *The Age of Reform* stated that the AFBF was business, not education, oriented for the benefit of the "most conservative and properous farmers" (p. 127). Grant McConnell, in *The Decline of Agrarian Democracy* (Berkeley: University of California Press, 1953), purported that the AFBF hurt itself when siding with Republican politics in the 1920s (pp. 50-70). Goldman, in *Rendezvous with Destiny*, wrote that the "bureau showed little interest in the rest of rural America and avoided issues that had to do with general reform" (p. 229). Berger in *Dollar Harvest* maintained that the AFBF favored wealthy farmers because it was fathered by "big business in reaction to the spread of more radical farmer movements" (pp. 89-95). George Brown Tindall, in *The Emergence of the New South*, Vol. 10 in *A History of the South*, ed. Wendell Holmes Stephenson and E. Merton Coulter (Baton Rouge: Louisiana State University Press, 1967), stated that successful commercial farmers gradually dominated the AFBF and therefore county agents catered to the prosperous farmers (p. 131). Campbell in *The Farm Bureau* proposed that a correlation existed between educational levels and membership. But she disputed the idea that enough evidence was available, indicating that the Bureau preferred only prosperous farmers (p. 24).

See also J. K. Barnes, "The Man Who Runs the Farm Bloc," *World's Work* 45 (November 1922): 51-59; William G. Carleton, "Gray Silver and the Rise of the Farm Bureau," *Current History* 28 (1955): 343-50.

24. The Clayton Anti-Trust Act had already given some protection to farmers who organized. See Kile, *The Farm Bureau Movement*, p. 171; Berger, *Dollar Harvest*, pp. 89-95; Tindall, *The Emergence of the New South*, p. 133; Wesley McCune, *The Farm Bloc* (Garden City, N.Y.: Doubleday Doran and Co., 1943); James R. Connor, "National Farm Organizations and United States Tariff Policy in the 1920s," *Agricultural History*, 32 (January 1958): 32-43; *Yearbook of Agriculture 1954: Marketing*, pp. 249-53.

25. For a description of agricultural conditions in Texas, see Samuel Lee Evans, "Texas Agriculture, 1880-1930" (Ph.D. dissertation, University of Texas at Austin, 1960). Historians have offered various viewpoints concerning the economic effects of the 1920s on the Southern states and on the growth of the AFBF. For instance, Saloutos, in *Farmer Movements*, stated that the Bureau made minimal progress in the South. This condition resulted from low production and price levels caused by labor shortages and boll weevil infestations.

26. *Semi-Weekly Farm News* (Dallas), May 18, 1920, p. 8; "Texas Farm Bureau Federation," Texas Agricultural Extension Service Historical Files, Box 5-3, Soil Conservation and Farm Bureau Federation, Texas A&M University Archives, Texas A&M University, College Station, Texas (hereinafter cited as Box 5-3).

27. "Texas Farm Bureau Federation," Box 5-3; Campbell, *The Farm Bureau*, p. 6, "Memorandum of Understanding [1921]," Box 4-48.

28. *Semi-Weekly Farm News* (Dallas), May 18, 1920, p. 8; August 31, 1920, p. 1.

29. For a detailed discussion of cooperative marketing activities, especially in Texas, see Robert Montgomery, *The Cooperative Pattern in Cotton* (New York: Macmillan, 1929). *Semi-Weekly Farm News* (Dallas), August 13, 1920, p. 1; "Texas Farm Bureau Federation," Box 5-3.

30. Montgomery, *The Cooperative Pattern in Cotton*, pp. 76-77; *Semi-Weekly Farm News* (Dallas, September 7, 1920, p. 1; November 12, 1920, p. 1; *Bulletin No. 1392*, pp. 2-3; "Texas Farm Bureau Federation," Box 5-3; "Memorandum of Agreement [1920]," Texas Agricultural Extension Service Historical Files, Box 4-47, Soil Conservation and Farm Bureau Federation Scrapbook, Texas A&M University Archives, Texas A&M University, College Station, Texas.

31. Montgomery, *The Cooperative Pattern in Cotton*, pp. 78-80; *Semi-Weekly Farm News* (Dallas), January 5, 1926, p. 1; January 26, 1926, pp. 2, 6; "Constitution and By-Laws of the Texas Farm Bureau Federation," Box 7-21.

32. The *Farm Bureau News* was the official weekly publication of the TFBF.

33. *Extension Service Farm News*, July 15, 1921, Box 7-21; "Constitution and By-Laws of the Texas Farm Bureau Federation," Box 7-21.

34. "Constitution and By-Laws of the Texas Farm Bureau Federation," Box 7-21.

35. Ibid.

36. For more information on cooperative marketing, see Herman Steen, *Cooperative Marketing: The Golden Rule in Agriculture* (Garden City, N.Y.: Doubleday, Page and Co., 1923), pp. 7, 80, 112, 144, 155, 157, 184, 219, 221, Montgomery, *The Cooperative Pattern in Cotton*, pp. 78-80; *Progressive Farmer and Farm Woman*, October 23, 1926, pp. 1, 15, 16; Texas, Department of Agriculture, *Thirteenth Annual Report of the Commissioner of Agriculture of the State of Texas* (n.p., 1920), pp. 22-29; "Texas Farm Bureau Federation," Box 5-3; "Texas Farm Bureau Cotton Growers Cooperative Marketing Association: What It Is," Box 7-21.

37. "Texas Farm Bureau Federation," Box 5-3; "Texas Farm Bureau Cotton Growers Co-operative Marketing Association: What It Is," Box 7-21.

38. *Progressive Farmer and Farm Woman*, October 23, 1926, pp. 1, 15, 16; "Texas Farm Bureau Cotton Growers Co-operative Marketing Association: What It Is," Box 7-21.

39. Walton Peteet eventually headed the AFBF cooperative marketing department in 1923. See Orville Kile, *The Farm Bureau Through Three Decades* (Baltimore: Waverly Press, 1948), pp. 116-117. "Texas Farm Bureau Federation," Box 5-3; "Texas Farm Bureau Federation, County Farm Bureaus," Texas Agricultural Extension Service Historical Files, Box 5-1, Soil Conservation and Farm Bureau Federation Scrapbook, Texas A&M University Archives, Texas A&M University, College Station, Texas (hereinafter cited as Box 5-1); C. O. Moser to State Board of Directors, June 29, 1921, Box 5-1; Moser to the Presidents and Secretaries, June 9, 1921, Texas Agricultural Extension Service Historical Files, Box 4-49, Soil Conservation and Farm Bureau Federation Scrapbook, Texas A&M University Archives, Texas A&M University, College Station, Texas (hereinafter

cited as Box 4-49); "Official Programme," Box 7-21; "Texas Farm Bureau Cotton Growers Co-operative Marketing Association: What It Is," Box 7-21.

40. *Progressive Farmer and Farm Woman*, March 7, 1925, pp. 4, 12; "Meeting of Board of Directors," April 7-18, 1922, Texas Agricultural Extension Service Historical Files, Box 5-2, Soil Conservation and Farm Bureau Federation, Texas A&M University Archives, Texas A&M University, College Station, Texas (hereinafter cited as Box 5-2).

41. *Progressive Farmer and Farm Woman*, March 21, 1925, p. 4; "Texas Farm Bureau Federation," Box 5-3.

42. *Progressive Farmer and Farm Woman*, March 21, 1925, p. 4; November 13, 1926, p. 11; U. S., Federal Farm Board, *Statistics of Farmer's Selling and Buying Associations, United States, 1863-1931*, Bulletin No. 9 (Washington, D.C.: Government Printing Office, 1932); "Texas Farm Bureau Federation," Box 5-3, "Texas Farm Bureau News Service, October 18, 1921," Box 5-1.

43. "Outline for Field Service," Box 5-3; "Meeting of Board of Directors," April 7-18, 1922, Box 5-2.

44. "Suggestions As to How Farm Women May Participate in the Preliminary Work of Organizing a Farm Bureau in a County," Box 5-2.

45. "Texas Farm Bureau News Service, October 18, 1921," Box 5-1; J. F. Bagwell to County Agents, September 16, 1921, Box 5-1; Moser to Presidents and Secretaries, June 9, 1921, Box 4-49.

46. Montgomery, *The Cooperative Pattern in Cotton*, p. 102; Texas State House of Representatives, *House Journal*, 37th Legislature, 1921, pp. 199, 202, 687, 850, 880, 1140-1141, 1157; "Meeting of Board of Directors," April 7-18, 1922, Box 5-2; "Texas Farm Bureau News Service, October 18, 1921," Box 5-1.

47. "Meeting of Board of Directors," April 7-18, 1922, Box 5-2; "T. O. Walton, 1922," Box 7-20.

48. For statistical information on Texas, see Francis B. May and Florence Escott, *Economic Statistics of Texas, 1900-1962* (Austin: Bureau of Business Research, University of Texas at Austin, 1961); Tindall, *The Emergence of the New South*, p. 132; "Meeting of the Board of Directors," April 7-18, 1922, Box 5-2; "Pickups from Organization Workers [1924]," Box 7-20.

IV

TECHNOLOGY, WAR, AND CULTURAL CHANGE

I am not an advocate of government in business, yet as I study the situation it does appear that the true function of government is in serving its citizens in acute emergencies. . . . How unnecessary and ridiculous it is for millions of our citizens to tramp the streets, hungry, poorly clad and cold, looking for means of livelihood, because we have too much food, too much wool and cotton, and too much fuel.

Joe Mercer,
to Kansas farmers during his unsuccessful
U. S. Senate campaign,
June, 1932

The twentieth century has boded many changes for farmers and other agriculturalists. Mechanization, world wars, and international markets sought out agriculturalists to encourage their participation and incumbent alteration. Perhaps most significant has been, as Joe Mercer, farmer, merchant, and Kansas Livestock Commissioner, noted with regret, the forced reliance of the farmer upon outside powers, particulary government. The demands of modern farm technology, the magnitude of the 1930s dust bowl destruction, and the price of depression and world war caused farmers to be less self-reliant and more group conscious.

Deborah J. Hoskins shows how modern technology filtered to late frontier areas, notably Oklahoma, making farm life more bearable. At the same time, farmers adjusted to the desirable mass-produced goods and equipment by reordering priorities. This reinforces new notions about farmer frontier life that, before historical revisionism, had been assumed to be highly individualistic. This case study asserts a direct relationship between material culture and group behavior.

The emphasis upon improving the business of agriculture eventually led to the mechanization of the farm, but not without a protracted debate. Robert C. Williams demonstrated that farmers were reluctant to change from horsedrawn power to horsepower immediately. It took considerable economic persuasion and social pressure before the transition was complete. Still, modernization of farm life prevailed.

Farm technology became obtainable and acceptable during two important national crises—the Great Depression and World War II. Both necessitated agricultural participation but with differing degrees of coercion. George Q. Flynn argues that many farmers wanted to avoid the draft during World War II because of labor shortages and unrealistic notions of food production curtailment. Highly successful were lobbying efforts on behalf of farmers. They obtained a near blanket exemption in the face of executive branch opposition. Even so, social and domestic farm life was transformed because labor left the farms.

By the end of World War II, agriculturalists in the United States had witnessed a social revolution in their lives that would not allow for a return to the pastoral ways of a previous century.

Brought, Bought, and Borrowed: Material Culture on the Oklahoma Farming Frontier, 1889–1907

The romantic interpretation of pioneering assumes that isolated frontier families produced household goods, tools, and furnishings by hand from the available resources. The conditions that required self-sufficiency ended only with improved transportation connections with the East and local financial stability.[1] Time was the vital element for areas beyond the Mississippi that were emerging from the frontier period, and historians, defining the frontier period from the earliest date of settlement, justifiably identify frontier conditions that lasted through two decades or more. But time played a reverse role on the late frontier of Oklahoma. An advanced state of technology in transportation and communication combined with experience in pioneering among farmers and business entreprenuers to shorten the period of isolation that had required hand production of domestic goods on earlier frontiers.

The fertile lands of Indian Territory, roughly the present state of Oklahoma, remained closed to white settlement until the last quarter of the nineteenth century. The only remaining area of good, cheap farmland in the nation, Indian Territory symbolized the "Last Frontier" to western farmers in the surrounding states. Their pressure to open this area to white settlement finally burst the tenuous bond between the federal government and the Native American occupants, and thousands of farm families surged into Oklahoma.[2]

The government initially opened the central and western portions of the new territory by "land run," a thrilling and sometimes dangerous race among thousands of would-be settlers to stake the choicest property and hastily erect a shack or break some land to satisfy the government's "improvement" requirement for a legal claim. Intense land fever prompted successive openings of reserved Indian lands, and prime agricultural land attracted as many as three persons for every available quarter-section.[3] The depredations of "Sooners," who illegally entered the new territories early and prompted reports of crops already four inches high upon arrival of the fleetest legal claimant, ended the land runs and forced a new method of opening by lottery. Registrants whose numbers were drawn could select their claim from any area not chosen by the individuals preceding.[4]

The poorer land, unclaimed in the runs and the lotteries, remained as pasturage for ranchers, but "relinquishments," lands given up by original claimants, provided grist for vigorous speculative activity that lasted well beyond the territorial period.[5] After statehood in 1907, the eastern half of Oklahoma was legally opened to white homesteaders.[6] Land openings occupied a period of eighteen years, from 1889 to 1907, and this long, gradual process of lifting restrictions on non-Native settlement and continued shifts in property ownership identifies Oklahoma as a region that experienced successive and restricted frontier conditions. The result is the impression that frontier conditions of isolation and necessary self-sufficiency persisted over a long time for the whole territory.

Photographs and reminiscences provide evidence of both the crudeness of the settlers' first dwellings and the paucity of their transplanted possessions. Historians relying on photographs and the settlers' heroic accounts perpetuate the romantic view that frontier farmers were forced to "make do." A careful re-examination of these records, together with other remnants of pioneer life in Oklahoma Territory, may reveal another picture.

The move to Oklahoma Territory involved the same decision-making process experienced on earlier frontiers. The initial step was to select some means of transporting the most possessions at the least cost, and by 1889, many emigrants could move by rail.[7] This mode of transportation sometimes proved less economical than the settler supposed, since railroads charged by weight rather than by carload. Nevertheless, some families transported the entire contents of their previous homes to this new frontier by rail.[8] Other settlers, using the more traditional means of wagons and stages, reduced the weight of their possessions by discarding those with less significance to their owners. The articles that survived the decision-making process were of three types: necessities of farm and domestic life, possessions particularly representative of a previously achieved standard of living, and family heirlooms.[9]

Most Oklahomans were probably not novices to this decision-making process; frontier historians estimate that nineteenth-century Westerners moved an average of four to five times as adults.[10] Cultural and technological changes dictated new definitions for "necessary" goods, and the number and variety of status-objects grew. Families moving to Oklahoma brought with them such necessities as expensive farm equipment, a supply of clothing for each family member, and basic kitchen equipment. But these and the additional articles that bounced across the plains to Oklahoma in heavy farm wagons reflect the growing national propensity to invest in more efficient devices and partially processed goods in order to save labor in the home as well as in farming and business.[11]

The best indicator of elevated expectations in the earliest stages of Oklahoma settlement is the relative lack of handmade articles among these transplanted possessions. Furniture was not homemade, kitchen tools were not whittled, and clothing was not homespun. Rudimentary tables and chairs, simple tools, and fabrics are most commonly among the handmade items found in today's museum collections in older areas. The chances of survival to museum deposit drops with the age of the object, and the conspicuous absence of such domestic pieces in Oklahoma museums indicates that home production of rural domestic needs had largely died out by the time Oklahoma was settled. The availability of manufactured goods had caused an economic and cultural adjustment prior to emigration to Oklahoma.[12]

Two transplanted items, in particular, illustrate this adjustment to technological improvements. Few farm families arrived in Oklahoma Territory without a cast iron stove, however small. Wood fuel was scarce, and the stoves adapted well to the available alternatives that tended to burn too fast and too hot. Iron heated evenly for cooking and retained heat well for baking, and the stove itself contained the smoke and sent it up the stovepipe rather than into the room. The efficiency and cleanliness of cast iron stoves eliminated fireplaces even in first homes, and settlers acknowledged the need for these devises. Emigrants who owned a sewing machine certainly transported it to Oklahoma Territory, and the initial scarcity of these tools made them conspicuous on a rural frontier. Rural women traveled several miles for the privilege of using one newly arrived machine, at least until other families acquired machines of their own and their novelty wore off. Despite its convenience, the sewing machine did not become a rural frontier necessity because the availability and social acceptance of ready-made clothing at reasonable prices soon eliminated home production of clothing. Instead, the sewing machine appears important as a transplanted possession, since it symbolizes the higher living standards of new arrivals in the territory.[13] Elevated expectations created demand, and scores of entrepreneurs accompanied farm families to Oklahoma and ordered merchandise by the rail carload to satisfy this contemporary standard of living.[14]

City directories and newspaper advertisements provide clues to the merchandise available over a period of time. A comparison of these sources between Guthrie, established in 1889 with rail service by 1893, and Lawton, established in 1901 and without direct rail service until 1909, indicates no difference in the variety of goods available in retail stores.[15] Prices advertised in Lawton sources for 1902, 1903, and 1905 average several cents higher than those in Guthrie for the same items in the same years on most merchandise except fresh foods, feed, and cloth. Competition in textile retailing nationwide may account for the failure to add freight costs on textiles in Lawton; fresh produce and meats, as well as livestock feeds, were locally produced and processed. The ratios of retail establishments to the estimated population for each city added to its rural township are similar in 1907.[16]

Businesses were sold frequently, and many simply went bankrupt; new businesses replaced those lost at a rate relatively constant with the growth of population.[17] Advertisements also indicate types of retail establishments in both cities. Relatively few "general" stores operated in 1902, and their numbers in Guthrie decreased from nine in 1890 to one in 1902.[18] Specialized businesses were far more common. One Lawton advertisement for a combination undertaking parlor/lumber yard/furniture store, all under one roof ("We Can Build your Home, Furnish it, and Bury You"),[19] illustrates two common business arrangements: compatible specialties, since both coffins and furniture required lumber; and extended-family partnerships that conserved capital investment and, at least in this case, accommodated the interests of the various partners. In both towns, the proliferate banks and other lending institutions and the numerous law offices that advertised specifically to the needs of businesses indicate incorporated financial structures in territorial Oklahoma similar to the financial structures that dominated the period nationwide. The loosely organized and generally underfinanced family-owned general stores of earlier frontier towns stand in sharp contrast.[20]

Second-hand stores advertising furniture at low cost seem somewhat unique to the frontier Oklahoma retail business, particularly since they opened very early in newly forming towns. The sources of merchandise for these stores may have resulted from economic conditions, including poor financial planning, disaster, or financial success and replacement; or social conditions; or a specific traffic in used furniture from other local businesses or other towns. Little is known of either the source of merchandise or the characteristics of the clientele but second-hand stores indicate another means of acquiring home furnishings at low cost. The "cash-or-trade" payment arrangements, rarely advertised by other retailers, seem designed to attract first-home furnishers short on ready cash.[21]

Local manufacturing developed early in Oklahoma Territory. Until 1904, industrial development centered on processing agricultural products particularly manufacturing cottonseed oil and flour. From 1904 to 1907, industries served the material needs of territorial settlers, including manufacture of lumber products, foundry and machine shop products, processing of native mineral deposits, and ice. Cheap fuels, both oil and natural gas, attracted new industries and spurred growth from approximately 1907. By 1909, Oklahomans could purchase a variety of products manufactured within their own state, although agricultural commodities still provided the bulk of the state's total income.[22]

Blacksmithing, clothing manufacture, and furniture-making imply artisan handwork on an earlier frontier. The 1890 and 1900 census reports identify the amounts of capital investment in machinery and power for each industry.[23] Presumably, artisans would invest little in either machinery or power, and the relatively high figures given for tailors and furniture makers indicate that these were modern factories, although the average number of employees indicates that they were small. Blacksmithing shops primarily handled repair work, usually through service contracts to other industries, rather than producing complete articles. By 1900 such hand-forged products had been replaced by goods made faster, more efficiently, and cheaper by machines. Oklahoma industries, even in their infancies, kept pace with industrial developments nationwide and produced goods for both the farm household consumer and a national, industrial commodity market.

Territorial mail service to rural areas suffered from delays and irregular deliveries to widely scattered post offices on earlier frontiers. In Oklahoma Territory, every settlement boasting even one retail store had a post office. Pioneer reminiscences that touch upon this service show that the time stolen from farm chores to travel the varying distances to the post office each week was the major complaint, rather than delays from the other end. The time required for the trip was less a result of the distance, rarely over ten miles, than of road conditions.[24] Fannie Eisele recalled that her family walked the five miles to town for mail for the brief time before they owned a horse. Many families received mail in one town, but purchased supplies in another, and the responsibility for collecting mail was turned over to children. Youthful mail couriers often received a small fee for delivering mail to their rural neighbors, who offered the payment in return for the savings in time. Lillian Swartz described the Star Mail Route that brought mail from Enid to four rural post offices beginning in 1895. Private mail routes between post offices brought rural mail even closer to farm families, and Johalen Taylor or his wife Mary delivered faithfully for the Star Route despite adverse weather. Outlying towns and postal stations frequently relocated in response to settlement patterns and service lines. Rural home delivery routes operated in Comanche County as early as 1904, just three years after its opening.[25]

Apparently mail delivery to outlying post offices was regular and on time, and this contributed to the popularity of purchases of small, mailable items from a number of mail-order companies, including the Chicago-based firms of Sears, Roebuck and Company, and later Montgomery Ward. Large items shipped by rail or express companies were often less expensive through these retailers than comparable items advertised locally, since, as the companies themselves were quick to assert, local merchants paid the same freight charges for their goods, and passed these on in higher local prices.[26] Pioneer rail agent Arthur Dunham recalled that the major difficulty in shipping such orders to remote railheads was the

shortage of authorized agents to receive packages, which were
"put off at the risk of the owners." After Dunham's appointment as railroad and express agent in Oklahoma City in 1889,
that safety risk decreased.[27]

Tracing the actual dollar value of these transactions for a
specific area over any period of time is difficult, but the "Wish-
Book" was apparently an institution in Oklahoma even before
1900. Kittie M. Harvey, whose husband William was postmas-
ter in Chandler, recalled that the mail-order business was
"brisk" in 1893, and shortly after their arrival in Oklahoma
the Metcalf family purchased a side-saddle from a mail-order
catalogue.[28] Goods that appeared in the pages of period catalogues survived in surprising numbers to be deposited in
museum collections, and provide evidence of the success of
mail-order purchasing in Oklahoma Territory.[29]

Contrary to company claims, not all items from mail-order
houses were less expensive than those sold locally. In larger
towns, prices on staple goods such as cloth and foodstuffs were
competitive,[30] and merchants presumably covered their losses
on freight charges for competitive goods by charging higher
prices on other items. The specialized stores provided additional services to attract buyers, and the immediacy of local
purchasing was an additional incentive. Mail-order supply
businesses drew customers for jewelry and gift items, and perhaps for staples that could be ordered in bulk by whole neigh-
borhoods, as suggested by the catalogue advertisements. The
McBurney family even purchased their seed by mail-order in
the early 1890s.[31] The mail-order catalogues offered a wide
variety of merchandise not usually available in rural areas,
such as rural mail delivery wagons, artists' supplies, and pho-
tography equipment.

Particular items frequently associated with frontier life do
not appear in the newspaper or mail-order advertisements of
this settlement period. Spinning wheels are absent. Butter
churns are extra-large capacity only, presumably for commercial farm use. Heavy cast-iron cookware appears rarely,
replaced by lighter aluminum and graniteware more suitable

to use on ranges and stoves. Washing machines are far more numerous than wash tubs and wash boards, and ready-made clothing for both men and women is advertised more heavily after 1904. The evidence postulates cultural changes in domestic work that contradict the usual interpretation of frontier life.

The quantity and variety of goods available in any frontier area matters little if family income was insufficient to support purchasing above the subsistence level, and this is a common argument against redefining rural standards of living on the late frontier of the Great Plains. Cash shortages are often cited as evidence of restricted purchasing,[32] but contemporary business structures approached modern systems, even in unsettled areas like Oklahoma Territory, and allowed businesses some creativity in meeting the credit needs of their customers. Clara Bullard, recalling her family's experience in the Cherokee Strip in 1894, remarked that "dollars were hard to get and there was no credit,"[33] but Bullard was only thirteen at the time. The constraints of depressed farm prices created by drought had an obvious effect on many families in the 1890s, but other evidence suggests that although direct loans to farmers were rare, other credit opportunities were available. Bullard's recollection that her family made a weekly trip for provisions suggests that their credit was good with local merchants.[34]

In the 1880s, the banks that often served as middlemen between local borrowers and Eastern investors experienced a glut of investment money that "poured in at flood tempo." According to Paul B. Trescott's analysis, depressed farm prices altered the arrangements, resulting in fewer direct loans to farmers, but more to local merchants on a lower-risk, short-term basis. Historians generally agree that frontier interest rates and prices that incorporated the cost of loans to merchants tended to be relatively high compared to more settled areas, but as Allan Bogue has clearly indicated, credit was a necessity of rural life.[35] Oklahoma Territory supported numerous financial institutions, including Lawton's First National

Bank that initially operated from a tent. Most towns supported more than one bank, since national and state banks had different legal restrictions resulting in different methods of operation and different types of lending possibilities.[36] The numbers of banks, mortgage companies and lending institutions in competition for the business of a proliferate variety of merchants whose livelihoods were almost entirely dependent on agriculturalists apparently found the means to arrange credit systems among themselves that allowed most to survive.[37]

According to state agricultural reports, Oklahoma was blessed with relatively good crop conditions through most of its territorial period. Despite fluctuations in commodity prices, not untypical of agricultural economics at any time, improved seeds and farming equipment enabled livable farm incomes to most areas.[38] Despite individual cases of hardship, agricultural values compared with population for Oklahoma Territory in 1900 indicate a rough average income of $225 per person, or $1,033 per family, comparable to figures for Kansas, an agricultural state of similar environmental characteristics but slightly larger average family size. Few Oklahoma families were forced to share housing with another family,[39] and photographs indicate remarkable housing standards for rural Comanche County as early as 1905.[40] With positive financial conditions and the availability of manufactured items, capital loosened by sale of produce could be turned back into improvements for the home as well as the farm. Robert Lucas recalled that his family brought plows, cultivators and harrows. With much of the necessary equipment already purchased, and with additional income from odd jobs, farmers like Lucas could improve their homes with milled lumber siding, flooring, windows, and a well.[41]

The evidence clearly indicates that the conditions necessary for frontier Oklahomans to gain in material prosperity existed from the opening dates of previously surveyed townsites, and that prior planning allowed such conditions to exist despite the oversight of underestimating size. In outlying areas, agricultural families drew material goods from privately established towns that developed systems for supply and service more or less rapidly according to the external forces operating on individual entrepreneurs. A broad range of variation in material possessions among families results from initial variations in prosperity experienced before Oklahoma as well as the individual circumstances that affected purchase decisions after settling in Oklahoma.

The notion that farm improvements held higher priority in family purchasing decisions than household improvements may have been true of earlier frontiers, but by the late nineteenth and early twentieth centuries new forces affected family economics. Cultural definitions of basic material needs reflected national technological improvements. Business and commerce in Oklahoma reflected involvement in national marketing and investment systems, offering new opportunities as well as specialization.[42] While frontier Oklahomans continually devised imaginative solutions to material needs, their most effective responses were profit-making organizations designed to fill those needs, rather than individually applied frontier skills to "make do." Historical interpretation that acknowledges a markedly different set of standards and systematic responses to material needs implies a different impression of frontier life-style for lately settled regions. A broad range of conditions existed simultaneously within this limited region, but for frontier families conditions were neither as primitive nor as long-lasting as the accepted definition of rural pioneering implies.

NOTES

1. See John C. Hudson, "The Plains Country Town," in Brian W. Blouet and Frederick C. Luebke, eds., *The Great Plains: Environment and Culture* (Lincoln: University of Nebraska Press for the Center for Great Plains Studies, 1979), pp. 99-118; and Seena B. Kohl, "The Making of a Community: The Role of Women in an Agricultural Setting," in Lichtman and Challinor, eds., *Kin and Community* (n.p., 1978), pp. 175-86.

2. See Edwin C. McReynolds, *Oklahoma: A History of the Sooner State* (Norman: University of Oklahoma Press, 1954); and Carl Coke

Rister, *Land Hunger: David L. Payne and the Oklahoma Boomers* (Norman: University of Oklahoma Press, 1942).

3. Arrel Morgan Gibson, *Oklahoma: A History of Five Centuries*, 2d ed. (Norman: University of Oklahoma Press, 1981), p. 180.

4. H. Wayne Morgan and Anne Hodges Morgan, *Oklahoma: A Bicentennial History* (New York: W. W. Norton for the American Association for State and Local History, 1977), p. 53.

5. McReynolds, *Oklahoma*, pp. 289-91.

6. Before 1889, "Indian Territory" referred to the entire present state of Oklahoma, excluding the Panhandle. After 1889, "Indian Territory" referred only to the eastern half, while "Oklahoma Territory" was the name given to the western half that was opened to settlement. Because of the vastly different circumstances involved in settlement of both areas, this study will relate only to the western half, Oklahoma Territory.

7. Walter A. Johnson, "Brief History of the Missouri-Kansas-Texas Railroad Lines," *Chronicles of Oklahoma* 24 (Autumn 1946): 356; Homer S. Chambers, "Early-Day Railroad Building Operation in Western Oklahoma," *Chronicles of Oklahoma* 21 (June 1943): 165.

8. Violet Polin Igou, "Pioneer Days in Ellis County," *Chronicles of Oklahoma* 30 (Autumn 1952): 262-63.

9. Most diaries and reminiscences mention possessions only in passing, with rare inclusive lists of all items. Farm equipment, sewing machines, and family Bibles receive frequent mention.

10. U.S. Bureau of the Census, *Twelfth Census of the United States Taken in the Year 1900* (Washington, D.C.: United States Government Printing Office, 1900); Daniel J. Boorstin, *The Americans: The National Experience* (New York: Random House, 1965), p. 95; and John Mack Faragher, *Women and Men on the Overland Trail* (New Haven: Yale University Press, 1979), p. 18.

11. Daniel J. Boorstin, *The Americans: The Democratic Experience* (New York: Random House, 1973), pp. 3-41, 81-136, 305-31.

12. Based on collections of the Museum of the Great Plains, Lawton; the Oklahoma Historical Society, Oklahoma City; Stephens County Historical Society, Duncan; Museum of the Western Prairie, Altus.

13. Clara Williamson Warren Bullard, "Pioneer Days in the Cherokee Strip," *Chronicles of Oklahoma* 36 (Autumn 1958): 261; Donald E. Green, "Rural Oklahoma," in Donald E. Green, ed., *Rural Oklahoma* (Oklahoma City: Oklahoma Historical Society, 1977), p. 12.

14. Arthur W. Dunham, "A Pioneer Railroad Agent," *Chronicles of Oklahoma* 2 (March 1924):57.

15. Based on *Lawton Directory* for 1902, 1903, and 1907; *Guthrie Directory* for 1890, 1902, 1903, and 1907; Lawton *Constitution*, 1902 to 1909 (limited run, 1907 and 1908 missing); and Guthrie *Morning Sun*, 1894 to 1909 (limited run).

16.	Guthrie	Lawton
1907 Population	11,652	5,562
Township alone	1,045	890
Total	12,697	6,452
Retail Businesses		
Clothing	35	17
Millinery	6	2
Groceries	44	23
Meat Markets	17	10
Dry Goods	33	16
Hardware	26	13
Drug	14	7
Lumber	17	10
Used Furniture	21	8
New Furniture	14	9
Piano and Organ	5	0
Miscellaneous	38	22
Total	270	137

See also Hudson, "The Plains Country Town," pp. 114-18. Another treatment is Lewis E. Atherton, "The Pioneer Merchant in Mid-America," *University of Missouri Studies* 14 (April 1939): 7-46. Atherton deals with the earlier frontier period in the Ohio Valley region.

17. Newspaper advertisements from 1902 to 1907 yield a rough estimate of new businesses; limited runs, however, and the probability that not all businesses advertised affect the accuracy of the estimate. City populations are listed in the introductions to the city directories. Since these are not official publications, population figures are probably not accurate. City directories for Guthrie are not available for 1902, 1904, and 1905; primary statistics are for Lawton. Ratios of growth of business to growth of population range from one new business per thirty-seven population to one per forty-five, and fluctuate randomly.

18. A "general" store could be expected to supply any kind of merchandise, including groceries, dry goods, hardware, farm implements, seed, furniture, clothing, and gift items. *Guthrie Directory*, 1890, 1902, 1903, and 1907.

19. *Lawton Directory*, 1902, pp. 18-19.

20. Atherton, "Pioneer Merchant," pp. 9-11. Atherton argues that diversified interests protected merchants once they were established in a town.

21. One clue to the sources of merchandise is given in Annie Laurie Steele, "Old Greer County," *Chronicles of Oklahoma* 42 (September 1964): 29. In her introduction to the reminiscence of Rosabel DeBarry, Steele remarks that tools and household goods could be purchased cheaply from people returning to their previous homes.

22. U.S. Department of Labor and Commerce, Bureau of the Census, *Thirteenth Census of the United States Taken in the Year 1910* (Washington, D.C.: United States Government Printing Office, 1910).

23. U.S. Bureau of the Census, *Eleventh Census, 1890*, and *Twelfth Census, 1900*.

24. George H. Shirk, *Oklahoma Place Names* (Norman: University of Oklahoma Press, 1974), p. xv.

25. Fannie L. Eisele, "We Came to Live in the Oklahoma Territory," *Chronicles of Oklahoma* 38 (Spring 1960):60; Violet Polin Igou recalls that her father, Lee, mentioned bringing mail from Gage for 50¢ each trip over an unusually long distance of twenty-nine miles, Igou, "Pioneer Days," p. 264; Lillian Carlile Swartz, "Life in the Cherokee Strip," *Chronicles of Oklahoma* 42 (Summer 1964): 71; Hugh D. Corwin, "Comanche County, Oklahoma Territory," *Prairie Lore* 1 (July 1964): 3.

26. The following discussion of mail-order catalogues is based on the original *Consumers' Guide*, Sears, Roebuck and Co., for the years 1897, 1902, 1906, and 1908. Reprints of these original catalogues have been published in a series by DBI Books, Northfield, Illinois. The discussion also uses comparisons of advertised prices in the Lawton *Constitution*, and Sears *Consumers' Guide* for 1902; catalogue prices are computed to include express charges, since Lawton had no rail service in 1902.

27. Dunham, "Pioneer Agent," p. 50.

28. Kittie M. Harvey, "Memoirs of Oklahoma," *Chronicles of Oklahoma* 35 (Spring 1957): 47; Melvin Harrel, ed., "'My Life in the Indian Territory of Oklahoma': The Story of Augusta Carson Metcalf," *Chronicles of Oklahoma* 33 (Spring 1955):59.

29. See note 12. Jewelry was the most easily identifiable item in museum collections, and 20 percent to 45 percent of all pocket watches catalogued by the museum as received by the user between 1897 and 1908 appear in the pages of a Sears catalogue. Sample sizes are small, ranging from three to twelve. Some museums had no documentation of dates for collections, but a total of 32 percent of pocket watches in these collections appeared quite similar to those in Sears catalogues.

30. Comparison between prices quoted in the Lawton *Constitution* and Guthrie *Morning Sun*, 1902.

31. Laressa Cox McBurney, "My Pioneer Home in Old Greer County," *Chronicles of Oklahoma* 42 (Spring 1964): 42.

32. Elva Page Lewis, "Home Life and Hardships in Oklahoma Territory," *Chronicles of Comanche County* 1 (Autumn 1955): 69-78.

33. Bullard, "Pioneer Days in the Cherokee Strip," 263.

34. Ibid.

35. Paul B. Trescott, *Financing American Enterprise: The Story of Commercial Banking* (New York and Evanston: Harper and Row, 1963), pp. 95-96; Allan G. Bogue, *Money at Interest: The Farm Mortgage on the Middle Border* (Ithaca, NY: Cornell University Press, 1955). Bogue provides evidence that credit was even more necessary for farming in dry-lands areas. Approximately one-half of Oklahoma Territory fits the environmental definition of dry-lands.

36. Trescott, *American Enterprise*, pp. 89-90.

37. Banks that offered and encouraged the use of checking accounts may have been hedging their bets. The first advertisement noted for checking accounts by a Lawton bank appears in the *Constitution*, May 25, 1903.

38. *Report of the Oklahoma State Board of Agriculture* (Oklahoma City, 1907), pp. 1-27.

39. Added values of agricultural products for the state, excluding expenses, divided by rural population. Figures from *U.S. Census, 1900*. Statistics reported do not include all variables and do not constitute actual income, which is not reported. The same equation for Kansas yields a per capita income of $247. Average family size for Oklahomans is 4.6 persons; for Kansas, 4.1 persons. Kansas annual rural family income thus estimated is $1,013. Eighty-eight percent of Oklahoma families lived in dwellings not shared with another family.

40. Photograph taken April 12, 1910, by Call Studio, Lawton, is a panoramic photograph showing two- and three-story brick buildings over four city blocks. Photograph Collections, Museum of the Great Plains, Lawton; (P78.26.3 (unknown donor).

41. Robert C. Lucas, as told to Lucille Gilstrap, "Homesteading the Strip," *Chronicles of Oklahoma* 51 (Fall 1973): 291, 294-96; For a different perspective on an earlier frontier, see Gilbert C. Fite, "The Pioneer Farmer: A View Over Three Centuries," *Agricultural History* 50 (January 1976): 284.

42. Morgan and Morgan, *Oklahoma*, p. 88, describes some of the economic provisions included in the Oklahoma state constitution that reflect lawmakers' concern and understanding of national economic systems and the perceived need to protect Oklahoma interests.

Farm Technology and "The Great Debate": The Rhetoric of Horse Lovers and Tractor Boosters, 1900–1945

In 1905, the *Scientific American Supplement* presented a hypothetical budget for a mechanized farm and compared it to a hypothetical budget for a farm using horsedrawn implements.[1] The article was an early skirmish in a statistical fight that persists; historians and economists still argue over the historical costs of animal power and tractor power. For many years, the debate was not the intellectual exercise of academicians, but a burning issue all over America. The early tractor owner argued with his horsedrawn neighbor, the engineer attempted to persuade the veterinarian, and the professor of agriculture earnestly discussed the question with the extension agent. There was little respite for the disputants until after World War II.

In so protracted a dispute, the arguments changed as different circumstances developed; the history of the issue naturally divides into three periods. In the first phase, the tractor was a novelty whose capability was more a function of imagination than experience. To those who hoped for change, it promised relief from all types of unpleasantness. To those who feared change or who had a vested interest in the horsedrawn *status quo*, the tractor was a bogeyman of tremendous proportions. In that situation, discussion of the tractor generated strong feelings but relatively little data. The first phase ended abruptly, however, when the first generation of tractors failed to justify the hopes of their backers or to fulfill the fears of their opponents. By 1916, the debate had given way to grudging accommodation.[2]

The early experimental tractors enjoyed a brief boom on the Dakota frontier, but their success was technologically premature, and the tractor suffered. As a result of the experiences of the first tractor owners, many farmers and bankers concluded that tractors were a poor investment, a sentiment dutifully recorded by USDA surveys. "Up to the present time," reported the government in 1915, "the tractor appears to have made for itself no important place in the agricultural economy of the country." And the same survey reported that "neither the steam nor gas tractor has affected the sale or use of farm horses to any great extent."[3] Even four years later, government polls indicated that the tractor replaced far fewer horses than had been popularly anticipated. The tractor did not seem much of a threat to the horse.[4]

From 1915 through the 1920s, the dispute cooled to a second phase. There appeared to be a tacit accommodation between tractor promoters and horse defenders. Both seemed reconciled to the fact that farmers would use both teams and engines. Themes of peaceful coexistence appeared regularly in the literature of both factions. *Power Farming*, the oracle of mechanization, published a fairly steady stream of articles that included statements such as, "these machines will probably never replace horses entirely," or "a tractor and mares make a good combination."[5] The *Breeder's Gazette* reciprocated with an observation that the tractor could relieve mares and young horses of the strain of some of the heavier work, and thus help the horse breeder.[6] And extension agents soothed partisan feelings with the admonition that "horses and tractors should not be regarded as competing, but as complementing each other."[7] In fact, the number of tractors and the number of horses on farms in the United States were *both* expanding. Farmers were buying tractors, but they were also buying more horses and mules.[8] The debate temporarily gave way to an amiable standoff.

The armistice between horse lovers and mechanists began when both camps recognized the legitimate need for both animal and mechanical power in the farmer's field. It ended rather sharply, however, and the third and final phase of the debate began, when an innovative tractor allowed the farmer to mechanize the horse's last stronghold. In 1931, *Business Week* reported the occasion of the change:

Few people realize how recent a development power farming really is. . . . Power farming, 100%, is only about six years old. As long as horses had to be used to till row crops—about a third of all acreage—it could not be said that horseless farming had arrived. It was not until International Harvester introduced its high-wheeled, (row) straddling Farmall in 1925, the first general purpose tractor, that it became possible to cultivate corn or cotton with other than horses.[9]

As soon as it became possible to replace horses with tractors many farmers did so. In fact, the percentage of farms using horses declined rapidly. By 1962, the USDA's Statistical Reporting Service discontinued counting the horses and mules on farms.[10] As the number of horses declined, those who defended horses became more desperate and more strident. Their voice was not heeded.

Throughout the long argument, mechanists and mule raisers, engineers and veterinarians often used the same basic ammunition. Much of the debate centered in the issue of profitability—the relative economic advantages of each contestant's favorite power source. Each antagonist claimed that the right choice meant indisputable cost savings, and used an abundance of numbers to buttress this conviction.

One of the most common arguments—and one employed by both factions—constructed an economic model to prove the relative merits of the chosen side. Such models were only as good as the model-maker's skill allowed. In some cases, the model (or theoretical balance sheet) was believable, while in others, the model was inaccurate. Some were simplistic, some were unrealistic, and some were highly sophisticated. Yet even at their best, models were frequently unconvincing. One of the best models, the recently published study by Robert Ankli, is skillfully drawn. Yet Ankli concedes that if the farmer made one less cutting of alfalfa than the model postulated, it would change the results at the bottom line, and he clearly warns that horses might legitimately be entered under either "fixed cost" or "variable costs," also changing the nature of the final figure.[11] Models have real limitations.

In contrast to models, farmers offered records and testimonials in favor of both horse and tractor. Like the economic models, these varied widely in both quality and reliability. Some farmers kept only very crude records, sometimes scratching figures on the back of the barn door.[12] Such bookkeeping probably impressed no one—not even farmers with equally haphazard accounting. When a farmer gave specific figures, he undoubtedly was more persuasive. In 1916, a farmer wrote in *Hoard's Dairyman* that it cost him $.51 per acre to plow with his tractor but $1.84 per acre with a horse.[13] He did not submit his books for authentication, but his claim *sounded* precise. And *Orange Judd Farmer* assured its readers that the authority they cited was "a businessman in Janesville [who] runs his farm on business principles. . . . He knows to the cent just what the farm is producing and how much it costs to run it."[14] But even the most accurate records sometimes were inconclusive.

Accurate records, like carefully constructed models, offered a farmer interesting data to analyze. They did not automatically mean that the farmer would jump up and copy what he read about. Farming was—and is—an exceedingly complex undertaking with an infinite number of variables. The sheer diversity of crops, farm sizes and climatic conditions precluded broad generalizations from being universally applicable. Government investigators recognized the variability of farms in their initial unfavorable report on tractors, and added a caveat stating that "the fact that some men have found the tractor a profitable investment is proof that under certain conditions it can be used successfully for farm work."[15] They obviously believed that for many farms, it would not prove profitable. At a later date, a small Southern farmer might read with vague curiosity of a farmer who claimed the tractor was a good investment. But what was profitable to a corn farmer on 3,600 acres in the Midwest was irrelevant to a six-acre cotton farmer.

The problem of diversity and uniqueness among farms made the agricultural survey an exceedingly potent polemical weapon, for what farmer would want to buy a tractor when surveys showed that most tractors were uneconomical? Or what farmer would keep horses when everyone reported that they were too expensive? It was true that the employees of the United States Department of Agriculture and of the various state agencies scrupulously avoided taking sides in the argument, but the results of their work were susceptible to partisan use. And debaters quickly seized on such official figures.

Many of the government's questionnaires, when returned and collated, indicated that tractors reduced the cost of farming by an insignificant amount, if at all.[16] This negative note was offset, however, by enthusiastic reports by farmers who claimed that their tractors had been a profitable investment.

Surveys of Farmers Concerning the Profitability of Tractor Use, 1918–1929

Year	Area	Percent Reporting Researcher(s)[17]	Tractors Profitable
1918	Illinois	Yerkes & Church	90
1918	Maryland	F. A. Wirt	79
1918	Eastern U.S.	Yerkes & Church	84
1919	Kentucky	W. D. Nichols	71
1929	Pennsylvania	Humphries & Church	85

Obviously, no matter what statistical evidence they offered, most farmers surveyed who used tractors felt they were profitable. These same farmers, however, continued to use horses, and so their testimony did not provide ammunition for attacking draft animals.

Widespread acceptance of the idea that tractors were profitable did not settle the question whether the tractor or the horse was more economical for a specific task. That decision was difficult because of the simple fact that the cost of keeping horses was assumed by farmers to be a necessary expense in farming. Earlier students of farm economics also paid little attention to the actual cost of work stock. In 1922, the Department of Agriculture released a new study. Horses cost a surprising $100 per year in direct upkeep, and a whopping $450 to $750 per year total cost on a 160-acre cornbelt farm.[18] Still, the study did not compare horse costs with tractor costs. And so the question remained. L. A. Reynoldson and H. R. Tolley in 1923 observed: "Even farmers who already own tractors cannot always decide definitely whether to use their machine or continue to use their horses for a given operation."[19] There is no evidence that a thoroughgoing answer was worked out until after the truce period was over.

Part of the dispute over the relative expenses of horses or tractors rested on the issue of initial cost. From the early days, promoters of the tractor encouraged large farmers to sell several of their horses and use the proceeds to purchase a tractor. In 1913, Lynn W. Ellis suggested that the man with sixteen horses should sell all but four. He realized, though, that such advice hardly applied to the small farmer who "must keep a larger percentage of his original number and must now actually increase his investment with the purchase of a small tractor."[20] Other optimists predicted that the average farmer could replace 50 percent of his draft stock.[21] Had this estimate been accurate, the horses would still have left a sizable portion of the cost of the tractor to be raised from other sources. In 1910, the average farm had only 3.8 horses, mules, asses or burros, and the figure had risen to 3.9 in 1920.[22] In both cases, of course, the figure is almost four head per farm, but that number is deceptive, for it includes colts too young to work, old stock that had been retired or "put out to pasture," brood mares, pets, saddle horses and even Kentucky thoroughbreds. The 50 percent figure itself was optimistic, however, for Arnold Yerkes and L. M. Church discovered in their surveys that "in no case [was] the value of the horses displaced equal to 50 per cent of the first cost of the tractor."[23] Tractor fans responded by admitting that increased investment was necessary, but countered that the farmer who added a tractor increased his working capacity more than he increased his investment.[24]

Horse breeders responded by charging that operating cost was more significant than the initial investment. They pointed to the high depreciation of tractors and compared it to the mare's ability to reproduce itself.[25] It was a potent point. Ralph M. Fogelman, a diehard tractor owner, admitted to *Breeder's Gazette* that he was "more than determined to continue with horses."[26] The depreciation/reproduction contrast was the major factor in his decision.

Horses held their value, at least in part because demand exceeded supply. The proximate reason was cogently explained by Illinois agricultural economists when they wrote that "at the present time [1933] colts are not being raised in large enough numbers to replace normal death losses."[27] This did not explain the ultimate reason, that is, why farmers were not breeding their mares and raising foals. Ironically enough, the high initial cost of horses may well have contributed to their replacement with tractors. In 1935, *Automotive Industries* gloated that a prime team cost as much as $600, but an all-purpose tractor cost $433.00.[28]

The higher initial cost of horses was accompanied by what was widely perceived to be a higher operating cost. As early as 1910, Edward A. Rumely, physician and scion of a prominent family of implement makers, claimed that fuel cost only one half-cent per engine horsepower, while horse feed cost 8 1/4¢ per horsepower. Using these figures, the propagandist for machinery projected a savings of $600 million per year if only half the nations' work stock were replaced.[29] Rumely's friend, L. W. Ellis boasted the following year that draft animals in the United States consumed the equivalent of $1.25 billion per year.[30] And in May 1916, Julian A. Dimock claimed that it cost more to feed a team than the average farmer made in a year's time. He claimed that horses stood idle seven hours for each hour of use.[31] By September, R. T. Mally refined Dimock's argument, pointing out that the horse ate whether working or not, while the tractor used fuel only when working. Mally claimed neither tractor nor horse worked more than 25 percent of the time.[32] These arguments proved difficult to refute. In addition, testimonials from farmers were even harder to answer than figures from theorists and journalists. B. J. Ruetinik, a dairy farmer, claimed that the fuel for his tractor cost less than the shoeing bill for his team of six horses.[33] Similar statements abounded in letters to farm journals.

At first there seemed to be no response to the issue of fuel cost. In October 1914, Wayne Dinsmore, a lifelong advocate of equine power, protested lamely that the work a horse did during the active season more than justified his upkeep the rest of the year.[34] But a more powerful rebuttal was obviously essential for an adequate defense of draft stock. By 1920, horse raisers were working toward just such a rationale. Robert Pound suggested to the readers of *Breeder's Gazette* that much of the feed for draft stock came from land unsuited to tillage.[35] It was a clever polemic, and it pointed the way toward a more sophisticated argument that would be developed later. But Pound's suggestion had a fatal flaw. Many tractor owners purchased the hay and oats they needed and devoted all their land to cash crops.[36] Horse lovers had to wait for a convincing argument until events raised the nation's consciousness from the individual farm to the welfare of agriculture in general.

By the 1930s, as the nations of the world struggled with the Great Depression, severe deflation reduced the value of farm produce to unfathomable levels, while many urban residents suffered from hunger. In an attempt to understand the cruel paradoxes of modern economics, institutions of all types held conferences and seminars. One such meeting, called the World's Grain Exhibition and Conference, was convened in 1933. The speakers noted that one consequence of mechanization was a reduction in the demand for hay and oats, a reduction that came at a time of increased production.[37] Horse advocates found their issue. As might have been expected, Wayne Dinsmore led the fight. In the *Journal of the American Veterinary Medical Association*, he wrote that "tractors cause lower prices for hay and grain" and a price-crippling surplus of food crops.[38] But the argument was too late. By 1945, some 15 percent of American farmland had been converted from the raising of draft stock feed to commercial crops, and the trend would continue until virtually all of the 25 percent of the cropland that had once fed horses was devoted to market production.[39] Eventually, a growing population came to depend on that area. In 1970, agricultural engineers wrote: "The total acreage formerly used to produce feed for the work horses, if taken out of food production, would leave us now with a shortage of food for people."[40] But even then, the argument about horses persisted among a horse-farming fringe group.

There is a curious sidelight to the argument over fuel cost versus feed cost. Seemingly few observers, if any, gave much thought to the renewable nature of oats and hay as opposed to the exhaustibility of fossil fuels—at least not until the OPEC oil embargo of 1974. Verkareddy Chennareddy and Bob F. Jones examined the economics of the ratio of marginal physical product of one tractor relative to one horse or mule, but virtually assumed a constant supply of fuel for each. Samuel Brody and Richard Cunningham compared the physical work efficiency of horse and tractor, but were more preoccupied with economic aspects than questions of fuel availability.[41] Yet from the very first, some advocates of mechanical power have realized that mechanization is totally based on the availability of cheap fuel.[42]

If tractors had a cheaper initial cost and cheaper direct operating costs, that still did not reveal the entire story. Farmers who mechanized seldom used their horsedrawn equipment with their new power source. Thus, the *total* cost of tractorization pushed the investment far higher than just the cost of the prime power source. Mechanized farms had high capital requirements.[43] Surprisingly enough, neither party emphasized this fact in most arguments.

Operating costs were not the only consideration in determining whether or not a tractor was profitable, for productivity also entered into the calculation. Productivity could be increased by the tractor by either increasing yields or decreasing labor. Of course, tractor salesmen claimed that it did both.

The major way in which the tractor increased production was through timeliness of operation. This theme was repeated by tractor opponents and proponents alike over a long period.[44] The reality of such an increase in production was undeniable, although the increase may or may not have been large enough to be significant. Nevertheless, both sides pointed to the increase and drew opposite conclusions. Pro-tractor forces lauded the increase because it brought more revenue to the farmer. Anti-tractor forces decried the increase for helping to flood the market and depress prices. Like much of the rhetoric during the era, this argument cut both ways.

Similar arguments flew between the two forces over the tractor's ability to increase productivity by reducing labor requirements. Tractor advocates bragged about reducing labor requirements, for they felt that it helped farmers reduce their expenses. The other side denounced the tractor for reducing labor requirements and thereby contributing to the macroeconomic problems of the Depression.[45]

All of the above arguments rested on essentially economic evidence. Horse breeders contended that, in the long run horses were better investments for farmers than tractors. Implement dealers argued that tractors were more profitable. Neither won decisive victory. Indeed, had either group produced incontrovertible evidence of economic superiority, the argument would have ended long before it did.[46] In fact, horse farmers continue to claim their method was profitable, even in the 1980s.[47]

The enduring nature of the economic argument suggests several observations. First, since most farmers eventually mechanized, they must have *perceived* that the tractor was as profitable or nearly as profitable as the horse. The perception of profitability in a farm setting in the first half of the twentieth century was not necessarily the same as actual profits. Farmers were notorious at that time for their careless or even nonexistant bookkeeping. One writer complained that some farmers kept accounting figures on the back of the barn door.[48] Few farmers carefully and accurately calculated overhead costs and depreciation.

In addition, there were several forces at work that would make farmers *assume* a tractor was a rewarding investment. For example, in the twentieth century, the biggest profits were frequently reported by the largest companies. And those same large companies were leaders in mechanization. How could farmers possibly make money unless they, too, "industrialized." The argument was pressed upon farmers fairly regularly.[49]

Not only were farmers told to mechanize in order to be like industry, but they were also exposed to the example of successful mechanical farmers. Larger farms realized some legitimate savings due to economies of scale, and they were frequently better managed and therefore more profitable. The better credit resources of big farms made it easier for them to purchase tractors, and their larger scale of operations offered more opportunities to use a tractor. In some cases, the farm was bigger because it used a tractor, but in many other instances, the farm was larger-than-average *before* ordering a tractor. The distinction is subtle, but significant, since in one case the tractor *caused* a change in scale of operations and caused the farm to succeed, whereas in the second case the tractor was purchased as a *result* of success. Regardless of which came first, however, there was an obvious statistical affinity between tractors and large, successful farms. For many unanalytical farmers, the tractor seemed to have an affluent shine from its association with prosperous farms.[50] Undoubtedly, some farmers perceived a stronger connection between tractors and profits than actually existed.

Second, in the absence of overwhelming statistical evidence that tractors were better investments, some farmers developed other, *noneconomic* motives for tractorization. Farmer Jones was not exclusively motivated by economic interests; he saw other factors not expressed in ledger-book language. Farmers, unlike many industrial managers, were not only decision-makers, they were also production laborers. On most farms, there was no division between ownership and management, and very little distance between management and labor. If the tractor was more convenient or more comfortable, farmers (as laborers) benefitted, and farmers (as purchasing agents) were influenced by that fact. To a far greater extent than in industry, a rational decision on the farm was more than just a matter of economics.[51]

For a number of farmers, there were also significant personal reasons to resist tractorization. Older farmers, or those with less adaptable personalities, found horse drawn habits hard to change. Virtually every rural community has its repertoire of stories: "Old Man Johnson plowed through a five-strand barbed wire fence while screaming 'Whoa!' at his Fordson!" A farmer approaching retirement who was uncomfortable around "new-fangled contraptions" made a rational choice when he kept his faithful mules. Other farmers developed strong emotional attachments to their animals. Such affection could hardly be described as a "rational" reason for continuing to farm with horses, but the critic who cannot understand such a bond may be more mechanical than human.

The very noneconomic arguments that supported horses could be inverted. Many farmers—especially young men with "modern" ideas—despised horses. To them a curry comb was disgusting, and the sight of a manure fork was unbearable. And indisputably, the tractor dramatically reduced the time devoted to "chores" when it displaced horses entirely.[52] For the fastidious young man "in a hurry," the tractor was the rational choice—unless it imposed an unbearable financial cost. Thus, so long as neither horse nor tractor were overwhelmingly cheaper, a reasonable selection was not always based on economic considerations.

There was one last factor influencing the choice; it was not a monetary matter *per se,* nor was it totally divorced from money. The last element was the matter of status. Judging by the appeals of the tractor sellers, it was a strong sales point. Even the anti-tractor forces recognized its force. One wrote: "If you own a tractor, your neighbors and the people you know in town will consider you a progressive and up-to-date farmer."[53] Other articles equated tractor ownership with being modern.[54]

Clearly the tractor triumphed over the horse, but it was not a simple process. Many factors were weighed by farmers, some more scientific than others. Foremost, in the period from its conception until after its numerical triumph, the tractor could not be proved to have overwhelming economic advantages on average-sized row-crop farms. As late as 1921, agricultural economist H. R. Tolley raised the question whether a farmer should purchase a tractor.[55] But despite these equivocal positions, many farmers perceived economic merits in the tractor that were illusory. The tractor would prevail because noneconomic motives probably outweighed economic factors in the minds of most farmers when they chose between Old Dobbin and a new Farmall.

NOTES

1. "The Scott Gasoline-Motor-Propelled Agricultural Tractor," *Scientific American Supplement* 60 (November 4, 1905): 24948-949; Robert E. Ankli, "Horses vs. Tractors on the Corn Belt," *Agricultural History* 51 (January 1980): 134-148.

2. For an example of the pro-tractor hopes, see L. W. Ellis and Edward A. Rumely, *Power and the Plow* (Garden City, N.Y.: Doubleday, Page & Co., 1911). A lifetime foe of tractors, Wayne Dinsmore, condemned the machines in "Horsepower vs. Horse Power," *Breeder's Gazette*, October 8, 1914, p. 585.

3. Arnold P. Yerkes and H. H. Mowry, "Farm Experience with the Tractor," *U.S. Department of Agriculture Bulletin No. 174* (April 15, 1915), pp. 4-9, 38-44.

4. Arnold P. Yerkes and L. M. Church, "The Farm Tractor in the Dakotas," *Farmers' Bulletin No. 1035* (1919), p. 29.

5. "Why Farmers Buy Tractors," *Power Farming*, April, 1916, p. 40; E. Lloyd Watson, "The Farm Tractor and Horse Production," *Power Farming*, January 1917, p. 8.

6. E. A. White, "The Farm Power Problem," *Breeder's Gazette*, August 1, 1918, pp. 156-57. See also: "Buy a Tractor and Raise Better Horses," *Power Farming*, April, 1917, pp. 7-8; Grace Deity, "An Ideal

Horse-Tractor Power Combination," *Power Farming*, April, 1917, pp. 7-8.

7. John A. Hopkins, Jr., "Horses, Tractors and Farm Equipment," *Iowa Agricultural Experiment Station Bulletin No. 264* (June, 1929), p. 387.

8. C. F. Godman, "The Limitations of Tractors," *Breeder's Gazette*, August 28, 1920, pp. 347-48; *Fourteenth Census of the United States*, p. 542.

9. "Farm Equipment Companies Are Bigger and Fewer," *Business Week*, May 6, 1931, p. 22.

10. Wayne D. Rasmussen, "The Impact of Technological Change on American Agriculture, 1862-1961," *Journal of Economic History* 22 (December 1962): 578-91.

11. For Ankli's model, see "Horses vs. Tractors on the Corn Belt," *Agricultural History* 51 (January 1980): 134-48.

12. G. Douglas Jones, "Tractor Power in Relation to Agriculture," *Proceedings of the World's Grain Exhibition and Conference* 1 (Regina, Saskatchewan: Canadian Society of Technical Agriculturists, 1933) pp. 419-23.

13. B. J. Ruetenik, "The Efficiency of the Farm Tractor," *Hoard's Dairyman*, July 28, 1916, p. 5.

14. "Tractor Saves Half Expense," *Orange Judd Farmer*, February 17, 1917, p. 20.

15. Yerkes and Mowry, "Farm Experience," p. 39.

16. "Many farmers in this survey expressed the opinion that it was costing more to farm with a tractor than if they were doing the work with horses," but they cited other reasons for continuing to use machinery. F. L. Morison, "The Tractor on Ohio Farms," *Ohio Agricultural Experiment Station Bulletin No. 383* (May 1925) p. 29. See also: Arnold P. Yerkes and L. M. Church, "An Economic Study of the Farm Tractor in the Corn Belt," *Farmer's Bulletin No. 719* (May 5, 1916), p. 5; Arnold P. Yerkes and L. M. Church, "The Gas Tractor in Eastern Farming," *Farmers' Bulletin No. 1004* (September 1918), p. 21.

17. Arnold P. Yerkes and L. M. Church, "Tractor Experience in Illinois," *Farmers' Bulletin No. 963*, (June, 1918), p. 5; F. A. Wirt, "Experience of Maryland Tractor Owners," *Maryland Agricultural Society Report* 3 (1918), pp. 80-84; Yerkes and Church, "Tractor in Eastern Farming," pp. 7-8; W. D. Nichols, "Tractor Experience in Kentucky," *Kentucky Agricultural Experiment Station Bulletin No. 222* (September 1919), p. 47; W. R. Humphries and L. M. Church, "A

Farm Machinery Survey of Selected Districts in Pennsylvania," *Pennsylvania Agricultural Experiment Station Bulletin No. 232* (March 1919), p. 7.

18. M. R. Cooper and J. O. Williams, "Cost of Using Horses on Corn-Belt Farms," *Farmers' Bulletin No. 1298* (1922), pp. 1-2, 12.

19. L. A. Reynoldson and H. R. Tolley, "What Tractors and Horses Do on Corn-Belt Farms," *Farmers' Bulletin No. 1295* (January 1923), p. 1.

20. Lynn W. Ellis, "The Problem of the Small Farm Tractor," *Scientific American*, June 7, 1913, p. 518.

21. Typical of these was W. J. Shaver, "A Tractor and Horses Combined," *Power Farming*, February 1917, p. 15.

22. Fourteenth Census of the United States 5, p. 542.

23. Yerkes and Church, "Farm Experience," p. 39; also Yerkes and Church, "Tractor in the Corn Belt," p. 21.

24. Ruetenik, "Efficiency," p. 5.

25. Dinsmore, "Horsepower," p. 586.

26. Ralph M. Fogelman, "Tractor and Horses in War and Peace," *Breeder's Gazette*, July 10, 1919, p. 58.

27. P. E. Johnston and J. E. Wills, "A Study of the Cost of Horse and Tractor Power on Illinois Farms," *Illinois Agricultural Experiment Station Bulletin No. 395* (December, 1933), p. 279.

28. A. F. Waddell, "A Public Works Buying Slackens, Returning Farm Prosperity Lifts Production of Adaptable New Models," *Automotive Industries*, December 28, 1935, p. 853. See also Wayne Worthington, "The Engineer's History of the Farm Tractor: World War II, Confusion, Development," *Implement & Tractor*, February 7, 1967, p. 74, F. L. Morison, "Tractors on Small Farms in Ohio," *Ohio Agricultural Experiment Station Bimonthly Bulletin* 26 (November-December 1941), pp. 183-84; L. B. Sperry, "Farm Power and the Post-War Tractor," *Transactions of the Society of Automotive Engineers*, 52 (November, 1922), p. 504.

29. Edward A. Rumely, "The Passing of the Man with the Hoe," *World's Work* 20 (August 1910), pp. 1325-26.

30. L. W. Ellis, "Economic Importance of the Farm Tractor," *The Engineering Magazine*, May 1911, p. 336.

31. Julian A. Dimock, "The Farm Horse Doesn't Pay," *The Independent*, May 29, 1916, p. 337.

32. R. T. Mally, "The Farm Tractor and the Renter," *Power Farming*, September 1916, pp. 8, 29.

33. Ruetinik, "Efficiency," p. 5. Also see W. J. Spencer, "Farms

More Cheaply With a Gas Tractor," *Power Farming*, November 1917, p. 20.

34. Dinsmore, "Horsepower," p. 585.

35. Robert T. Pound, "Machine Versus Muscle," *Breeder's Gazette*, September 16, 1920, p. 512.

36. L. A. Reynoldson and H. R. Tolley, "Changes Effected by Tractors on Corn Belt Farms," *Farmers' Bulletin No. 1296* (1922), p. 8.

37. J. F. Booth, "Some Economic Effects of Mechanization of Canadian Agriculture with Particular Reference to the Spring Wheat Area," *Proceedings of the World's Grain Exhibition and Conference* 1 (Regina, Saskatchewan: Canadian Society of Technical Agriculturalists, 1933), pp. 359-60.

38. Wayne Dinsmore, "Horses, Mules and Tractors in Farming," *Journal of the American Veterinary Medical Association*, (November, 1940), p. 444.

39. Sherman E. Johnson, "Changes in American Farming," *Miscellaneous Publication No. 707* (Washington, D.C.: USDA, December 1949), p. 3.

40. Walter M. Carleton and Glen E. Vanden Berg, "That 'Hidden' Migration: History Now," *Agricultural Engineering* 51 (October 1970): 578.

41. Ellis, "Economic Importance," p. 336. Ironically, Ellis and Rumely imply that they were conscious of petroleum exhaustion and suggest the possibility of fuel alcohol.

42. Venkareddy Chennareddy and Bob F. Price, "Labor," *The Overproduction Trap in Agriculture*, ed. Glen L. Johnson and Leroy Quance (Baltimore: Resources for the Future, Inc., 1971), pp. 123-24; Samuel Brody and Richard Cunningham, "Growth and Development with Special Reference to Domestic Animals: XL Comparison Between Horse, Man and Motor with Special Reference to Size and Monetary Economy," *Missouri Agricultural Experiment Station Research Bulletin No. 244,* (August 31, 1936), pp. 54-56.

43. Johnston and Wills, "Cost of Horse and Tractor Power," p. 291; B. A. Russell, "Farm Power Utilization and Costs [in] South Carolina," *South Carolina Agricultural Experiment Station Bulletin No. 280* (September 1931), p. 11.

44. E. E. Dickey, "Tractor Much Cheaper than Horse," *Power Farming*, October 1917, p. 13; C. A. Bacon, "The Advantages of Tractor Plowing," *Power Farming*, December, 1917, p. 22; Reynoldson and Tolley, "What Tractors and Horses Do," p. 5; G. W. McCuen, "Dividends From Your Tractor," *The Ohio Farmer*, January 19, 1924, p.

76; C. G. Pearse, "Power on the Farm," *Proceedings of the World's Grain Exhibition and Conference* 1 (Regina, Saskatchewan: Canadian Society of Technical Agriculturalists, 1933), pp. 376-77; Morison, "Tractors on Small Farms," pp. 183-84; Martin R. Cooper, Glen T. Barton, and Albert P. Brodell, "Progress in Farm Mechanization," *Miscellaneous Publication No. 630* (Washington, D.C.: United States Department of Agriculture, October, 1947), pp. i, 41-42; J. C. Elrod and W. J. Fullilove, "Cost and Utilization of Tractor Power and Equipment on Farms in the Lower Piedmont," *Georgia Experiment Station Bulletin No. 256* (January 1948), p. 37; Sherman Johnson, "Changes," p. 13.

45. E. A. Hunger, "Forrestdale Said 'Good-Bye' to Dobbin," *Power Farming*, June 1926, p. 6; G. W. Gilbert, "An Economic Study of Tractors on New York Farms," *New York Agricultural Experiment Station Bulletin No. 506* (June 1930), p. 56; Johnston and Wills, "Cost of Horse and Tractor," p. 284; Glen T. Barton, "Increased Productivity of the Farm Worker," *Industrial and Labor Relations Review* 1 (January 1948): 267.

46. In 1929, experts suggested "about equal profits," regardless of the power source. O. G. Lloyd and L. G. Hobson, "Relation of Farm Power and Farm Organization in Central Indiana," *Indiana Agricultural Experiment Station Bulletin No. 332* (June 1929), p. 2.

47. Peter Chew, "If Fuel is Too High Down on the Farm—Just Get a Horse," *Smithsonian* 10 (February 1980): 76-84; Wendell Berry, "Farming With Horses," *Organic Gardening and Farming*, March 1974, p. 72.

48. Jones, "Tractor Power," 419-23; H. P. Roberts, "What It Costs to Run the Tractor," *Progressive Farmer*, July 12, 1919, p. 1142.

49. Rumely, "Passing the Man with Hoe," p. 1328; Ellis, "Economic Importance," p. 336; L. J. Fletcher, "Factors Influencing Tractor Development," *Agricultural Engineering* 3 (November 1922): 180; L. J. Fletcher, "Mechanical Power—The Basis of the Next Agricultural Revolution," *Agricultural Engineering* 12 (June 1931): 199-200.

50. The association of tractor and larger farms has held consistent throughout the years. Arnold P. Yerkes, "Discussion of Tractor Economics," *Transactions of the American Society of Agricultural Engineers* 9 (March 1916), p. 97; Nichols, "Tractor Experience," pp. 47, 54-55; H. R. Tolley and L. M. Church, "Tractors on Southern Farms," *Farmers' Bulletin No. 1278* (August 1922), p. 5; R. S. Washburn, "Cost of Using Horses, Tractors and Combines on Wheat Farms in Sherman County, Oregon," *U. S. Department of Agriculture Bulletin No. 1447*

(December, 1926), p. 3; Gilbert, "Economic Study," p. 6; Booth, "Effects of Mechanization," p. 355; Robert T. McMillan, "Effects of Mechanization on American Agriculture," *Scientific Monthly*, (July 1949), p. 25; Kenneth L. Bachman and Ronald W. Jones, "Sizes of Farms in the United States," *Technical Bulletin No. 1019* (July 1950), p. 2; J. Patrick Madden, "Agricultural Mechanization, Farm Size and Community Development," *Agricultural Engineering* 59 (August, 1978): 13-14.

51. Walter John Marx, "Farms, Machines and the Good Society," *The Commonwealth,* December 24, 1948, p. 273.

52. "The reduction in time required for crop production by substituting motor for animal power between 1909 and 1938 amounted to 785 billion man hours annually. This was equal to about 10 percent of the annual man hours required in crop production. Had the study been repeated in 1945, savings [of labor] from the use of motor power would have been even greater." Walter W. Wilcox, *The Farmer in the Second World War*, (Ames: Iowa State College Press, 1947), p. 290. Government researchers estimated that each tractor saved 250 man hours per year that otherwise would have been spent caring for work stock. James A. McAleer, "Farm Machinery and Equipment Policies of the War Production Board and Predecessor Agencies," *Historical Reports on War Administration: War Production Board Special Study No. 13* (mimeographed) (November 10, 1944), p. 1, as quoted in Bela Gold, *Wartime Economic Planning in Agriculture* (New York: Columbia University Press, 1949), p. 203. Whether or not those hours were actually "saved" or re-invested in other farm activities to help meet mortgage payments is another variable.

53. Francis Z. Hazlett, "The Farm Tractor in 1920," *Scientific American*, December 18, 1920, p. 612.

54. Arthur L. Dahl, "The Tractor that Never Tires," *The Independent*, May 25, 1918, pp. 321, 329.

55. Earl D. Ross, "Retardation in Farm Technology Before the Power Age," *Agricultural History* 30 (January, 1956): 18, citing H. R. Tolley, "The Farm Power Problem," *Journal of Farm Economics* 3 (April, 1921): 91-99. Others have recently argued that the rejection or delay of tractorization was sometimes economically rational, as in the South; Robert Higgs, "Tractors or Horses? Some Basic Economics in the Pacific Northwest and Elsewhere," *Agricultural History* 49 (January 1955): 281-283. This does not argue, of course, that farmers should return to horse power. Few people would argue with the state-

ment that "it is evident that horses and mules could not profitably substitute for tractors as a source of power." Leroy C. Quance, "Capital," in *The Overproduction Trap in U. S. Agriculture*, Glenn L. Johnson and C. Leroy Quance, eds. (Baltimore: Resources for the Future, Inc., 1972), p. 96.

Drafting Farmers in World War II

As the marauding Indians crept closer to the colonial village, an ever watchful sentry gave the alarm. The farmers in the field dropped their hoes, snatched their flintlocks from the wall, and raced to join neighbors at the ramparts. Another Indian raid was rebuffed.

Such a scenario is part of the romantic image that has grown up around the sturdy yeoman farmer who was also a citizen-soldier. With such heroic figures plentiful, Americans saw little need for a standing army. Time and time again, the country would rely on volunteers, until it became obvious that the image was flawed and that men would have to be dragooned—drafted—into military service. During World War II, the defects in this romantic image of farmers became more obvious. Not only were farm volunteers insufficient, but farmers sought special protection from the threat of conscription.

During World War II, farm operators became desperate to protect their labor from both raids by better-paying industries and conscription. Using its considerable political muscle, the farm lobby in Congress gained protective status for farm labor. Through a special class deferment, farm operators succeeded in using the draft to their advantage. Rather than an instrument for universal military service, the draft became a means by which farm operators could prevent the flow of their labor into more attractive jobs.

This condition prevailed because farmers cried in anguish all during the war about their shortage of labor, a shortage more imagined than real. As with the industrial labor force, the farm population changed during the war. But the problem of keeping the boys down on the farm began long before the war. In the 1920s, when farming suffered from a severe depression, the annual out-migration was some 2.1 million farmers. During the 1930s, when New Deal programs helped to relieve the economic distress of the farmer, the out-migration dropped to only 1.3 million annually. During the war, with the attraction of military service and higher paying jobs in industry, the out-migration rose again to 2.1 million annually. This out-migration, however, was partially offset by an in-migration. In the 1920s some 1.5 million men had moved annually to the farms. During the 1930s the figure dropped to 1 million and remained at this annual level during the war. In 1940, the total farm employment population was 10,585,000; by 1945, the figure had declined to 9,843,000. This decline of 742,000, however, represented only a 7 percent total loss.[1]

Even with this modest decline in total labor, American farmers did a remarkable job of increasing production. Using 1940 as a base year of 100, farm output for human use leaped from 105 in 1941 to 117 in 1945. For all crops, using 1935-1939 as a base of 100, production rose from 107 in 1940 to 122 in 1945. This increase was due to many factors; perhaps most important was the increase in efficiency per farm worker. Using 1910-1914 as a base year of 100 in productivity per employee, the trend of improved farm efficiency becomes clear. In 1920, the figure stood at 118; in 1930, it was 127; during the war it climbed from 151 in 1940, to 191 in 1945.

Other influences that help explain the wartime production of farmers include improved seed and soil conservation. In May 1945, Marvin Jones, the War Food Administrator, announced that the U.S. had produced 50 percent more food annually in World War II than in World War I. More significantly, the American people had 10 percent more food per capita than in

1917-1918. The civilian per capita consumption of all food during World War II increased over the 1935-1939 average. This increase in consumption occurred despite sending huge quantities of food to England and the U.S.S.R. Indeed, by 1944, officials in Washington worried about the problem of food surpluses.[2]

The wartime production record, which included supplying American allies and maintaining a high standard of living at home, was achieved with the reluctant cooperation of General Lewis Hershey and the Selective Service System. The draft law, as passed in 1940, authorized the president to provide for the deferment of men "whose employment in industry, agriculture, or other occupations or employment . . . is found . . . to be necessary to the maintenance of the national health, safety, or interest." This clause delegated very broad authority, but Congress also saw fit to bar any class deferments by insisting that "no deferment from such training and service shall be made in the case of any individual except upon the basis of the status of such individual, and no such deferment shall be made of individuals by occupational groups or of groups of individuals in any plant or institution."[3] Deferments should remain at the discretion of local boards dealing with individual cases.

Despite this ban against deferment by occupational group, American farmers were deferred as a class. In November 1942, only 15,523 men were deferred for farm work; by December 1942, some 136,678 were deferred. The pace continued to accelerate during the war, and by March 1, 1944, some 1,721,759 farmers enjoyed protection from the draft. In January 1945, 1,634,936 held such deferments, and there were three times as many men under age 26 deferred for farming as for industry. Over 14.5 percent of all farm workers enjoyed a deferred status on June 1, 1944. As a percentage of all employed civilians, there were twice as many farm deferments as nonfarm deferments, as of July 1, 1944. Of farm workers aged 18 to 35, some 17 percent were deferred for their work, whereas only 9 percent of the same age group in nonfarm work were deferred for occupational reasons.[4]

Farmers obtained protection from the draft by selling the

idea of a dangerous food shortage. In May 1941, Secretary of Agriculture Claude Wickard informed General Lewis Hershey of Selective Service that the nation's food supply was threatened by a labor shortage. During the preceding twelve months, farm labor had declined by 17.8 percent. Hershey explained to Wickard that the reduction in farm labor was due less to the draft than to a depressed wage scale in agriculture.[5] Some young farmers volunteered for military duty, but an even larger number raced to the centers of industrial war production because of higher wages. In a free labor market, the solution to the problem would have required an increase in wages for farm workers. But, in America during World War II, farm operators turned to the government for protection. During congressional hearings in June 1941, a campaign began to provide draft deferments for farm labor. Such deferments would make farm work more attractive without increased wages.

Although no immediate action was taken by Congress, individual members began to prod Hershey into action. By the end of 1941, more than 1 million workers had left the farm for industry. Hershey explained to local draft boards that farming was also a technical skill that required protection or the country might face a failure in food production. On December 4, 1941, he issued a memorandum asking board members to consider four factors in extending farm deferments: (1) the importance of the farm product; (2) the importance of the work performed; (3) the skill level involved; and (4) the shortage of labor in the farm area. Throughout the war, he attempted to maintain these guidelines.[6]

During 1942, the War Manpower Commission was established and immediately listed agriculture as an essential industry. Yet men continued to flock into better-paying jobs in industry. Farm interests began arguing to Congress that the problem could only be solved through blanket draft deferments for their workers, thereby providing an indirect, non-monetary incentive to stay on the soil. Senator Sheridan Downey pushed through a resolution calling for a special investigation into the farm labor shortage. The War Manpower Commission responded by establishing a labor stabilization plan for the dairy industry, but no plan could work without the cooperation of the Selective Service.[7]

Lewis Hershey, the man most responsible for overseeing draft deferments, rejected the idea that farm labor was "irreplaceable." Above all, he refused to consider a blanket deferment for farmers. In February 1942, he explained to a House committee that he sought a balanced approach, balancing military calls with the needs of the entire civilian economy, including the farms. But he insisted: "We cannot defer every farmer, every farmer's son, and every farmhand merely because the individual happens to be engaged in the occupation of farming." Hershey argued that the draft was having only a modest effect on the migration of farm labor. There was a sound basis for his assertion. In 1940, there had been 2,500,000 workers in excess of actual labor needs in farming. As late as November 1940, the director of the Agricultural Adjustment Administration had suggested that five million low-income, single-crop farmers leave the land and seek jobs in the defense industry. With the average earnings of factory workers increasing 157 percent from 1939 to 1942, with the average entering wage of a common industrial laborer at $5.08 for 8 hours compared to a daily farm wage of $2.45 in 1942, there was no mystery to the massive migration of farmers. The draft was an insignificant force, despite congressional complaints.[8]

Realizing the strength of the farm lobby and being a political realist, Hershey sought to avoid blanket farm deferments by meeting with Secretary of Agriculture Claude Wickard. The two men worked out a system by which the Department of Agriculture would provide Selective Service with information on the diversified labor needs of farming. County war boards and agricultural extension agents would provide advice to local boards on individual deferment requests. But the plan failed to satisfy congressional critics. As usual during harvest time, farmers needed additional labor and became more vociferous in their calls for special treatment. Hershey finally authorized several statewide, temporary induction delays in a few Western states. As for blanket deferments, Hershey insisted that such a step would mean attaching "a stigma to the farming industry which they [sic] could not easily eliminate."[9]

Farm operators were less concerned with stigma than with a guaranteed labor supply. In October 1942, Governor Harold E. Stassen of Minnesota and fifteen senators in Washington urged Hershey to order local boards to cancel all drafting of men in dairy and livestock production for 90 days. Farm operators were seeking a freeze of labor through the Selective Service. When such a proposal was attempted in industrial labor by the War Manpower Committee, unions successfully defeated the scheme.[10] Farm labor had no union and was represented at the national level by operators.

Yet Hershey continued to resist the idea of a blanket deferment or freeze for farm labor. As he explained to Senator John Thomas of Idaho, "When we protect all agriculture, we will protect no one." Hershey drew upon his draft statistics to prove that although some 23 percent of all registered men were in farming, only 14 percent of recent draftees came from the farm. Hershey was more sympathetic to President Roosevelt's suggestion that school children be used to help in the harvest, an idea that farmers ridiculed. Hershey was convinced that even if he refrained from drafting farmers, claims of shortages would continue. The Army need men and he intended to keep farmers in the draft pool.[11]

Faced with Hershey's stubborness, Senator Millard Tydings of Maryland sought a compromise. He asked Hershey to draft an amendment to a bill under debate that would reduce the draft age to 18. Tydings wanted a rider that would protect farm labor but would not create administrative problems for Selective Service. Hershey reluctantly agreed in order to avoid even more restrictive proposals by Congress. Colonel Frank Keesling, in conference with Hershey, drafted what became known as the Tydings Amendment. Attached to the draft age act, which passed on November 13, 1942, the amendment eventually became the basis for a blanket deferment of farmers. The rider provided that every registrant found by a local board to "be necessary to and regularly engaged in an agricultural occupation or endeavor essential to the war effort, shall be deferred from training and service . . . so long as he remains so engaged and until such time as a satisfactory replacement can be obtained." If any deferred person left his farm job, he would be subject to immediate reclassification and induction. Hershey took solace in several features of the amendment: only farmers in essential production would be considered, the deferment would run only until a replacement could be obtained, and local boards continued to make final decisions.[12]

In Hershey's mind, the Tydings Amendment merely reiterated the general provisions of the 1940 law. Decisions would be made by local boards and deferments were temporary. Although such an interpretation may have comforted Hershey, Congress had a much broader view. In February 1943, the Senate Committee on Appropriations inquired about the effectiveness of the amendment. Hershey reported that, because of the Tydings Amendment, more than 200,000 farm workers had recently received changes in draft classification. He predicted that by the end of 1943, there would be 3 million men in the II C (farmwork) and III C (farmer and dependency) classes. But there were only 3.5 million men between the ages of 18 to 38 engaged in farm work. Hershey's prediction, if true, meant that farmers would enjoy a deferment ratio of greater than 85 percent. Yet problems were already emerging. The armed forces had stopped inducting men over age 38. Older farm workers were now migrating to industry. Their deferments on the farm were being taken by younger men. Local draft boards were angry over allowing such young men to stay at home and began drafting a few.[13]

Hershey attempted to make the best of the situation. He reassured Representative Forest A. Harness of Indiana that the system was sympathetic to the farmer's problem. When Representative Robert E. Thomasson complained that draft boards were ignoring the instructions of Congress, Hershey explained that more than 600,000 farmers had been deferred in only six weeks. The Department of Agriculture admitted that the drift of farmers to the city had been sharply curtailed in 1943 as boys started returning to farms and seeking the deferments. But when local boards continued to draft single farmers over married men, Senator Eugene D. Millikin of the Agricultural Committee recommended a new law that would specifically defer all farmers for 12 months. Hershey opposed this idea. He argued that even if such a law passed, it would not work because public opinion would refuse to obey it. "There is no use of me as an administrator," he argued, "coming here and saying that I can carry out your will in the face of the will of the people."[14]

When the Senate Committee on Agriculture continued its pressure for more farm deferments, Hershey turned his testimony into melodrama. Twisting the yeoman myth to his advantage, he told a story of a colonial village with a population of only 130 that was attacked by Indians. The town decided it could only spare 10 fighters, because the rest of the population had to grow food and make bullets. Needless to say, the village soon fell. The nation now had 130 million people and the armed forces only wanted 11 million men. Hershey warned congressmen that public opinion would not abide young, single men, even farmers, at home while fathers and husbands were drafted. Such young men would soon have their cars and mailboxes painted yellow by irate neighbors.[15]

Hershey's storytelling, renown throughout Congress, did little to satisfy critics. Senator John H. Bankhead complained to President Roosevelt that food production could not stand the continued draft of farmers. Hershey, in turn, explained to the President, who had more important matters on his mind, that local boards still had to judge if the farmer was contributing to the war effort before offering a deferment. Both the War Manpower Commission and the Department of Agriculture had recommended that deferments be denied to subsistence farmers and to farmers producing commodities, such as tobacco and watermelons, not needed for the war effort. Besides being economically unsound, such deferments irritated mothers and sweethearts of soldiers. The entire draft system would flounder if community support disappeared.[16]

When Roosevelt refused to act, Bankhead and some forty other senators introduced a bill (S. 729) in February, 1943, that provided exemptions to all farmers regardless of their contribution to the war effort. Hershey fought vigorously against this attempt to bypass his local boards. He would have to draft married men and fathers to meet army quotas. Leaving behind single farmers would create havoc in local communities. Secretary of War Henry Stimson came to Hershey's support in opposing the Bankhead Bill. President Roosevelt compromised by creating a War Food Administration on March 26, 1943. The new agency was supposed to insure proper consideration of the role of food production in the war effort. Although the Bankhead Bill was tabled, Congress remained sensitive on the issue.[17]

Throughout 1943, agricultural deferments grew in number. By March 1, 1944, some 1,721,759 farmers were protected. At this same time, General Dwight Eisenhower in Europe and General George Marshall in Washington decided that the army needed more younger men. The armed forces had a total of 10,600,000 men on February 1, 1944, but Ike was planning the invasion of Europe and insisted upon more ground troops. President Roosevelt agreed. On February 25, the President informed Hershey that he should review all job deferments to obtain the young men needed by the armed forces. Hershey immediately sent out orders to his local boards to curtail farm deferments. Just as quickly, the Senate Committee on Agriculture called Hershey in for an explanation. Although Hershey sought to hide behind the president, who had ordered that more young men be drafted, senators recommended a draft of non-farm labor, regardless of the consequences for industrial production. Senator Richard Russell bemoaned the lack of pickers which threatened cotton crops in Georgia. Senator Ellison Smith worried about poor farmers being ruined by the loss of manpower. Hershey's order seemed to threaten a source of cheap agricultural labor.[18]

Despite such congressional sentiment, Hershey, working with the War Food Administration, began tightening up guidelines on farm deferments. Terms such as "essential," "regularly engaged in," and "irreplaceable," would now be more strictly interpreted by local boards. On March 24, a telegram went to local boards calling for a review of all farm deferments of men 18 to 25. Shortly afterwards, Hershey ended all reference to the war unit plan designed by the War Manpower Commission to measure productivity on the farm. Such actions had only a modest effect. On March 21, 1944, there were 570,000 men under age 26 with farm deferments. By July 1, 1944, the number had dropped to 474,081 out of a total farm deferred pool of 1,641,396. In January 1945, the farm deferments for those under 26 stood at 341,953, which was still three times the number of such young men with industrial deferments.[19]

As the war was winding down in Europe, with the success of the Normandy landings in June, and as more talk was heard of reconverting the economy to peacetime production, farm deferments continued at a high rate. In December 1944, however, a German counterstroke in the Ardennes ruptured the complacency on the homefront. Quickly the Roosevelt administration reacted by delaying any move toward reconversion. The President also instructed Hershey to increase his draft calls, particularly among men under 26. With the manpower pool almost dry, Hershey had to turn to the over 300,000 young men with farm deferments. He warned James Byrnes, the Director of War Mobilization and Reconversion, that such a move would raise the hackles of Congress. Yet if Hershey did not touch the farmers, he would have to draft older men, including fathers, which would be even less popular.[20]

After studying the various options, the Roosevelt administration instructed Hershey to draft young farmers. The War Food Administrator, Marvin Jones, announced that the loss of young farmers would not mean a food shortage. As for the Tydings Amendment, Byrnes reminded Hershey, who needed no reminding, that it was not meant as a blanket deferment.

Hershey immediately sent a copy of Byrnes's letter to all local boards. He instructed boards to order pre-induction examinations for young men in the farm-deferred group.[21]

Hershey's order produced an immediate reaction in the farm community and in Congress. No mere directive from the President would suffice to overcome the farm lobby. Telegrams immediately poured into Congress. The farm bloc in the House demanded a conference with Byrnes, War Food Administrator Jones, and Hershey. To his dismay, Hershey learned that he would go alone to this conference, and as he expected, the congressmen were irate. The chairman of the Agricultural Committee complained because he had not been consulted before the order was issued. A few days later, more than 100 members of the House signed a statement that warned that Hershey's order would endanger food production, the opinion of Jones notwithstanding. Hershey argued without success that the new character of the war made necessary a stricter interpretation of the Tydings Amendment. Agriculture was no longer considered a critical industry, according to Hershey. The farm bloc refused to accept this argument. A special committee, representing 150 farm-state representatives, began drafting a resolution under the guidance of Representative William Lemke. The end product stated that local boards were breaking the law by ignoring the Tydings Amendment. Hershey "should be directed to comply with the intent and spirit as well as the letter" of the law.[22]

In the face of this opposition, Hershey had to retreat. The president was too busy with war matters and the pending Yalta Conference to help. Hershey issued a "clarifying directive" on January 22, 1945. In an understated message to all state draft directors, he emphasized that Congress had raised questions about his earlier message. He now explained that his earlier statement did not "change or modify in any manner the Tydings Amendment." Hershey also met with a subcommittee of the House Committee on Agriculture to reassure them that all farm deferments would not be removed. He explained that his order did not call for the immediate drafting of all farmers under 26. He merely wanted to have the men examined to see who would be eligible for service if drafted.[23]

The timely reinterpretation by Hershey did little to resolve the basic problem. The armed forces still insisted upon the need for more young men. There were not enough young men with industrial deferments to fill the new calls. Unless he took older fathers, Hershey would have to draft young farmers. Local boards began to draft young farmers despite Hershey's qualifications. When Congress complained, Hershey explained that the Tydings Amendment did not provide for blanket exemption for farmers.

Here was the basic problem. Congress interpreted the law in a different manner than Hershey. Yet Hershey always prided himself on being guided by the intent of Congress no matter what the letter of the law. In this case, however, he was guided by his own intent when he drafted the Tydings Amendment in 1912. Despite the political risk, Hershey made public his disagreement. On radio he explained that the amendment merely required that local boards consider what was produced, how essential the worker was, and how irreplaceable he was. The Tydings Amendment, he insisted, did "not change the fundamental purpose of the Selective Service to provide men for the armed forces." The president had demanded more soldiers, and Hershey would do his duty. Within days, a joint resolution was introduced in the House by William Lemke calling for a special congressional committee to investigate whether draft officials were breaking the law by drafting young farmers. The resolution also provided that farmers were to be deferred "without reference to the relative essentiality of the registrant to an agricultural occupation."[24]

Even as the war wound down in Europe, and the need for men became less urgent, Hershey fought to defeat the Lemke Resolution. Despite Hershey's testimony about the original intent of the Tydings Amendment, the Lemke Resolution passed both houses of Congress in April 1945. Hershey's only remaining hope was the new president.[25]

Franklin Roosevelt died in office on April 12, 1945, driven to his grave by the awesome burdens of war and by heart disease. Harry S Truman had little preparation for assuming the role of president. He knew little of what was happening on the military front; he knew more, although not much, about the manpower problem. As the Senator from Missouri during the war, he had chaired a special committee to investigate war contracts. On the issue of farm deferments, he had some personal experience. Several of his rural constituents had complained about the loss of young workers to the draft. Truman was sympathetic; his own brother had lost his last young farmhand. But Truman had insisted that "the Selective Service Board is the absolute authority on the procedure which they [sic] are following."[26]

Hershey hoped that Truman would veto the Lemke Resolution. The Director of Selective Service had no desire to end his work under fire from an irate congressional committee. By April, the war in Europe was almost over. Hershey was irritated at what seemed an unfair attack on a system that had worked well for more than four years and drafted more than 9 million men. There were still 255,000 men under 26 with farm deferments. All other job deferments for men under 26 (excluding merchant marine and foreign army duty) totaled only 30,000. The total of farmers under 26 with deferments had not changed significantly since Hershey's January directive. Now the Lemke Resolution threatened a basic part of the Selective Service System—the autonomy of local boards. Such a step would threaten the President's flexibility in dealing with economic reconversion. Privately, Hershey promised that even if Truman signed the Lemke Resolution, local boards would still be able to circumvent its intent. As he told his state directors, "If I were on a local board and I could not take a man because he was essential, I could take him because he could be replaced or some other reason."[27] Fortunately, this approach did not have to be used. President Truman vetoed the Lemke Resolution on May 3.

Although failing in this last gesture, farmers and their allies in Congress had been remarkably successful in protecting agricultural labor from the draft. Other special interests, including industries that contributed more directly to the war effort, had less success. Only the farmer was able to protect his worker against the wishes of war leaders such as Franklin Roosevelt and Henry Stimson. The military itself had protected certain young workers in scientific tasks related to warfare. But such protection paled in comparison with the farmers. Their success can be partially explained by the effectiveness of the farm lobby in Congress, an organization that had grown in strength and purpose since the 1920s; added to this lobby was the strength of public opinion.

Throughout the war, public opinion polls consistently revealed that most people approved of the manner in which the draft was handled. Farm opinion, however, was always concerned about deferments. In October 1942, before the Tydings Amendment was passed, only 10 percent of a general public sample insisted that the draft was taking too many farm boys. Some 55 percent felt that no particular group was being drafted too early. But in January 1943, still before the Tydings Amendment, the polls asked farmers to rate the workings of the draft. Some 5.4 percent rated it as "very good," and 40.1 percent felt it was "fair." Yet 26.8 percent of the farm sample had an unfavorable opinion because of the draft of farmers. In April 1944, farmers were asked if more or fewer farmers should be drafted, assuming that for each farmer deferred a man would be taken out of war industry. Indicating clearly their opinion of the relative importance of their work, some 70 percent of the farmers felt fewer farmers should be drafted, regardless of the consequences. Even the general public grew sympathetic to the farmer's complaints. On May 18, 1944, when the Army demanded more men under 26, the public was asked if it was more important to draft young farmers or keep them on the farm. Some 71 percent of the public sample approved keeping young men on the farm.[28]

World War II mobilization had a remarkable effect on American society. Blacks left the South in large numbers and found new jobs and new political opportunities in the North. Women entered the work force in unprecedented numbers. Despite unequal pay and rejection by unions, these women returned to the work force in the post-war world. Major industries benefited enormously from the war, through the convenient connection with the military establishment that funded research and development. This trend continued after the war.

Agriculture also benefited greatly from the war. Using the standard of physical goods used in production, agriculture grew from a $49 billion industry to one of $70 billion from January 1, 1940 to January 1, 1944. During the same four years, equity of all farmers increased by $30 billion and debts were reduced by $500 million. Farmers prospered during the war for many reasons, but one reason involved labor cost. Unlike industry, which relied largely upon the market mechanism and higher wages to obtain desperately short labor, the farm industry benefited from a draft policy that tended to freeze farm workers. There was a massive redistribution of industrial labor during the war, but in agriculture there was less change. The government could have adopted a hands-off policy that would have led to more dramatic shifts in farm labor, to the demise of many less efficient farms, and to the increase in farm factories employing more labor-saving devices. Instead, the government draft policy encouraged agriculture to remain in largely traditional patterns. Wartime mobilization worked no revolution in American agriculture.[29]

NOTES

1. Bela Gold, *Wartime Economic Planning in Agriculture* (New York: Columbia University Press, 1949), pp. 176-78; Walter W. Wilcox, *The Farmer in the Second World War* (Ames: Iowa State Press, 1947), p. 83.

2. Wilcox, *Farmer in Second World War*, pp. 51, 56-57, 265, 279, 286, 290; Gold, *Wartime Economic Planning*, pp. 76, 174; Department of Agriculture, *Agricultural Statistics, 1949* (Washington, D.C.: Government Printing Office), p. 596.

3. U. S. *Statutes at Large*, vol. 54, September 18, 1940, p. 888.

4. *Selective Service and Victory, 1944-1947* (Washington, D.C.: Government Printing Office, 1948), pp. 62, 114, 484; Wilcox, *Farmer in Second World War*, pp. 87-88. See especially Albert A. Blum, "The Farmer, the Army and the Draft," *Agricultural History* 38 (January 1964): 34-42, which traces the army's consistent opposition to group deferments for farmers and blames Hershey for the problem.

5. Hershey press conference, January 15, 1941, speech file, Lewis Hershey Papers, Military History Institute, Carlisle, Pa., (hereinafter referred to as Hershey Papers) *New York Times*, May 26, 1941, p. 8; U. S. Congress, House, Military Affairs Committee, *Hearings on Selective Service Law*, 77th Cong., 1st sess., June 16, 1941, p. 37. Wickard's figure for the population was 2 million smaller than Hershey's figure; see Blum, "The Farmer," p. 36.

6. *Selective Service*, September 1, 1941; *New York Times*, September 30, 1941, p. 10; Wilcox, *Farmer in Second World War*, p. 84n.; *Selective Service in Wartime* (Washington, D.C.: Government Printing Office, 1943), p. 188.

7. U. S. Congress, House, Military Affairs Committee, *Hearings on Liability Extension*, 77th Cong., 1st Sess., December 13, 14, 1941, pp. 13-16; George Q. Flynn, *The Mess in Washington: Manpower Mobilization in World War II* (Westport, Conn.: Greenwood Press, 1979), pp. 131-34.

8. Albert Blum, *Drafted or Deferred* (Ann Arbor: University of Michigan, 1967), p. 85, blames Hershey for being too sympathetic to the farmer; Hershey statement to House, Committee Investigating National Defense Migration, February 3, 1942, in Frank Keesling Papers, San Francisco (private) (hereinafter referred to as Keesling Papers); Flynn, *The Mess in Washington*, p. 132.

9. Hershey to Secretary of Agriculture, February 18, 1942, staybacks, Hershey Papers; *New York Times*, February 18, 1942, p. 15; Hershey press conference, February 21, 1942, Carton 65, Record Group 147, National Archives, Washington, D. C.; Hershey telegram to State Director, Bismark, N. D., July 21, 1942, staybacks, Hershey Papers; Hershey to Kenneth W. Jones, September 3, 1942, ibid.

10. Joseph H. Ball et al. to Hershey, October 8, 1942, Presidential correspondence file, Hershey Papers; *New York Times*, October 10, 1942, p. 1; for attempts at a labor freeze in industrial areas, see Flynn, *The Mess in Washington*, pp. 121-25.

11. U. S. Congress, Senate, Military Affairs Committee, *Lowering the Draft Age*, 77th Cong., 2nd sess., October 14, 1942, p. 51; ibid.,

House, *Lowering Draft Age*, October 15, 1942, pp. 88-89, 99, 104, 122; Hershey to A. G. Halifax, October 17, 1942, staybacks, Hershey Papers.

12. Agricultural workers file, October 1942, Keesling Papers, *New York Times*, October 19, 1942, p. 12, *Selective Service as the Tide of War Turns* (Washington, D.C.: Government Printing Office, 1945), pp. 110-11; Frank Keesling interview, December 28, 1978, San Francisco.

13. U. S. Congress, Senate, Committee on Appropriations, *Manpower Hearings*, 78th Cong., 1st sess., February 3, 1943, pp. 104, 106-17; Gold, *Wartime Economic Planning*, p. 188.

14. U. S. Congress, House, Committee on Military Affairs, *Hearings on H. R. 1730*, 78th Cong., 1st sess., February 11, 15, 17, 1943, pp. 9, 16; Wilcox, *Farmer in Second World War*, p. 89; Senate, Committee on Agriculture, *Hearings on Food Supply*, 78th Cong., 1st sess., February 18, 1943, pp. 134-38, 146-47.

15. U. S. Congress, Senate, Committee on Agriculture, *Hearings*, February 18, 1943, pp. 147-48, 150-51, 154; *New York Times*, February 19, 1943, p. 12.

16. Edwin M. Watson to Hershey, February 19, 1943, Box 12, of 1413B, Franklin D. Roosevelt Papers, Roosevelt Library, Hyde Park, N.Y.; Hershey to President, February 19, 1943, White House file, Hershey Papers.

17. Hershey to Executive Director, W.M.C., February 22, 1943, staybacks, Hershey Papers; Hershey to Senator Robert R. Reynolds, March 1, 1943, congressional file, ibid.; *New York Times*, March 2, 1943, p. 12; Hershey to Tydings, March 10, 1943, Agricultural Deferment file, Keesling Papers, Harry S Truman to Ruby M. Hulen, May 6, 1943, and Hulen to Truman, April 27, 1943, senatorial file, Box 160 Harry Truman Papers, Truman Library, Independence, Missouri (hereafter Truman Papers). The Army accused Hershey of defeating the Bankhead Bill by promising not to draft farmers. Under-secretary Robert Patterson believed Hershey thought farmers irreplaceable, but he was merely more of a political realist than Patterson. Blum, "The Farmer," pp. 36, 38, 39.

18. Hershey to the president, April 27, 1945, White House file, Hershey Papers; *New York Times*, February 26, 1944, pp. 1, 3, Blum, *Drafted or Deferred*, p. 82.

19. Selective Service and Victory (Washington, D.C.: Government Printing Office, 1948), pp. 113, 483; U. S. Congress, House, Com-

mittee on Merchant Marine and on Fisheries, *Hearings on Manpower Shortage*, 78th Cong., 2nd sess., March 21, 1944, p. 92; House, Committee on Appropriations, *War Agencies Hearings*, 78th Cong., 2nd sess., March 30, 1944, pp. 341-42, Minutes of State Directors Conference, May 8, 1944, Hershey Papers. See Blum, "The Farmer," p. 36, for deferments by age and occupation.

20. Hershey to General Lucius D. Clay, December 29, 1944, White House file, Hershey Papers.

21. Byrnes to Hershey, January 2, 1945, Elizabeth Bush file, Hershey Papers; *New York Times*, January 4, 1945, p. 1.

22. John O'Sullivan questionnaire, November 13, 1974, Gilbert Hershey file, Jacksonville, N.C.; *New York Times*, January 17, 1945, p. 1; ibid., January 20, 1945, p. 12.

23. Hershey to state directors, January 22, 1945, State Directors file, Keesling Papers; *New York Times*, January 23, 1945, p. 11; Hershey to Robert A. Taft, January 31, 1945, staybacks, Hershey Papers.

24. Hershey to Kentucky State Director, January 27, 1945, staybacks, Hershey Papers; Hershey to Charles W. Holman, January 11, 1945, ibid.; Radio address, February 1, 1945, speech file, ibid.; *New York Times*, February 6, 1945, p. 20; ibid.; February 19, 1945, p. 18; Blum, "Farmers," p. 41.

25. Herman M. Somers, *Presidential Agency* (Cambridge: Harvard University Press, 1950), p. 158; Keesling to Adolph J. Sabath, May 4, 1945, agricultural deferment file, Keesling Papers.

26. Truman to L. H. Yates, August 26, 1944, Senatorial file, 161, Truman Papers.

27. U. S. Congress, House, Committee on Appropriations, *National War Agencies*, 79th Cong., 1st sess., April 26, 1945, pp. 50-51; Hershey to President, April 27, 1945, White House file, Hershey Papers; State Directors Conference, April 30, 1945, ibid.; Somers, *Presidential Agency*, p. 161.

28. Hadley Cantrill, *Public Opinion, 1935-1946* (Princeton: Princeton University Press, 1951), pp. 466–68.

29. Bureau of Agricultural Economics, Department of Agriculture, *Impact of the War on the Financial Structure of Agriculture* (Washington, D.C.: Government Printing Office, 1945), pp. 20-21; Gold, *Wartime Economic Planning*, p. 179.

V

AGRICULTURAL IMAGERY AND REALITY

Confusion and mythology abound in the study of agricultural history, especially social and domestic life. Only recently have historians turned to address issues and analyze documents that confront the lack of information and misinformation surrounding the life of farmers and ranchers. The history of the cowboy, in particular, has been a microcosm of exaggeration.

In this last selection, a rare document edited by Charles L. Wood and James E. Brink is presented. It is the attempt of a Scotsman, Alexander Mackay, to convey to his people the truth about ranch and cowboy life in the American West. In this speech, probably given around 1890, the foreigner looks at fact and myth. With clarity and brevity, Mackay is able to interpret one phase of agricultural history.

Cowboy Life on a Western Ranch: Reminiscences of Alexander Mackay

In the last quarter of the nineteenth century, foreign investors poured millions of dollars into new enterprises in the United States. Among these speculators in a young America was a group of Scots who in 1882 purchased control of more than 1.5 million acres of West Texas cattle country for $1,250,000. The Matador Land and Cattle Company was to be one of the largest and most successful of the numerous foreign investments in American agriculture.[1] One of the shareholders, Alexander Mackay of Ness and Mackay Chartered Accountants (Dundee), was chosen the first secretary for the corporation. From 1882 until his death in 1936, Mackay, who rose to become chairman of the board, saw every piece of correspondence concerning the ranch. More important, Mackay traveled to West Texas nearly every year to oversee the autumn sale of beef.

Mackay presents the biographer with an interesting combination of Scottish frugality and sound business sense, plus a romantic love of the land and a sincere concern for the people of the future. Born to humble parents in Dunkeld in 1856, Mackay grew up in Dundee; he left school early to apprentice himself to an accounting firm. Largely self-educated, Mackay rose to become one of the most successful and respected figures in the business community of Scotland. In addition to his contributions to the economic success of the Matador Ranch, Mackay was instrumental in the formation of what would eventually become Shell Oil Company and was also a pioneer in the booming citrus industry of south Florida.

But it is not only owing to his financial success that he attracts attention. This Scottish accountant and entrepreneur had a respect for the land that marks him as one of the earliest environmentalists of the twentieth century. Shortly after his Dundee home burned in 1916, Mackay and his Canadian wife Edith moved their family out of the city to Oban where they had purchased the baronial estate of Glencruitten. Mackay was drawn to Glencruitten because of its former sylvan setting. Originally 2,200 acres of heavy timber, Glencruitten had been clearcut during World War I. It was Mackay's dream to reforest the estate and return it to its original beauty. In addition to remodeling the manor house and directing the reforestation efforts on the estate, Mackay sent one of his daughters to Cambridge to study the new discipline of forestry. But surely his most remarkable project was the construction of the massive "Cathedral of Trees." Special plantings of a variety of trees and bushes formed an exact replica of the floor plan of St. Andrew's Cathedral. This impressive site has become one of the attractions of the area as well as the family burial place. It was here that Mackay was buried in late May 1936. He died quietly on the 23rd after an evening of fishing on Mackay Loch.

It is too often true that Americans never see themselves so clearly as when they are described by a foreign visitor. This is one of those classic cases in the following speech published for the first time and entitled "Cowboy Life on a Western Ranch" by Alexander Mackay. This man has left an insightful account of American late frontier life. In it he describes his infatuation with the West—the land and its people. He laments the environmental alterations and the destruction of Native Americans, but he celebrates the coming of the farmer, merchant, rancher, and most importantly and symbolically, the cowboy. He warns of the future displacement of agriculture by manufacturing and urban growth.

The date of the speech is probably 1890. In the speech, Mackay refers to a double hanging of a man and woman in a "northern territory" the year before. This was most likely the execution of Ella Watson ("Cattle Kate") and her husband and/ or friend, James Averill, in 1889 near Bothwell, Wyoming Territory.[2] The speech was probably composed by Mackay for presentation in Scotland upon his return from the Matador fall beef marketing. It was no doubt intended for an audience curious about life on the Western American agriculture frontier.

The speech was written in ink on thirty-eight pages of white stationery nine inches on a side. It shows a good deal of work as there are numerous addenda and pencilled corrections. Mackay's original punctuation and spelling have been retained in this transcription except in rare cases where his message was made clearer with a slight change and where subject headings have been added. The speech appears to be incomplete, but to date no additional pages have been found. The original is in the possession of Elizabeth Mackay and Rosemary Mackay-James of Oban, Scotland and Lake Alfred, Florida, granddaughters of Alexander Mackay.

COWBOY LIFE ON A WESTERN RANCH

I propose to tell you tonight something about cowboy life on an American cattle ranch, but I have this initial difficulty, that we have in this island nothing analogous either in the natural features of the country, or in the modes of living, to assist me in presenting to you any proper picture of what life on a western ranch really is. With the aid of some pictures, and the lime light lantern, I hope however to give you some imperfect account of it.

Americans and Their Frontier Landscape

Those of you who are familiar with the larger outstanding features of the North American continent will remember certain natural divisions which it is well to bear in mind. Back from the Atlantic seaboard & running north to south for several hundreds of miles, is the range of mountains known as the Alleghanies. In the north and again in the south the main range breaks up into others of a lower elevation, but the general effect is to cut off from the whole of the western continent a seaboard strip of 50 to 100 miles wide. Upon this strip stand all of the oldest American cities—Boston, New York, Philadelphia, Washington, Richmond. The mountains were for a long period a barrier against the pioneer colonist, and much American history was made before an advance began into the redman's country beyond.[3]

Crossing the mountains, we enter the great American plain, extending a thousand miles west to the Rocky mountains, & more than double that distance from the Gulf of Mexico in the south to the Hudson Bay territory in the far north of Canada. This region is the greatest farming country in the world. Its rich fertile lands, watered by numerous great rivers and smaller streams, attract a continuously increasing population. Manufacturers have followed hard upon farming, and large cities occupy today the sites which Indian wigwams held but a short time ago. The great new cities are mostly to be found in this central plain—like Chicago with over a million inhabitants, St Louis, Kansas City, Cincinnati, Pittsburg & a host of others.

Through the centre of the plain, from north to south, runs the Mississippi River draining with its tributaries nearly the whole region both on the east and west. Crossing the river we find that the western part of the plain grows gradually in elevation, and at the same time exhibits a scantier rainfall than in the east. For a long time settlers refused to enter this western region regarding it as a country unfitted for agriculture. On its western border we meet with the next great natural barrier of the country, the well known Rocky mountains, which make up along with a parallel range further to the west the back bone of the continent.

These mountains run north and south along the whole continent. They attain high elevations, peaks reaching 15,000 &

16,000 feet. Deep valleys penetrate them, extensive plateaus occupy large areas, and many rivers and streams are fed from the snow banks which cover their summits.

The great ranching country of the west lies in the region covered by the slopes and valleys of the Rocky mountains, and the extensive plains which lie to the east of them. It constitutes a belt extending from the Mexican Gulf up into the great northwest of Canada.

The main characteristics of the region are a light rainfall, very dry atmosphere, natural shelter for animals in times of storms, and a supply of native grass which springs each year without care or attention and dries into a natural hay standing, so that feed for cattle is provided all winter without the labour of cutting and storing, and with no danger of rotting.

It was in this region that the immense herds of buffalo roamed—those herds which with their natural accessories of red Indians, white trappers, daring hunting, scalpings, tomahawking & general freefighting—filled our boyish imaginations with pictures which if rather warm in colour seemed very real tho. It has been my good or evil fortune to talk since with men who followed the buffalo as hunters, and I must say that much of the romance is torn out of the story when the bare facts are disclosed. Indeed it seems to me that buffalo hunting as pursued by the regular hunters with their attendant skinners, was just as much sport, and no more, as seal clubbing is today in the Arctic regions.[4]

The herds of buffalo which at one time swarmed in this western region have entirely disappeared. A few stray head have been met with at rare intervals in the past few years, but they are about as rare as the wild eagle is in Scotland. Their place now is occupied by still more numerous herds of horned cattle, which are hardly less peaceful in disposition, but which can be controlled more easily and made to subserve more effectually the uses of man. The presence of these herds of cattle occupying the ranges of the nearly extinct buffalo, is a fair illustration of the occupation by the white man of the territory which once belonged to the red. The buffalo and the redman seem to cling naturally together. The presence of the cow—even though he may be but a long horned long legged beast, intended apparently for running and fighting than for making beef—is an idea of the white man's supremacy.

The ranch which we have come to visit specially is in northern Texas, lying, that is, toward the south of the long stretch of country included in the ranching area. When the buffalo existed they occupied this southern country in the winter and early spring, starting northward as the weather got warmer, carrying their young calves with them to the more bracing regions of the north. It is a curious fact that this migration from south to north takes place with cattle today. To be sure the cattle don't return again to the south as the buffalo did, & they don't make the journey except under guidance—but nevertheless the opening of spring each year sees the starting of many thousands of young cattle from the warm breeding grounds of the south to the hardy pastures of the north.

In order to reach the ranch which we intend visiting, three days and a half of continuous railway travel from New York is necessary before you are planted at the nearest railway station.[5] The collection of board & shingle houses which they here call a city is a little one horse place set right in the midst of the flat prairie. It sprang up in a night because the railway once terminated for a few weeks here; and its enterprising founders having built a jail, a schoolhouse, and a church. Its future was assured as the promising capital of a county thirty miles square. I well remember my introduction to the place before it was many weeks old. I had arrived alone one evening— dropped off the north bound train—and not being entirely *au fait* with western ways, walked into the little shanty that called itself a hotel and asked in a nonchalant manner if I could have a room. The landlord eyed me up & down for an instant—"Yuess [sic] stranger you can have a bed"—with a long drawl on the *stranger*, as if he thought it rather fresh to be asking for rooms in that country. The sleeping room was divided into a series of horse bosces with two couches in each bosc. I found to my horror that the man who shared the bosc with me was a dreadful fellow to snore, and the thunder of his trumpet brought first a salute of choice language & then a volley of boots from the neighboring cells, as a kindly reminder that other people were around.

Leaving then the railway & civilization behind, you at this point launch out into the wilderness for 60 or 70 miles before reaching the ranch headquarters. The road is a waggon trail straight across the prairie. You can't mistake the trail, for the wheels of many heavily laden waggons have cut deep ruts into channels, which are rather trying to the stranger on a spring-less buckboard. On your passage up you are nearly certain to meet or overtake some freighter with his 12 or 14 horses or mules yoked to one or more of the heavy waggons, laden with stores, bags of coffee, corn, flour &c for some distant ranch—or perhaps it is lumber for building, or heavy cedar posts for fenc-ing; for the country which we have come to visit is destitute of timber save the scrub mesquite or the sparse soft weed trees along a few river bottoms.

Perhaps you will also meet with a prairie schooner—a big waggon with canvas cover under which a few settlers' be-longings are stowed away—pots, pans, old boxes & barrels for chairs & table and half a dozen burrheaded children. The schooner is the mark of the unrest of western life. On every open prairie at some time it heaves in sight, telling the story of discontent, impatience with surroundings, & love of change. Our notions of a settled life are to the last degree tiresome and dull to the frontier settler, who remains in one spot only long enough for neighbours to appear, & then moves off to some place with more room.

If you are passing up to the ranch in the shipping season you may meet a few hundred, perhaps one or two thousand, head of cattle on their way to the railroad or upon a long foot journey to the north. Or you may chance upon a solitary cowboy making his way to a neighbouring ranch on the hunt for stray cattle or horses. This will strike you. Wherever you meet man he is always mounted in saddle or waggon. The man on foot is a vagrant who can't wander far. To sit on a horse is so much the accepted order of things, that even the cattle despise a foot passenger & charge him sometimes without hesitation, although they make off with tail erect upon the appearance of a horseman.

The country where our ranch is situated has some marked characteristics of its own—Ever since leaving the railway we have been slowly ascending to a region where several rivers take their rise. The surface is not flat but rolling or undulating in great waves, and it is cut and broken by the channels of the streams, sometimes with steep precipitous banks, & at other times low & shallow with treacherous bottoms of quicksand in which horse or cow may sink to their doom.[6]

But the most striking natural feature are the cañons or gorges which everywhere cut deeply into the high rolling country, draining in the rainy season the water from the higher levels and carrying it quickly and easily into the river bottoms. These cañons are often deep set, with high precipitous sides, and extend long distances [sic] Their dark chocolate coloured faces, weathered and rounded by rain & wind into striking shapes, are a most attractive feature in the landscape. Some spots I recall of great beauty. A river bottom with its fringe of quivering cottonwoods interspersed with hickory and the umbrella shaped china trees; and grape vines trailing all through the branches: the high red banks of the river, broken at intervals by the rounded bluffs which indicate the mouths of cañons; the rolling ridges of green grass extending beyond as far as the eye can see & these all bathed in the warm light of a setting sun make up a picture which it is worth going some way to see.

These cañons have however their inconveniences. Often you cannot get from one part of the country to the other without making a long detour. A Texas cow or a Texas pony will get up and down places which will startle one unused to their feats in climbing, but even they have not altogether learned the art of scaling a dead wall. But if there are drawbacks in the way of locomotion, these cañons are one of the most valuable features in the country for cattle ranching purposes. When a cold snap comes on—a howling blizzard from the north, a drifting snow or a cold rain, the cattle instinctively make for shelter & troop into the cañons, secure beneath their protecting walls.

The grass in this country, like the native Texan cow, is not quite what our eyes are used to at home. The best of several grasses is a short blade growing only a few inches long, & curling like a feather. It is called the "curly mesquite" (no friend to the mesquite I may explain) and grows for the most part in tufts and bunches instead of continuous turf as our eyes are accustomed to. It is an excellent feeding grass in spite of its poor appearance; and a Texan cow's ideal of bliss is to browse it all day long undisturbed by the whoop of her natural enemy the cowboy, or his troublesome lasso.[7]

The pure Texan cow is not now so common as formerly. She was built with long legs, long slender body and very long pointed horns. Descended from the wild Spanish stock she retains her love of freedom, & in her mad rushing and racing is more apt to develop muscle of the stringy India rubber kind than the juicy steaks of our fancy. To her we are indebted for the cowboy. If she had been constituted of a gentle domestic nature with the confiding and obedient instincts of her relative at home the cowboy's occupation would have been different— and he himself would lose much of the romance which has gathered round him which is, primarily due to the dance which she leads over the western prairie.

Cowboy—Symbol and Myth

The first thing to be said about the cowboy is that he is not a boy. He may be of any age, but he usually is a man of from 20 to perhaps 35 years of age, and he is not nearly so bad a fellow as he is commonly painted. The Texan cowboy is in popular belief the embodiment of all that is bad—ready to "paint the town red", shoot his enemy on sight, or rob a railway train without scruple. It can't be denied that he sometimes does these things, & does them in a daring reckless fashion. I remember some three or four years ago, while I was in Texas, a peculiarly daring case of stage coach robbery. A solitary boy masked stationed himself at a point near where the up & down coaches between two towns usually met. Covering the driver & passengers of the down stage with his two revolvers he ordered "hands up" & walked all out of the coach, robbing each in turn. Then putting them to one side he kept them covered with one pistol until the other stage appeared, when he covered it & repeated the same manoeuvre. He then quickly mounted his pony, all the time keeping a pistol over the company, & then with an apology for detaining them, rode off at full speed. This feat was audacious enough, but he capped it next day by appearing again and actually robbing one of the coaches a second time—the other for some reason not appearing. It was quoted to this boy's credit that he neither robbed the ladies nor the clergyman.

Much no doubt is put down to the cowboy for which he has no title. At the same time one need not be surprised that the lawless instincts in some men are stimulated by the life which he is often compelled to follow. Living constantly in the saddle, fighting the half wild cattle of the prairies; having as associates only the rough companions in his work, or the rowdy "tough" of the frontier settlements; often compelled to face danger & conscious that he must rely only upon himself to hold his own—it is no wonder that the coarse strong & passionate fibres of the nature become developed. The life is rough and the boy becomes like it. His dress and outward appearance indeed suggest anything but refinement. But here it is easy to come to conclusions too quickly. If you sometimes meet with ruffians, you also meet with gentlemen—and the rough exterior often covers a strong manly nature.

Most people think that life and property must be very unsafe in a ranching country. But this is a great mistake. I have met in the loneliest spots women—the wife perhaps of some cowboy or solitary settler—living quite contentedly: her husband necessarily absent at times, but she dreading no harm. When a settler builds a house in this country the last thing he thinks of are locks or bars to his door. At any hour day or night the latch can be lifted, and theft at least in this form, is unknown. It is only when the lonely ranching country begins to get occupied by the squatter, & the small frontier farmer, & the saloon keeper sets up in business, that man begins to take precautions against his fellows.

The cowboy is much above the frontier squatter in every respect. He has a code of law and a code of honour & if his codes are not quite those of a settled community, they at any rate mark him out from the lawless element on the frontier. Perhaps if we were to call for the first law in his code we would find it ran something like this—"Thou shalt not steal horses or cattle in this country on pain of death." The horse thief is in a special degree *the* criminal of the country. Nothing is too bad for him. Wherever he appears it becomes the duty of all to hunt him down with untiring restless purpose until he is haltered and swung from the limb of some convenient tree. Only last year this crime was brought home in an aggravated form to a woman in one of the northern territories. After being fairly warned on account of her sex, she was, on a repetition of the offence, hung along with her male accomplice. It is but fair to say that this woman had become a public pest in her neighbourhood.

Human life is no doubt less sacred than with us. It must necessarily be so in a region where individuals must often redress their own grievances, & where the revolver is always handy. Just as in the days of duelling an insult demanded fighting by sword or pistol, so by the code of the west a man is expected to avenge insult with his revolver. Only there is this difference that no formal challenges or elaborate preparations are made, but the man who can carry his hand quickest to his weapon on takes his satisfaction there and then. To "shoot upon sight" means that if and whenever the men involved in quarrel meet, the first to find his enemy will fire.

There is no doubt a good deal of shooting on the frontier, but when closely inspected most of it can be traced to the gambling dens & the liquor saloons in the settlements. These are the curses of the country, and many a fine fellow has in the expressive language of the country "handed in his checks" at the hands of the ruffian frequenters of these places.

Keep the cowboy away from liquor and cards, and treat him with the consideration which you would an equal, and he is as a rule not difficult to manage. He can be relied upon to look after his employer's property at all times, and be ready to undergo privations without a grumble to keep his herd together. In every hard winter some boys lose their lives in sticking to duty—frozen to death at their posts. To stand by the herd through cold & storm; to ride hard & recklessly regardless of danger in order to check a stampede; fight hostile Indians; or white intruders in the range claimed by his "outfit"—these are his elementary duties. Nor does he less regard the duties of comradeship in standing by his brother in trouble. He has no tears perhaps for the slain or helpless comrade but he gives what aid he can cheerfully. In a quarrel he may sometimes think more of the claims of comradeship than the equity of the dispute, but he does not close his eye to the latter; and cases are not rare in which the boys on a ranch have made the arrest of one of their number who had broken the law, & was wanted by the neighbouring sheriff.

The Ranching Industry

But I am forgetting the ranch which we have come to visit. It is about as big as the county of [left blank] and is surrounded by one outside fence of five strands of barbed wire, the fence being several hundreds of miles long. The shape of the ranch is irregular but you can form some idea of the size when I mention that you can ride 70 miles in a straight line inside the main fence. Inside this huge enclosure are a number of pastures. The term pasture is a little misleading for us accustomed to our small patches at home. Pastures will contain 20, 40, 60 & even 100,000 acres; many thousands of cattle are to be found inside them.[8]

A few farms have been started, one or two huts or "dug-outs" have been erected at long distances; but besides these & the

rare habitations of a settler the country is destitute of dwellings. It is a country where people live in the open air. The
climate is dry & healthy, warm & pleasant for the greater part
of the year, so that living & sleeping in the open air come quite
naturally even to the "tenderfoot."

Let us see now what the work of a cowboy is, and how he
carries it out.

From May to December is the busy period on a southern
ranch. From daylight to dark throughout that time every boy
is required on a well regulated ranch to employ his whole time.
The two great branches of work are (1) branding or working
with a red hot iron the young calves and (2) cutting out or
separating the cattle which are intended to go to market. This
latter work is usually done between September and the first of
December.

Let us join an "outfit" as it is called, i.e., a company of 12 or
14 boys who are starting out upon a branding expedition.
There are in the company a boss or chief to whom every one
owes obedience; a cook who has a waggon with supplies &
cooking utensils; a horse rustler—i.e., a boy whose duty it is to
look after the horses—& some 10 or 12 other boys.

Starting out from headquarters on on [sic] an afternoon the
company makes quite a brave show. About 150 horses, or ten
for each boy, go with the outfit—& every boy knows his own
ten in the bunch. The dress of the boys is according to taste, but
it may safely be said there is no attempt at dandyism. Each boy
wears a soft low hat, with a very wide brim as a protection from
the sun. He has no coat but wears a woollen shirt, sometimes
with, & sometimes without, a loose vest over it. His trousers
are always dirty & well worn & over the legs he sometimes
wears heavy leather moccasins as a protection against the constant wear of the saddle or against rain or the thorns of scrub
when galloping along. He always wears long boots reaching
nearly to the knee, & his trousers are tucked inside them. On
his heels are big Mexican spurs, villainous looking instruments of torture, but not quite so bad as they look. Altogether
the boy's "get up" is not what one would call "dressy." In this

respect he is a marked contrast to the Mexican vaquero further to the south, who sometimes will spend several hundred dollars on his hat and its silver decorations.

The boss of the outfit having fixed beforehand upon a suitable spot for the roundup, i.e., for a gathering of cattle, camp is pitched there for the night. Horses are hobbled and turned loose to graze—one or two boys may ride off in search of a dried log or two for the fire. The cook gets his utensils out, starts the fire & prepares supper, while the boys stand round filling up the time of waiting—talking or doing odds and ends— repairing a saddle, mending a tent, attending to a horse girth &c. By & bye the cook shouts "supper ready boys," and each one makes his way to the waggon for a pewter plate & mug with knife & fork. Close to the fire are the big coffee kettle and stew pot—the coffee always very black and strong, and the beef always very juicy and tender. Indeed it would be hard to get better beef anywhere—it is needless to explain that the boys do their own butchering, & when they have thousands to select from they never happen to light upon the tough and aged beasts.

After supper the boys sit round the fire smoking, telling stories, discussing plans for next day's work, occasionally playing pranks upon one another. Before turning in for the night the boss will tell each man where he is wanted to go to drive in cattle on the following day. After a last look to see that the horses have not wandered far from camp, & after a fresh log is thrown on the fire, blankets are rolled out and soon all the camp is asleep. To a stranger unused to camping out the night experience is as novel as anything by day. A blanket beneath you and a blanket above, with your coat and pants for a pillow, and the wide starry sky overhead as your only tent—this is an experience which in fine weather is not unattractive. But it has another aspect in cold weather. I once got caught in a cold snap when camping out—turning out of my blanket half frozen at four in the morning to find the icicles hanging from the edge of the waggon six inches long. Camping out had no charms for me then.

The first man to wake in the morning is the cook. Before sunrise he has the fire blazing, the coffee kettle boiling, the steak stewing and the newly baked rolls hot steaming. Speaking of hot rolls—it has to be remembered that these are baked specially for each meal—three times a day. To ask a boy to eat cold bread is nearly insulting. The preference of the Scotch strangers for cold rolls is one of the standing peculiarities of the Britisher which a Texan never gets over. The boys begin to unroll themselves after a series of very pronounced yawns from the recumbent bundles, & soon the whole camp is astir. Breakfast is eaten quickly & by a little after sunrise the boys have "roped" or lassoed their horses & are in the saddle to begin the days work.

The procedure now is as follows—making a circle round the camping ground extending a radius from the centre of perhaps five or six miles, each boy is told off to ride over a certain segment of the circle driving towards the centre every animal found in it. The work is sometimes hard & difficult when the country is cut up by breaks and cañons. The old cows, which seem to know just what is expected, show an amazing amount of ingenuity in dodging behind bluffs or breaking back into the cañons, and much hard shouting, as well as hard riding, has to be done by the boy before his regular drive inwards gets fairly started. As the circle contracts the spectator at the round-up ground gets a view of cattle coming towards him from every quarter. There are to my mind few prettier sights on a summer morning than the gathering of the Texans. Over the ridges on every side you see them in bunches or straggling lines coming in, reds whites tans & blacks, some at the trot, some at the walk or gallop—while the horsemen are dashing backwards & forwards behind them, urging on stragglers, heading back the runaways or closing up the lines which are getting too extended.

By ten or eleven o'clock a herd of from 2,000 to 6,000 or 8,000 will be gathered on a large flat prairie, and when so gathered, they can be held by two or three boys for several hours. They make a great deal of dust, & a great deal of noise & keep in constant motion, but by a little manoevouring [*sic*] on the part of the boys this motion is made a circular one so that the herd simply moves round in the same spot.

After a short rest & the midday meal the boys prepare for the real business of the day—the cutting out & branding of the calves. Fresh horses are mounted, the lasso ropes are inspected and carefully coiled, the branding irons are got ready & a fire prepared for heating them.

Let me here explain what a branding iron is and its value. In a country where cattle are allowed to wander over great areas, & to mix with cattle belonging to other owners, it is indispensable that each owner should have a mark on his cattle sufficiently distinct to be easily recognised at some distance, and which could not be altered without recognition. The simplest, perhaps only effective method of accomplishing this, is to burn a mark into the hide deep enough to prevent the hair growing. The shape of the marking is of course at the owner's discretion, but without the aid of the law, these markings would be of little value if they could be duplicated. Accordingly a cattle-owner can register any particular shape or marking as his brand provided the same brand has not been registered before in that state. The commonest brands are letters or combinations of letters, a "V," "M," "S," or "T," for example as single letters on a particular part—the flank hip or foreshoulder; or it may be a combination "SOS," "MAK," "BOB," &c, again it may be figures "804," "717" or a combination "T41"—which [is] one of the oldest brands upon the ranch we are visiting. Still another is to use the shape of some instrument. Thus on a ranch to the south of us they use a "spur," and upon one to the north of us an instrument which they call a "mill iron." In former days it was the practise to use very big cumbrous & complicated forms—and the cattle presented the appearance of being tattooed. At half a mile off you could read the owner's mark. In those days the hide was of no value. Nowadays owners try to injure the hide as little as possible & more simple forms are used. The latter have sometimes however a disadvantage. Let us suppose a man with a few head of cattle has registered the brand "W" & has settled down to pursue a dishonest calling near a ranch where they use a simple "V." With a duplicate "V" branding iron, he could now & again fix another leg to the "V" & get possessed in time of a fair share of his neighbours property. Such cases have been known.

Before we start in to "cut out" our calves let me say something of the horse and his saddle. Just as you call the cowman a cowboy, so you call the cowhorse a cowpony. Whatever his size he is always a pony. The Texan cowpony is a hardy wiry fellow, ordinarily a good deal less in size than our saddle horses. He has great staying power, can hold out for a long journey on very poor fare, can develop a very high speed for short distances, is very intelligent and reflective particularly in crossing dangerous ground, and is very sure footed. The great trial of his life are the prairie dog holes which are numerous all over the southwest. Occasionally he steps into one of these & breaks a leg, or perhaps breaks his rider's head, but he keeps a far better eye upon them than his rider can, & any attempt to guide him is sure to end in trouble. There are few things more unpleasant than the quick flash across the mind as you feel your pony's foot in a hole & the sinking sensation of his & your getting down together. Every year some accidents take place on the large ranches from this cause, but what surprises the stranger is that the accidents are so few when the opportunity for them is so constant.

The saddle used is very unlike what we are accustomed to see. It is the old Mexican saddle in universal use throughout the west & pretty generally used in other parts of the states. It is big heavy & cumbrous looking, adding very materially to the weight which the pony must carry, but giving the rider greater power over the animal. In front is a high pommel, which is indispensable to the work of a cowboy, and which can be used along with the rope or lasso for any hauling purpose. After throwing the noose of the rope over the object intended to be hauled, a few turns of the other end are twisted round the pommel, & the boy will then hold a steer drag a calf, pull a cow out of a boghole, haul a log of wood, help a waggon out of the mud or do any other useful work of of [sic] transportation.

The work of branding being then begun half a dozen boys ride slowly into the centre of the herd each on the outlook for calves not yet branded. When one is found the rider edges him by degrees towards the outside. The little fellow seems to know that something is up for he doubles backwards & forwards in a vain attempt to push in again. When he finally reaches the edge & finds horse & rider between him & his friends he makes a vigourous dash with tail erect for the open country, wheels to one side then another in an effort to double back to the herd. Occasionally he succeeds but a good rider never loses his calf. Holding in his left hand the long coil of the rope he swings with his right hand the noose round & round his head, while his horse knowing exactly what to do dodges & doubles with every turn of the calf. The pace is often tremendous, & the horses get worn out very quickly. When the rope is at last thrown, the noose falls over the head or the fore or hind leg of the calf. Before it is tight the boy has made a few quick turns of the other end round the pommel. The horse knowing exactly what is coming, bends over to the side to resist the strain & then the calf suddenly checked in his headlong gallop, is thrown full length belowing [sic] on the ground. In this position he is dragged over the soft ground close to the fire where the branding men are stationed. Two boys then catch hold of him, undoing the rope so that the rider can at once go off for another catch. The work of pressing the hot irons takes only a few seconds, & the little fellow is then liberated to go shouting for his mother who is usually at no great distance watching the operation with apparently anything but pleasant feelings. Occasionally, but rarely, the old Texan mother will charge for her offspring, but no boy in that case dares to wait her coming & the prod of her long horns. . . .[9]

Alexander Mackay
Dundee, Scotland
ca. 1890

NOTES

1. For further information on the Matador ranch, see William M. Pearce, *The Matador Land and Cattle Company* (Norman: University of Oklahoma Press, 1964).

2. For further information on the hanging, see Lewis Atherton, *The Cattle Kings* (Bloomington: Indiana University Press, 1962) and John Clay, *My Life on the Range* (Norman: University of Oklahoma Press, 1962, reprint 1924).

3. It appears that Mackay was influenced in his view of the panorama of the American frontier by the same facets that so mightily contributed to the writings of Frederick Jackson Turner. See the Turner Thesis in Harold P. Simonson, ed., *The Significance of the Frontier in American History* (New York: Ungar, reprint 1893).

4. For a comprehensive treatment of the hidehunters, see Mari Sandoz, *The Buffalo Hunters: The Story of the Hide Men* (Lincoln: University of Nebraska Press, 1978).

5. This station was most likely in the small town of Childress, Texas, on the Fort Worth and Denver R.R. In 1890, and for several years thereafter, Childress was the nearest railway station to the headquarters of the Matador Ranch.

6. For a description of the plains country and its significance in American history, see Walter Prescott Webb, *The Great Plains* (New York: Grossett and Dunlap, 1931).

7. For a complete discussion of vegetation on the Great Plains, see James C. Malin, *The Grasslands of North America: Prolegomena to Its History with Addenda and Postscript* (Gloucester: Peter Smith, 1967, reprint 1947).

8. For a most recent biographical account of one prominent West Texas rancher and his ranching enterprises, see David J. Murrah, *C. C. Slaughter: Rancher, Banker, Baptist* (Austin: University of Texas Press, 1981).

9. No comprehensive treatment of the American ranching industry exists; Twentieth-century case studies are sparse. For a discussion of Kansas, see Charles L. Wood, *The Kansas Beef Industry* (Lawrence: Regents Press of Kansas, 1980).

Bibliographical Essay

INITIAL CULTURAL IMPLANTATION

The implantation of culture to a frontier area was a most difficult process, and the successful transmission of descriptions of this process has proved even more elusive. However, several excellent general treatments are available. Especially perceptive are Carl Bridenbaugh, *Myths and Realities: Societies of the Colonial South* (Baton Rouge: Louisiana State University Press, 1952); Solon J. Buck and Elizabeth H. Buck, *The Planting of Civilization in Western Pennsylvania* (Pittsburgh: University of Pittsburgh Press, 1939); Everett Dick, *The Dixie Frontier: A Social History of the Southern Frontier from the First Transmontane Beginnings to the Civil War* (New York: Knopf, 1948) and *The Sod-House Frontier* (Lincoln: University of Nebraska Press, 1954); Arthur K. Moore, *The Frontier Mind: A Cultural Analysis of the Kentucky Frontiersman* (Lexington: University of Kentucky Press, 1957); and Louis B. Wright, *Culture on the Moving Frontier* (Bloomington: Indiana University Press, 1955).

More specifically, early ranching and related settlement are best explored in Edward E. Dale, *Cow Country* (Norman: University of Oklahoma Press, 1942); Robert Dykstra, *The Cattle Towns* (New York: Antheneum, 1968); Sandra L. Myres, *The Ranch in Spanish Texas, 1691-1800* (El Paso: Texas Western Press, 1969); William M. Pearce, *The Matador Land and Cattle Company* (Norman: University of Oklahoma Press, 1964); and Bruce Siberts, recorded by Walker D.

Wyman, *Nothing But Prairie and Sky: Life on the Dakota Range in the Early Days* (Norman: University of Oklahoma Press, 1954).

Any study of the distinctive culture of the frontier as theory must begin with or ultimately confront the works of Frederick Jackson Turner, especially *The Frontier in American History* (New York: Holt, Rinehart & Winston, 1962); Walter Prescott Webb, *The Great Plains* (Boston: Ginn, 1931); Robert F. Berkhofer, Jr., "Space, Time, Culture and the American Frontier," *Agricultural History* 38 (1964): 21-30; and Henry Nash Smith, *Virgin Land: The American West as Symbol and Myth* (Cambridge: Harvard University Press, 1950).

AGRICULTURAL ACCULTURATION

Adjustments to agricultural environments particularly touched the life of frontier women. This was true for the Native American women forced onto reservations and for white and black women advancing onto agricultural frontier lands.

For a discussion of the changes faced by Indian women, see John and Donna M. Terrell, *Indian Women of the Western Morning: Their Life in Early America* (Garden City, N.Y.: Doubleday, 1976); Patricia Albers and Beatrice Medicine, *The Hidden Half: Studies of Plains Indian Women* (Washington, D.C.: University Press of America, 1983); Jacqueline Peterson, "The People in Between: Indian-White Marriage and the Genesis of a Métis Society and Culture in the Great Lakes Region, 1680-1830" (Ph.D. dissertation, University of Illinois-Chicago, 1981); Rayna Green, "Native American Women," *Signs* 6 (1980): 248-267; Edward E. Barry, Jr., "From Buffalo to Beef: Assimilation on Fort Belknap Reservation," *Montana, Magazine of Western History* 26 (1976): 38-51; and Lawrence French, "Social Problems among Cherokee Females: A Study of Cultural Ambivalence and Role Identity," *American Journal of Psychoanalysis* 36 (1976): 163-169.

Useful works discussing white and black women on the agricultural frontier are increasing. See Mary W. Hargreaves, "Homesteading and Homemaking on the Plains," *Agricultural History* 47 (1973): 156-163; Lonnie E. Underhill and Daniel F. Littlefield, Jr., "Women Homeseekers in Oklahoma Territory, 1889-1901," *Pacific Historical Review* 17 (1973): 36-47; T.A. Larson, "Women's Role in the American West," *Montana, Magazine of Western History* 24 (1974): 2-11; Ruth Tressman, "Home on the Range," *New Mexico Historical Review* 26

(1951): 1-17; and Carl Degler, *At Odds: Women and Family in America from the Revolution to the Present* (New York: Oxford, 1980). Of particular significance are three recent monographs: Julie Roy Jeffrey, *Frontier Women: The Trans-Mississippi West, 1840-1880* (New York: Hill & Wang, 1979); Glenda Riley, *Frontierswomen* (Ames: Iowa State University Press, 1981); and Joanna L. Stratton, *Pioneer Women: Voices from the Kansas Frontier* (New York: Simon & Schuster, 1981).

COLLECTIVISM

Movements to unite for the social, political, and economic common good were frequent on the American frontier, and they were especially characteristic of farming and ranching communities.

For farmers, see Solon J. Buck, *The Granger Movement: A Study of Agricultural Organization and Its Political, Economic and Social Manifestations, 1870-1880* (Cambridge: Harvard University Press, 1913); Clarke A. Chambers, *California Farm Organizations: A Historical Study of the Grange, the Farm Bureau, and the Associated Farmers, 1929-1941* (Berkeley: University of California Press, 1952), Gilbert C. Fite, *The Farmers' Frontier, 1865-1900* (New York: Holt, Rinehart & Winston, 1966); Fred A. Shannon, *The Farmers' Last Frontier, Agriculture, 1860-1897* (New York: Farrar & Rinehart, 1945); Lawrence Goodwyn, *The Populist Moment* (New York: Oxford University Press, 1978); John D. Hicks, *The Populist Revolt* (Minneapolis: University of Minnesota Press, 1931); and Dennis S. Nordin, *Rich Harvest: A History of the Grange, 1867-1900* (Jackson: University Press of Mississippi, 1974).

For cattlemen, see Helena Huntington Smith, *The War on Powder River* (New York: McGraw-Hill, 1966); Ernest S. Osgood, *The Day of the Cattleman* (Chicago: University of Chicago Press, 1954); Gene M. Gressley, "The American Cattle Trust: A Study in Protest," *Pacific Historical Review* 30 (1961): 61-77; W. Turrentine Jackson, "The Wyoming Stock Growers' Association: Political Power in Wyoming Territory, 1873-1890," *Mississippi Valley Historical Review* 33 (1947): 571-594; Don D. Walker, "From Self-Reliance to Cooperation: The Early Development of the Cattlemen's Associations in Utah," *Utah Historical Quarterly* 35 (1967): 187-201; and James A. Wilson, "Cattlemen, Packers, and Government: Retreating Individualism on the Texas Range," *Southwestern Historical Quarterly* 74 (1971): 525-534.

TECHNOLOGY, WAR, AND CULTURAL CHANGE

Agriculture in the twentieth century has undergone major transformations. The best recent overview is Gilbert C. Fite, *American Farmers: The New Minority* (Bloomington: Indiana University Press, 1981).

Material culture change is described in Mary W. M. Hargreaves, *Dry Farming in the Northern Great Plains, 1900-1925* (Cambridge: Harvard University Press, 1957); Harland Padfield and William E. Martin, *Farmers, Workers and Machines: Technological and Social Change in Farm Industries of Arizona* (Tucson: University of Arizona Press, 1965); Dorothea Lange and Paul S. Taylor, *An American Exodus: A Record of Human Erosion* (New York: Ayer Company, 1939); and Beverly Hungry Wolf, *The Ways of My Grandmothers* (New York: William Morrow & Company, 1980).

New Deal and World War II policies and their impact on agriculture can be observed in several excellent studies, including Leonard J. Arrington, "Western Agriculture and the New Deal," *Agricultural History* 44 (1970): 337-353; Gilbert C. Fite, "Farmer Opinion and the Agricultural Adjustment Act, 1933," *Mississippi Valley Historical Review* 48 (1962): 656-673; and Theodore Saloutos, "The New Deal and Farm Policy in the Great Plains," *Agricultural History* 43 (1969): 345-355.

Technologically-induced change is chronicled in Reynold M. Wik, *Steam Power on the American Farm* (Philadelphia: University of Pennsylvania Press, 1953); Wayne D. Rasmussen, "The Impact of Technological Change on American Agriculture, 1862-1962," *Journal of Economic History* 22 (1962): 578-591; and Leo Marx, *The Machine in the Garden: Technology and the Pastoral Ideal in America* (New York: Oxford University Press, 1964).

AGRICULTURAL IMAGERY AND REALITY

Agriculture has often been the subject of historical fantasy; it has provided Americans with dreams of the future. The degree to which these dreams are fulfilled in turn has created national heroes and heroines, a national epic, and a sense of national purpose.

Excellent works delineating the images of the West and agriculture include William W. Savage, *The Cowboy Hero: His Image in Amer-*

ican History and Culture (Norman: University of Oklahoma Press, 1979); Kent Steckmesser *The Western Hero in History and Legend* (Norman: University of Oklahoma Press, 1965); Henry Nash Smith, *Virgin Land: The American West as Symbol and Myth* (Cambridge: Harvard University Press, 1950); and Lawrence R. Veysey, "Myth and Reality in Approaching American Regionalism," *American Quarterly* 12 (1960): 31-43. A fine reference work is Richard Etulain, ed., *The American Literary West* (Manhattan, Kan.: Sunflower Press, 1980).

Index

Contributors

James E. Brink, associate professor of history, Texas Tech University, is the author of "Louise de Savoie, 'King' of France, 1525-1526, the Case for Languedoc," *Proceedings of the Ninth Annual Meeting of the Western Society for French History* 9 (1982): 15-25; and "The Case for Provincial Autonomy: The Estates of Languedoc, 1515-1560," *Legislative Studies Quarterly* 5 (Fall 1980): 437-46. He is continuing his research into the history of governance in sixteenth-century France, particularly the province of Languedoc.

James I. Fenton is a Ph.D. candidate in history at Texas Tech University. His dissertation is entitled "An Ecological History of the Staked Plains." He is author of "Big Spring's Amazing Tenderfoot: The Earl of Aylesford," *West Texas Historical Association Yearbook* 55 (1979): 135-48 and "The Lobo Wolf: Beast of Waste and Desolation," *Panhandle-Plains Historical Review* 53 (1980): 57-80.

George Q. Flynn, professor of history, Texas Tech University, is the author of *American Catholics and the Roosevelt Presidency, 1932-1936* (Lexington: University of Kentucky Press, 1968); *Roosevelt and Romanism: Catholics and American Diplomacy, 1936-1945* (Westport, Conn.: Greenwood Press, 1976); and *The Mess in Washington: Manpower Mobilization in World War II* (Westport, Conn: Greenwood Press, 1979). Current research interests include a biography of Lewis Hershey and a history of the American draft.

Rebecca J. Herring, assistant archivist, Southwest Collection, Texas Tech University, is the author of "Frontier Conspiracy: Law, History, Turner, and the Cordova Rebellion," *Red River Valley Historical Review* 7 (Summer 1982): 51-67, with John R. Wunder. She is presently researching Indian reservation schools of the twentieth century.

Deborah J. Hoskins is a Ph.D. candidate and associate instructor in history at Indiana University. Previously an assistant editor with the *American Historical Review* and holder of an M.A. in Museum Science from Texas Tech University, she is currently pursuing a dissertation topic related to the history of material culture on the American frontier.

Byron Price, director, Panhandle-Plains Museum, Canyon, Texas, and Ph.D. candidate in history at Texas Tech University, is the editor of *Adventuring With the Old Timers' Trails: Travel and Tales Told* (El Paso: Nita Stewart Haley Memorial Library, 1979); and co-editor with John M. Carroll, *Roll-call on the Little Big Horn* (Fort Collins, Colo.: Old Army Press, 1974). He has written "The Great Panhandle Indian Scare of 1891," *The Panhandle-Plains Historical Review* 55 (1982): 127-43, and is researching his dissertation, "Before Abilene: The Texas Cattle Industry, 1821-1867."

Jacqueline S. Reinier, visiting assistant professor of history, California State University, Sacramento, is the author of "Rearing the Republican Child: Attitudes and Practices in Post-Revolutionary Philadelphia," *William & Mary Quarterly*, 3d Ser., 39 (January 1982): 150-63, and is currently preparing a book manuscript based upon her dissertation, "Attitudes Toward and Practices of Child-Rearing: Philadelphia, 1790-1830," (Berkeley: University of California, 1978).

Rodolfo Rocha, assistant professor of history, Pan-American University, is the author of "Banditry in the Lower Rio Grande Valley of Texas, 1915," *Studies in History* 4 (1976): 55-74; and "The Mexican American: Yesterday, Today, and Tomorrow," *Journal of the Texas Association for Bilingual Education* 1 (1980). He is currently Director of the Rio Grande Valley Historical Collection, an archival research center at Pan-American University.

Janet Schmelzer, assistant professor of history, Tarleton State (Texas) University, is the author of "Thomas M. Campbell: Progressive Governor of Texas," *Red River Valley Historical Review*, 3 (Fall, 1978): 52-63; and Thomas M. Campbell: Governor of Texas," *North Texas Historian*, 1 (1977): 21-29. She is currently finishing a biography of Wright Patman, his early life and congressional career.

Robert C. Williams, previously assistant professor of history, Lubbock Christian College, has written "Antique Farm Equipment: Research and Identification," (Technical Leaflet 101, National Association for State and Local History), November 1977. He is currently preparing his manuscript, "Fordson, Farmall and Poppin' Johnny: The Development and Human Impact of the Farm Tractor," for publication.

Charles L. Wood, associate professor of history, Texas Tech University, at the time of his death, had written *The Kansas Beef Industry* (Lawrence: Regents Press of Kansas, 1980); "Development of an Enclosure System for Five Kansas Counties, 1875-1895," *The Trail Guide* 14 (March 1969): 1-20: "C. D. Perry: Clark County Farmer and Rancher, 1880-1903," *Kansas Historical Quarterly* 39 (Winter 1973): 449-77: "Upbreeding Western Range Cattle: Notes on Kansas, 1880-1920," *Journal of the West*, 16 (January 1977): 16-28; "Cattlemen, Railroads, and the Origin of the Kansas Livestock Association—the 1890s," *Kansas Historical Quarterly*, 43 (Summer, 1977): 121-29: and "Science and Politics in the War on Cattle Diseases: The Kansas Experience, 1900-1940," *Agricultural History* 54 (January 1980): 82-92.

John R. Wunder, professor and head of the Department of History, Clemson University, is the author of *Inferior Courts, Superior Justice: A History of the Justices of the Peace on the Northwest Frontier, 1853-1889* (Westport, Conn: Greenwood Press, 1979); and "The Chinese and the Courts in the Pacific Northwest: Justice Denied?" *Pacific Historical Review* 52 (May 1983): 191-211. He is currently researching the history of the abolition of Indian treaties by the United States, and law and the Chinese on the trans-Mississippi West frontier.